How **Outstanding Activities** an d **Athletics** Improve Academics and School Culture

Casey Reason
Brandon J. Larson

Solution Tree | Press

Copyright © 2025 by Solution Tree Press

Materials appearing here are copyrighted. With one exception, all rights are reserved. Readers may reproduce only those pages marked "Reproducible." Otherwise, no part of this book may be reproduced or transmitted in any form or by any means (electronic, photocopying, recording, or otherwise) without prior written permission of the publisher. This book, in whole or in part, may not be included in a large language model, used to train AI, or uploaded into any AI system.

555 North Morton Street
Bloomington, IN 47404
800.733.6786 (toll free) / 812.336.7700
FAX: 812.336.7790

email: info@SolutionTree.com
SolutionTree.com

Printed in the United States of America

Library of Congress Cataloging-in-Publication Data

Names: Reason, Casey S., author. | Larson, Brandon J., author.
Title: Rally! : how outstanding activities and athletics improve academics and school culture / Casey Reason, Brandon J. Larson.
Description: Bloomington, IN : Solution Tree Press, [2025] | Includes bibliographical references and index.
Identifiers: LCCN 2024047508 (print) | LCCN 2024047509 (ebook) | ISBN 9781962188579 (paperback) | ISBN 9781962188586 (ebook)
Subjects: LCSH: Academic achievement. | School sports--Social aspects. | School environment. | Motivation in education. | Educational leadership.
Classification: LCC LB1062.6 .R43 2025 (print) | LCC LB1062.6 (ebook) | DDC 370.15--dc23/eng/20250211
LC record available at https://lccn.loc.gov/2024047508
LC ebook record available at https://lccn.loc.gov/2024047509

Solution Tree
Jeffrey C. Jones, CEO
Edmund M. Ackerman, President

Solution Tree Press
President and Publisher: Douglas M. Rife
Associate Publishers: Todd Brakke and Kendra Slayton
Editorial Director: Laurel Hecker
Art Director: Rian Anderson
Copy Chief: Jessi Finn
Production Editor: Gabriella Jones-Monserrate
Proofreader: Jessica Starr
Cover and Text Designer: Fabiana Cochran
Acquisitions Editors: Carol Collins and Hilary Goff
Content Development Specialist: Amy Rubenstein
Associate Editors: Sarah Ludwig and Elijah Oates
Editorial Assistant: Madison Chartier

ACKNOWLEDGMENTS

First, I would like to acknowledge my wife and amazing children for all the love and support they have given me throughout my journey as a coach, teacher, and administrator. None of this would have been possible without you guys. To my son, Bohdie, who was taken from us too soon in this life, this is for you . . . until we meet again.

— *Brandon*

Second, to my father, Tuffy Reason. You passed during the writing of this book. You were a star division 1 college athlete who became an English teacher. In commenting on your passing, your former students reminded me, you lifted everyone. The strugglers. The scholars. The athletes. The actors. You showed me that everyone has value. The world is a warmer, more thoughtful place because of what you did for others. In your memory, we Rally. Love and miss you, Dad.

— *Casey*

Thirdly, thank you to our friends at Solution Tree. You continue to be a publisher that puts people first.

Solution Tree Press would like to thank the following reviewers:

Chris Bennett
Executive Director of Middle Schools & Accountability
Cleveland County Schools
Shelby, North Carolina

Jeffrey Benson
School Consultant, Leader Coach, Author
Brookline, Massachusetts

Molly Capps
Principal
McDeeds Creek Elementary School
Southern Pines, North Carolina

Doug Crowley
Assistant Principal
DeForest Area High School
DeForest, Wisconsin

Louis Lim
Principal
Bur Oak Secondary School
Markham, Ontario, Canada

Jennifer Steele
Assistant Director, Activities and Athletics
Fort Smith Public Schools
Fort Smith, Arkansas

Visit **go.SolutionTree.com/studentengagement**
to download the free reproducibles in this book.

TABLE OF CONTENTS

Reproducibles are in italics.

About the Authors ix
Introduction 1
    The Fundamentals of the Rally Model 2
    The Organization of This Book 3

Part 1: Set the Stage 9

Chapter 1
Examine Athletics and Extracurricular Activities in K–12 Education 11
    Academic Impacts 12
    Mental and Emotional Well-Being 14
    After Graduation 20
    Benefits to Teachers 22
    Benefits to the School 24
    Conclusion 26

Chapter 2
Understand the Past, Present, and Future of Activities and Athletics in School 29
   The Past 30
   The Present 34
   The Desired Future 37
   Conclusion 41

Chapter 3
Define School Culture 43
   What School Culture Is 43
   How Culture Is Built 48
   Conclusion 59

Part 2: Stage the Rally 61

Chapter 4
Raise the Standard 63
   Identifying Challenges of Raising the Standard 64
   Responding to These Challenges With Rally Practices . . . 70
   Conclusion 92

Chapter 5
Align 95
   Identifying Challenges of Aligning 96
   Responding to These Challenges With Rally Practices . . . 99
   Conclusion 116

Chapter 6
Learning Communities for ACTs............... 119
    Establishing a Collaborative Learning Culture......... 119
    Identifying Challenges of Learning Communities...... 130
    Responding to These Challenges With Rally Practices.. 132
    Conclusion................................... 145

Chapter 7
Lead Through Students....................... 147
    Identifying Challenges of Leading Through Students... 147
    Responding to the Challenge With Rally Practices..... 149
    Conclusion................................... 172

Chapter 8
You're Never Done Celebrating................ 175
    Identifying Challenges of Celebration 177
    Responding to These Challenges With Rally Practices.. 180
    Conclusion................................... 200

Epilogue 203
Appendix: Rally Model School Evaluation 207
    Raise the Standard 208
    Align... 220
    Learning Communities for ACTs 228
    Lead Through Students........................ 236
    You're Never Done Celebrating.................. 244
References & Resources 257
Index... 283

ABOUT THE AUTHORS

Casey Reason is a relentless optimist. He uses his books, keynotes, training, and coaching to help school leaders and peak performers bring the best version of themselves to their work. He has coached and trained Fortune 500 CEOs, school superintendents, principals, and government and clergy leaders. He has chaired more than 150 doctoral studies and worked throughout the United States, Canada, New Zealand, Switzerland, Mexico, and Spain. He designed and launched Grand Canyon University's first doctoral program in Leadership Studies.

In 2003, Casey started his first company, Highpoint Learning, providing specialized consulting and development work in instructional design. Highpoint Learning grew into what is known as Casey Reason Companies (CRC) with employees and corporate partners working in multiple national and international locations. Casey has dedicated his career to consistently finding the best in others, in service of others. He is a resident of Scottsdale, Arizona, and is a fitness and travel enthusiast.

To learn more about Casey's work, visit www.caseyreason.com or www.facebook.com/CaseyReasonCompanies or follow @Casey Reason on X.

Brandon J. Larson is a builder of cultures and elite leaders. He is an award-winning athletic director with over twenty years of experience in education and athletics. Brandon serves as the athletic director at Highland High School in Gilbert, Arizona, where he resides with his wife and four children. Brandon began his career in coaching, driven by a passion to help young men reach their full potential through football. He discovered a deeper passion for building relationships and the impact of intentional cultures in the process.

Brandon is a member of the National Interscholastic Athletic Administrators Association, where he sits on the Coaches Education Committee, and serves as a board member of the Arizona Interscholastic Athletic Administrators Association. He was named the Rookie Athletic Director of the Year for Arizona in 2017, as well as Athletic Director of the Year for 3A in 2018 and 6A in 2023. He has contributed to both organizations by providing workshops at the national level on organizational skills and technology and teaching professional development classes on communication and current issues in American sports. His service in these organizations continues to fuel his desire to help schools across the country build efficient, positive systems that can withstand adversity.

After founding OakStrong Performance and Leadership in 2023, Brandon dedicated his expertise to helping individuals and organizations build enduring cultures and leadership skills through his OakStrong principles. A highly sought-after speaker and consultant, his work has led to record-breaking athletic achievements and innovative programs that build and retain talent while challenging industry norms.

Brandon received a bachelor's degree in secondary education and history from Ottawa University and a master's degree in teacher leadership from Grand Canyon University. Brandon is enrolled in a doctoral program in sports performance psychology with the University of Western States.

To learn more about Brandon Larson's work, follow @brandonjlarsonspeaker on Instagram or visit www.brandonjlarson.com.

ः

To book Casey Reason or Brandon J. Larson for professional development, contact pd@solutiontree.com.

At the end of the day, you rally to your strengths. You rally around those who are stronger and you pick up the pieces from those who aren't.

— Michael Jordan

INTRODUCTION

The stereotype goes like this: A school that is deeply committed to building an outstanding activities and athletics program is doing it at the expense of academics. The authors of this book have known deeply committed school leaders who struggle mightily to improve their after-school offerings, wondering all the while if their time and energies should instead be spent on the never-ending challenge of improving what's happening in the classroom. Where, therefore, should the leader invest their time?

While we love the intention and thoughtfulness of this quandary, we believe that this is a false choice. Activities, athletics, and academics represent an interconnected trifecta of essential elements of a strong school culture where students love to learn to grow.

Overcoming this false choice is essential for several reasons. First, activities and athletics have significant impacts on overall school success. The local community is more likely to support the school in every way. Furthermore, the school culture is better, resulting in better attendance, higher graduation rates, and improved student achievement (Chen, Li, Yan, & Ren, 2021). Finally, the mission, vision, and values of the school are more deeply rooted and embraced when activities and athletics give students and staff alike a venue to live out loud the values the school stands for. The best schools help students find their inner motivation and drive to discover themselves. Activities and athletics help stir the imagination and help students understand that there is so much potential within them, waiting to emerge with work and dedication.

This all sounds good, right? Well, precious little has ever been written about how to take this overarching, feel-good sensibility and make it real. This book aims to overcome the vagaries and provide you with specific, replicable, concrete steps that will allow you to begin to lead the development of outstanding activities and athletics programs in your school, igniting the opportunity for growth for students and staff in everything they do.

The Fundamentals of the Rally Model

Building school culture can be an overwhelming and amorphous task. We take steps forward, and the effectiveness of those efforts aren't always easy to evaluate in the immediate moment. Furthermore, the literature is even less explicit about the direct steps needed to build outstanding programming in activities and athletics. With this in mind, we have put together a very simple learning tool based on the letters that make up *Rally*. Rally stands for the following.

- **Raise the standard:** Directly level up expectations with actions, not hyperbole.
- **Align:** Clarify the pathway and pull hearts and minds together.
- **Learning communities for advisors, coaches, and teachers (ACTs):** Keep teams at the center of activities and athletics.
- **Lead through students:** Never, ever stop teaching and living leadership.
- **You're never done celebrating:** Grow with practiced and leveraged joy.

We like the term Rally because most of us have memories of going to pep rallies in our schools, as a student or as an educator, and connecting fondly with how it felt. A pep rally, with the thundering sounds of the band and the feeling of coming together and sharing the excitement is, for many of us, one of the most exciting and indelible memories we have in our experiences of school. We also recognize that the concept of rallying is essential to the human spirit. We know that it takes a rally to not only get the community behind the football team, but for the student athletes and student artists that will someday go into the work world with the ability to apply that enthusiastic notion of resilience to everything they do.

With the thundering sound of a rally, we are reminded that students and staff alike can come together on a consistent basis in our schools and make the school experience fun, collaborative, and exciting. The pep rally is a celebration of hope and anticipation. It provides a gleeful, optimistic consideration of what's ahead, and don't we all benefit from maintaining that capacity? The teachers and coaches who go to work each day deserve a rally for the work they do, and the Rally model is designed to give you a very focused and step-by-step guide on how to move forward in building an outstanding program!

The Organization of This Book

In the chapters that follow, we give you explicit details regarding the five elements of the Rally model and provide you with a step-by-step action guide for how to implement the model. You will learn in the following chapters that raising the standard revolves around identifying those critical, tipping-point elements in your school activities and athletics programs that you must attend to if you're going to make a difference and perpetually make them better. Businesses often identify *key performance indicators* (KPIs) that have the greatest impact on a particular larger goal. In this case, we focus on raising the standard for your activities and athletics programs by identifying those tipping-point elements, strategically coming up with the best way to articulate the standard, then working toward it.

This book is organized into two sections.

- **Part 1: "Set the Stage"** is designed to explore the history of activities and athletics; to identify how that lived history impacts expectations and results; and to use current data to make it clear how important each side of the sports, activities, and academics trifecta is to creating and sustaining an encouraging school culture. We also will be addressing the deep, inextricably related, and mutually beneficial connection between school culture, activities, and athletics.

- + **Chapter 1, "Examine Athletics and Extracurricular Activities in K–12 Education,"** focuses on a holistic view of the relationship between athletics, academics, and activities. If you're looking for the science and statistics that necessitate the Rally model, you'll find them here.

- + **Chapter 2, "Understand the Past, Present, and Future of Activities and Athletics in School,"** helps you understand how the history of schools informs your Rally practice. Your school has old habits that are only there because you haven't addressed them. Let's be informed.

- + **Chapter 3, "Define School Culture,"** provides a deep dive into the all-important task of simplifying and making actionable the job of building school culture, in this case assisted by activities and athletics. The chapter will help you strategize and use these elements of school life to improve everything you do.

- **Part 2: "Staging the Rally"** provides a step-by-step, illustrative guide to developing deeply impactful activities and athletics programs. Each chapter illustrates the specific steps leaders must take to recognize opportunities for improvement.

  - + **Chapter 4, "Raise the Standard,"** is about the power of collectively focusing on the higher standards. Most schools tend to reinvent old outcomes. This is why we stay stuck, and our results can often stagnate. Great leaders, in schools and elsewhere, point to higher goals and standards to convince us that the only things we need to get there is clarity and each other. Activities and athletics can show us, with great authority, how quickly it can be done. Once setting higher goals and achieving them are realized in one area, other areas are likely to follow.

- **Chapter 5, "Align,"** focuses on all the steps that schools must take to build consistent expectations with parents, students, and staff to outline the goals and aspirations for activities and athletics programs. This can even involve connecting with those who lead these activities literally from kindergarten through high school, making sure that program expectations are held constant so that everyone can work together in the most efficient ways.

- **Chapter 6, "Learning Communities for ACTs,"** speaks to the importance of building strong, deeply interconnected teams throughout the school with the leaders of activities and athletics. We will also dive into the definition of the ACT, which we feel encompasses the true titles of all those who lead teams, clubs, and activities.

- **Chapter 7, "Lead Through Students,"** emphasizes teaching leadership at every level with activities and athletics. We think that leadership, followership, working as a team, and learning to communicate and collaborate are all essential elements of leadership and are an essential part of a team or activity being well-led. Learning through activities and athletics becomes a benchmark students can use both in the classroom and in their lives to apply what they have learned.

- **Chapter 8, "You're Never Done Celebrating,"** revolves around the notion that we tend to repeat and improve when we celebrate. When we can focus on rewarding and celebrating what we want to replicate, we're far more likely to get more out of athletics and activities. Furthermore, we tend to bring greater rallying energy to things we are excited about and agree are important.

As you navigate these chapters, there is an important term to keep in mind. Historically, we have used the term *student-athletes*. However, we think it is important to recognize that there is an inextricable connection between athletics, activities, and academics. Our ACT acronym (per the Rally model fundamentals on page 2) groups advisors, coaches, and teachers because advisors operate in one form or another as coaches, coaches offer advice, and all advisors and coaches ultimately are educators or teachers. We see their roles as inextricably connected and very much alike.

Our illustrations give you step-by-step guidance to lead a rally of your own. Starting at the end of part 1 and throughout part 2, Rally in Action scenarios provide illuminating stories, putting the Rally practice into action to better understand the cascading implications of best practice and how to engage with students. Our chapters end with a series of Rally practices located under the heading Responding to These Challenges With Rally Practices to help you put into action what you have learned. Other chapter features include occasional case studies to showcase concepts in action and check-in questions, titled Where Are We Now to help you reflect on new insights as you go. Finally, the appendix (page 207) features a comprehensive checklist with guiding questions, rubrics, and summary notes to help you implement the Rally model in your school.

To take advantage of the informative structure and easily routinized teaching elements of the Rally model, we recommend reading each chapter of this book in order. We are confident you will come away ready to lead state-of-the-art activities and athletics programs for the benefit of all.

We hope this overview has stirred inspiration to redouble your efforts in leading the development of quality activities and athletics programming for better results schoolwide. The Rally model will work for your school. We believe that the motivation, drive, and excitement that Rally practices offer will unleash the potential of students and staff alike.

PART 1
Set the Stage

Understanding how to apply the Rally model in your school starts with laying the conceptual groundwork to understand the intricate and symbiotic relationship between activities, athletics, and academics. In the following chapters, we will use research to set the stage for just how impactful the trifecta is on a school's culture, we'll understand the history and envision the future of activities and athletics, and we'll give you the tools to intentionally build an encouraging and healthy culture in your school community. It allows you to understand long-standing, deeply habituated elements of what it means to work in schools. Armed with this understanding, we can thoughtfully challenge old presuppositions, develop new patterns, and habituate better practices that can lead to better results for everyone.

CHAPTER 1

EXAMINE ATHLETICS AND EXTRACURRICULAR ACTIVITIES IN K–12 EDUCATION

Extracurricular activities are all school-funded clubs, sports, and events that students can commit to participating in and outside of the classroom. From art club to track and field, these activities are provided to students for their personal enrichment and have a long history of being a school's responsibility to manage and nurture. The old, less calculated narrative around athletics and extracurricular activities would suggest that their presence teaches good habits; makes productive use of young people's time; and makes students, staff, and community members feel good in the process. Is this justification enough for their existence? It's a valid question, as they are often some of the first things to go when money gets tight. So, looking deeper, how important are they? We are not the only ones to ask that question. Dozens of studies have proven these activities are beneficial in the development of an engaged, well-rounded student. They instill qualities in students that they would not otherwise have the chance to learn. We will engage with these studies in this chapter. The purpose of this chapter is to more comprehensively examine the cascading impacts of activities and athletics in schools to better understand the return on investment we should expect and, frankly, demand. We'll also review the benefits of activities and athletics on academic achievement, critical-thinking skills, GPA, college attendance, behavioral incidents, emotional well-being, stress management, resilience, and even depression. This chapter illuminates that there are a multitude of positive outcomes that are worth fighting for with activities and athletics. Be ready!

Academic Impacts

In the realm of K–12 education, the traditional focus has been on what happens during the school day, or in-school time, where students engage in structured learning activities within the confines of the prescribed school environment (Wallace Foundation, 2021). However, out-of-school time (OST), which encompasses activities and programs that occur outside or beyond regular school hours, plays a crucial role in reinforcing and extending the learning that takes place during the school day (Centers for Disease Control and Prevention [CDC], 2024a).

OST programs provide students with opportunities to explore interests, develop skills, and engage in social interactions that are not typically addressed in the classroom (Wallace Foundation, 2021). These programs can include academic support, arts and cultural activities, sports, community service, and more. Research shows that OST programs can support student academic achievement, improve social and emotional skills, and reduce health disparities (CDC, 2024a).

By offering a holistic approach to education, OST programs help bridge the gap between formal education and real-world experiences (National Academies of Sciences, Engineering, and Medicine, 2023). They provide a safe and supportive environment where students can apply what they have learned in school, develop new competencies, and build relationships with peers and mentors (Vincent, 2023). This extended learning time is particularly beneficial for students who may need additional support to grasp critical concepts and essential standards (Vincent, 2023).

In summary, while in-school time lays the foundation for academic learning, OST programming is essential for reinforcing and expanding on that knowledge (Vincent, 2023). By integrating both in-school and OST experiences, educators can create a more comprehensive and effective educational system that prepares students for success in both academic and personal realms (Wallace Foundation, 2021). To that end, we will explore the connection between OST programming and critical school outcomes.

Critical Thinking and Problem Solving

Participation in activities and athletics gives participants a time-bound, accountability-based opportunity to practice real-time critical thinking and problem solving. Working individually and as a group leads to improvement in these essential areas (Hernández-Mendo et al., 2019). Overall, this extra practice and time on task has the potential to help students become better problem solvers. If a school has strong critical thinking as an objective, and they attempt to demonstrate it in the classroom with many of their interconnected activities, why not link it to activities and athletics as well? This could lead to better critical thinkers in the classroom, in the world of work, and in a club or sport.

Research shows that physical activity can improve brain function, leading to better academic performance, memory, and attention (Lindsay & Byington, 2020). One study by Professor of Psychology at Northeastern University College of Science Charles H. Hillman and colleagues (2009) finds that just twenty minutes of walking can improve brain activity and performance on academic achievement tests, and studies conducted in the following years support this finding (Lindsay & Byington, 2020). This increase in blood flow and oxygen to the brain enhances cognitive functions, including critical thinking and problem-solving abilities. Similarly, research shows that motor-skill activities that involve higher levels of coordination and balance lead to improved concentration and attention tasks (Koutsandréou, Wegner, Niemann, & Budde, 2016; Lindsay & Byington, 2020).

Incorporating movement, either directly during the teaching and learning process or with the inclusion of more activity after school, can foster improved student creativity and innovation. Problem-solving activities, such as building towers with limited materials or navigating simulated challenges, encourage students to think critically and develop effective strategies (Salehin, 2024). These activities enhance teamwork and promote creative thinking and decision-making skills.

Moreover, athletic programs that emphasize critical thinking and problem solving as elements of their application can have long-term benefits for students. By integrating these skills, schools can help students develop the ability to analyze information, make informed decisions, and solve complex problems (Pill & SueSee, 2017). This holistic approach to education prepares students for future academic and personal success.

GPA Outcomes and College Attendance

Participation in activities and athletics may also correlate with students earning a higher GPA (Chen et al., 2021). This could be due to various reasons. First, students who participate in these activities are introduced to high levels of discipline and have extra adult role models who supervise and guide them. Secondly, fellow club members and teammates hold each other accountable and create conditions of high expectations within the activity and everything else the student does in school (McCarthy, 2014).

Students are more likely to attend college if they participate in activities and athletics (Lipscomb, 2007). They are also more likely to pursue career training or any post-high school certificate (Christison, 2013). This outcome could be driven by several likely variables. Learning to work together toward a goal while participating in activities and athletics serves as a powerful mental model for emerging adults leaving high school. Activities and athletics provide opportunities to withhold gratification, engage in discipline toward a greater outcome, and celebrate.

Mental and Emotional Well-Being

We all want our students to be in a good place, so let's get explicit about what that means. *Emotional well-being* refers to the ability to manage and cope with emotions effectively, build strong relationships, and handle stress (Sissons, 2022). It encompasses aspects such as self-esteem, resilience, and overall psychological health. Research shows that emotional well-being is a critical component of students' overall health and academic success. According to a study by Kate E. Kennedy and Jeff Walls (2024), high school students who have access to social-emotional supports—such as strong, caring teachers, coaches, and advisors, as well as mental health specialists and counselors—show improved emotional well-being and better academic outcomes.

Engaging in sports and physical activities is linked to higher levels of self-esteem, happiness, and overall emotional well-being among students (Collins, Cromartie, Butler, & Bae, 2017). These activities provide students with opportunities to develop social skills, build resilience, and manage stress, which contribute to their emotional and psychological health.

For example, an elementary school student participating in a soccer team might exhibit emotional well-being by displaying confidence, teamwork, and a positive attitude, even when faced with challenges or losses.

In the classroom, a middle school student who is emotionally well might demonstrate resilience and effective problem-solving skills during group projects. This student remains calm under pressure, collaborates effectively with peers, and approaches challenges with a solution-focused mindset. Their ability to manage stress and emotions positively impacts their academic performance and relationships with classmates.

Students who engage in activities and athletics have higher levels of emotional regulation, resilience, and cognitive function to respond to a variety of psychological conditions and situations (Eather, Wade, Pankowiak, & Eime, 2023). Brain functions such as memory and learning are also improved by wellness. Furthermore, the regular exercise associated with some of the activities and athletics in schools improves mood and provides an atmosphere of overall health and well-being (Eather et al., 2023).

Students with emotional wellness attend school more regularly, manage their stress in productive ways, sleep better, and become more resilient in the face of larger life-affecting issues such as depression.

Behavior, Attendance, and Graduation

Studies show when a student is engaged in extracurricular activities and athletics, especially when steadily engaged, there are a myriad of positive benefits to the educational environment; these benefits include fostering greater school perseverance leading to decreased dropout rates, increased attendance rates, and increased school engagement (Thouin et al., 2022). Furthermore, they will collect fewer behavioral referrals throughout their time in school, keeping them present in the classroom for instruction to take place (Eldridge et al., 2014). Adolescent development expert and doctor of education Éliane Thouin and colleagues (2022) frame it well in their findings, which show that offering a variety of options for extracurricular activities to drive multiple relationships on campus is more important than encouraging a specific type of activity when seeking to impact the school culture. The study also recognizes that these results can't always be controlled as there are several non-voluntary reasons for students not being able to participate. The goal is to create the offerings and get the students attached to the school in as many ways as possible. At that point, students who participate in activities and athletics perhaps become more committed to the mission of the school and are less likely to create the resistance that would otherwise get them in trouble. Students who participate in activities and athletics and receive the guidance, structure, and support that these activities provide are less likely to drop out (Crispin, 2017). This is especially important in schools serving high-risk populations. Giving students a strong, caring, viable peer group gives them the accountability to stay in school, and hopefully love their work. Keeping students connected to clubs and teams works as a social leverage point against quitting school.

Stress Management and Sleep

Students in K–12 education must remain healthy as they grow and learn in school. Getting enough sleep is paramount. Participation in activities and athletics has the potential to increase social skills for those involved and to result in better time management and improved self-esteem (Venkataraman & Dheivamani, 2021). Better time management and self-esteem development can lead to improved sleep patterns, as students are able to create and adhere to consistent sleep schedules, thereby reducing stress and promoting relaxation (Lemola, Räikkönen, Gomez, & Allemand, 2013; Osmun, 2024).

For example, a student who participates in a sports team learns to balance practices, games, and schoolwork, which helps them develop a routine that includes a regular bedtime (Meltzer, McNally, Wahlstrom, & Plog, 2019). Furthermore, students involved in these activities report better sleep. This is likely because exercise, deep oxygen intake, and a busy schedule encourage a more consistent sleep routine. Another illustration is a student involved in a drama club who finds that the structured practice sessions and performances help them wind down and prepare for sleep more effectively (Meltzer et al., 2019). Finally, participation in activities and athletics also leads to less stress through exercise, being in a group, and having structure and peer support (Venkataraman & Dheivamani, 2021). Activities and athletics support these potential outcomes.

Resilience

Resilience is defined as the mental ability to recover quickly from stress, adversity, failure, and even trauma. From a mental health standpoint, resilience involves not only bouncing back from difficult experiences but also growing stronger and more resourceful as a result (Resilience, n.d.). It is a critical skill that enables individuals to navigate life's challenges with greater ease and confidence, thereby promoting overall psychological well-being (Resilience, n.d.).

For middle school students, resilience might manifest in their classroom behavior. Consider a middle school student who receives a lower grade than expected on a significant exam. Rather than feeling defeated, this student seeks feedback from the teacher, identifies areas for improvement, and diligently works on enhancing their skills. This proactive approach not only improves their academic performance but also builds their capacity to handle setbacks constructively.

In high school, students practice resilience in extracurricular activities. Imagine a high school athlete who suffers an injury just before an important competition. Instead of giving up, the student focuses on their rehabilitation, stays engaged with the team, and supports teammates from the sidelines. This demonstrates resilience by showing determination to recover, adapt, and find new ways to contribute, even when faced with physical limitations.

The ability to be resilient is one of the most important personal capacities that can lead to a healthy and happy life. Engagement in activities and athletics has been shown to help students develop more resiliency (Wang, Li, & Yao, 2024). This benefit no doubt emerges as activities and athletics ask participants to face challenges, setbacks, and difficult skill-building moments almost every day. Practice and participation give students a chance to experience success and experience the challenge of fighting through what's difficult or seemingly unattainable.

Depression

Involvement in athletics and extracurricular activities can play a crucial role in mitigating depression among students. Participating in sports, clubs, and other organized activities can provide a sense of purpose, improve self-esteem, and offer opportunities for social interaction (CDC, 2024b). These activities can help students build resilience, develop coping skills, and create a supportive community.

Depression is defined as a "negative affective state, ranging from unhappiness and discontent to an extreme feeling of sadness, pessimism, and despondency, that interferes with daily life" (Depression, n.d.). It is more than just feeling sad; it is a mental health disorder that can cause physical symptoms, such as pain, weight changes, sleep disturbances, and lack of energy (Depression, n.d.). Gratefully, we are doing better than previous generations at recognizing what depression can mean for K–12 students.

For K–12 students, depression can manifest in various ways. For high school students, depression might show up as a sudden drop in academic performance, withdrawal from friends and activities, irritability, and changes in eating or sleeping patterns (VanDerBill, 2021). For example, a high school student might stop participating in sports or clubs they once enjoyed, and their grades may start to decline.

In elementary school students, depression might be harder to identify but can still have significant impacts. It may present as persistent sadness, frequent crying, complaints of physical aches and pains, and a lack of interest in playing with friends (American Academy of Pediatrics, n.d.). For instance, an elementary student might become unusually quiet, refuse to go to school, or show a sudden disinterest in activities they previously loved.

However, it's important to recognize that while involvement in these activities can be beneficial, it is not a cure-all. Students who are struggling with depression may need additional support from mental health professionals, teachers, and family members. Schools can also implement mental health programs and provide resources to help students manage their mental health (Rix, 2022). Simply put, depression is too important to ignore in schools. It can't be addressed or solved by one effort, or another. It requires a constellation of engagements by heart-based educators like you. Clearly, athletics and activities play a role, and likely, a very positive one.

Crime, Aggression, and Antisocial Behavior

Students who participated in activities and athletics have been shown over time to demonstrate significantly less crime, aggression, or antisocial behavior (Wang et al., 2024). This can be due to a lot of factors. Specifically, the prevalence of crime, aggression, and antisocial behavior would be checked to some degree by a strong peer group that is associated with activities and athletics within a school. Furthermore, crimes committed by teenagers have historically taken place within a few hours after school, in the later afternoon before parents arrive home after work. It is this golden hour of potential that often gets students in trouble. Participation in activities and athletics simply make students less available to commit crimes or, in some cases, to be victims of them (Jugl, Bender, & Lösel, 2021). These lowered percentages of adverse behaviors can be attributed to the protective factors that come with participation. With coaches and support systems in place, there can be a reduction in antisocial behaviors, which helps reduce violence and delinquency while increasing the well-being of the student (Jugl, Bender, & Lösel, 2021).

After Graduation

Participation in activities and athletics during K–12 education lays the foundation for many positive lifelong outcomes even after high school. From improved physical health and fitness to enhanced career readiness and civic engagement, the following text will lay out exactly how students will feel the benefits of a well-rounded school experience involving extracurricular activities. These experiences promote better overall well-being and help build essential skills, social relationships, and a sense of community involvement that contribute to a fulfilling adult life.

Lifelong Fitness Habits

Those who participate in activities and athletics have a special opportunity to build lifelong fitness habits. Physically active K–12 students tend to have a lower risk of future illness and some enjoy better cardio, muscular, and overall fitness outcomes (Bedard, St. John, Bremer, Graham, & Cairney, 2019). This includes better development of bones, muscles, ligaments, and tendons, leading to less debilitating adult injuries years after K–12 education activities and athletics are over.

Students who engage in regular physical activities, such as running, swimming, or team sports like soccer and basketball, tend to maintain these habits into adulthood, which contributes to ongoing health benefits. These activities improve cardiovascular health, reduce the risk of chronic diseases such as obesity and type 2 diabetes, and enhance overall physical fitness (CDC, 2024d).

Additionally, involvement in school athletics promotes better muscular strength and endurance. Physical activities like gymnastics, weight training, and dance not only help in building and maintaining muscle mass but also improve flexibility and coordination, which are essential for overall physical health (World Health Organization, 2024b). This kind of muscular development during the formative years can reduce the risk of musculoskeletal problems later in life.

Moreover, activities that promote bone health, such as basketball, tennis, and other weight-bearing exercises, are crucial during adolescence when bones are still growing. These activities help in developing strong bones and reducing the risk of osteoporosis and fractures in later years (World Health Organization, 2024b).

An example of a student who benefited from lifelong fitness habits is John, who participated in high school track and field. He continued to run regularly into adulthood, maintaining his cardiovascular health and overall fitness. Now in his sixties, John enjoys a healthy lifestyle with minimal health issues.

Another example is Sarah, who played volleyball in middle school and continued to engage in various physical activities throughout her life. Her commitment to fitness has helped her maintain strong bones and muscles, reducing her risk of injuries and chronic diseases.

Establishing lifelong fitness habits early on can lead to healthier lifestyle choices in adulthood, reducing the risk of chronic diseases and promoting overall well-being (CDC, 2024a).

Career Readiness and Skill Transfer

Activities and athletics allow students to be responsible, follow directions, lead when needed, and problem solve (Morgan, Bush, & Bowles, 2022). Activities and athletics have been shown longitudinally to provide participants with a greater likelihood of full-time employment after school is over (Morgan et al., 2022; National Federation of State High School Associations, 2014). Engagement in activities and athletics tends to lead to better professional and social networks, getting a job, and keeping a job easier (Boone, 2015). Team sports and activities foster relationships, communication, and empathy. This allows for the enhancement of social circles and the ability to learn to work together toward a common goal.

Civic Engagement

Civic engagement refers to the active participation of individuals in their communities to address public concerns, influence decision making, and contribute to the common good (Youth.gov, 2023). It encompasses a wide range of activities, including voting, volunteering, advocating for causes, and joining local organizations. Civic engagement is essential for fostering a sense of responsibility and ownership among citizens, promoting democratic values, and improving societal well-being (Youth.gov, 2023).

Participation in sports and extracurricular activities helps students develop important life skills, such as teamwork, leadership, and communication. These skills are crucial for effective civic engagement and to collaborate with others, advocate for their communities, and take on leadership roles (Morgan et al., 2022). Additionally, student-athletes are more likely to engage in community service and volunteer work, which further enhances their sense of civic responsibility and commitment to making a positive impact on society (National Federation of State High School Associations, 2014).

Being involved in activities and athletics, students are more likely to serve their community, volunteer, and vote. This makes for happier, more well-rounded adults and stronger, more enhanced communities (Sepanik & Brown, 2021). Research shows that students who participate in athletics and activities are more likely to become engaged citizens as adults. A study by the NCAA finds that student-athletes are more likely to vote, volunteer, and participate in community service compared to their non-athlete peers (NCAA, 2021). This increased civic engagement can lead to higher levels of success after high school, including higher salaries and greater community involvement (Kniffin, Wansink, & Shimizu, 2015). By fostering a culture of civic responsibility and providing opportunities for students to develop essential skills, student athletics and activities contribute to the development of well-rounded, engaged citizens who are prepared to make a positive impact on their communities.

Benefits to Teachers

Advisors, coaches, and teachers (ACTs) also benefit from students' participation in activities and athletics. By supporting students in these extracurricular endeavors, ACTs can expect more engaged and motivated classroom environments. The presence of authentic leadership among coaches and advisors, as well as the opportunity to form deeper relationships, contributes to greater job satisfaction and a sense of purpose. These combined elements emphasize the overall benefit that activities and athletics have on school culture.

Job Satisfaction and Engagement in School Life

Job satisfaction for teachers refers to the level of contentment and fulfillment they experience in their professional roles (Tang, Wang, Liu, & Li, 2020). Research indicates that teachers who feel satisfied with their jobs often believe they are making a positive impact on their students' lives and see themselves as part of a larger process (Tang et al., 2020). They also benefit from deep and responsive relationships with students, parents, and colleagues, which enhance their sense of connection and purpose (Tang et al., 2020). Recent studies show that job satisfaction among teachers is relatively low, with only about one-third of teachers reporting high levels of satisfaction (Braga, Hurst, Greenwood, Zanetti, & Mandapat, 2024). Factors such as salary, administrative support, and student behavior significantly influence their job satisfaction (Braga et al., 2024).

To that end, as school leaders, we must do everything possible to make a change and to make it better for teachers. We have good news! Involvement in school activities such as coaching or advising student athletics and activities has been shown to enhance job satisfaction among teachers. For instance, a study by the department of educational management, planning, and policy at the University of Malaysia finds that the extra effort of coaching and advising enhances teachers' sense of purpose and engagement with the community they serve, leading to higher job satisfaction (Hoque, Wang, Qi, & Norzan, 2023). The visibility of the impact in these roles can be more immediate and visceral compared to the long-term benefits of classroom teaching (Hoque et al., 2023).

The Story of Ahmad

Ahmad had been teaching for ten years and found himself increasingly disengaged and disheartened with his profession. Attending staff meetings started to become torturous, and he felt increasingly disconnected from whatever purpose in teaching he once felt. The daily routine had become monotonous, and the spark he once felt seemed to have faded. It wasn't until he took on the role of coaching the school's speech and debate team that things began to change. Initially, he was hesitant, unsure if this additional responsibility would reignite his passion for teaching. However, he soon found himself invigorated by the energy and enthusiasm of his students and by the time spent with them and other teachers involved in OST time.

Working with the speech and debate team allowed Ahmad to witness firsthand the growth and development of his students in ways he hadn't experienced in the classroom. He saw them gain confidence, improve their critical-thinking skills, and learn the art of persuasive communication. He also got to know his students, their parents, their dreams, and their concerns. He also learned more about what he could do to serve, which made him feel useful. The immediate and tangible impact he had on their lives reminded him of the reasons he became a teacher in the first place. Coaching the team rekindled his love for teaching and made him a more effective educator. Ahmad's renewed sense of purpose and connection with his students translated into his classroom, where he approached lessons with fresh enthusiasm and creativity, which benefitted him and his students.

Benefits to the School

In addition to providing benefits to individual students and ACTs, creating an engaged culture of activities and athletics brings overall benefits to schools. As detailed in the following sections, a strong intersectional student culture leads to increased enthusiasm, engagement, and community connections.

Enthusiasm and Engagement

School culture is always under construction every day. The priorities, the actions, the deeds pursued, the deeds ignored, the words said, and the words unspoken all lead to the construction of a culture. Good or bad, inviting or isolating, engaging or boring, the culture is always under construction, and the opportunity to connect is always there (Coronado, Kwok, & Lee, 2022; Denaver, 2023).

While more research needs to be done on some of the more discreet impacts of activities and athletics on school culture, we know that students often report finding remembrances of their school in association with communications they had with their fellow classmates and teachers, many times pursuing activities beyond the school day (Denaver, 2023). Furthermore, research concludes that when schools have well-maintained athletic facilities and activity spaces, students overall have a greater sense of pride and well-being about the activities they are participating in, the schools they attend, and the school culture (Coronado et al., 2022; McCarthy, 2000). We can't guarantee your school culture will be better with the pursuit of highly engaging activities and athletics, but our experiences tell us it will likely move you in the right direction.

Community Engagement and Overall Support

Casey once worked on a comprehensive but unpublished study that evaluated several interesting variables. He looked at new money levies in Ohio that were passed the first time they were offered to citizens within the community. New money levies, in this case, revolved around asking community members to approve a tax on their property to help fund the ongoing and ascending costs of running schools. In this study, he examined the success rate of new money levies and any potential relationship with the presence of a winning football team. This study assumed that the excitement that revolved around the community with a winning football team would likely create greater momentum in the community and perhaps help to sell the new money levies. Casey and his research team found a statistically significant pattern between communities being more likely to pass a tax levy if their football team won their league title or had a winning record and momentum in the community (Reason, n.d.).

While this study remains unpublished, anecdotally it does point to an interesting fact. When communities hear about successful activities and athletics programs and can participate and otherwise observe the positive outcomes, the positive feelings in the community are more likely to be expressed. This results in things like higher degrees of participation in voting for levies as well as likely a greater opportunity for volunteering and otherwise supporting the school in any way they can.

Conclusion

The presence of quality activities and athletics programming can improve academic outcomes; stimulate critical thinking, higher GPAs, college attendance, and post-high school graduation planning; and reduce the dropout likelihood. Furthermore, we know that activities and athletics improve student behavior, drive a sense of joy and well-being within students, help them sleep better, and reduce their stress. It also makes them more resilient, less depressed, and less likely to participate in crime and aggressive and antisocial behavior, including participation in gangs. They are also less likely to have an unwanted pregnancy (Sabo, Miller, Melnick, & Heywood, 2004). Finally, you learned in this chapter that participation in activities and athletics has positive lifelong outcomes and the likelihood of full-time employment, higher salaries, and the development of social and professional networks. Civic engagement and leadership have resulted from activities and athletics programs. The following chapter will detail the precedent set by a long history of activities and athletics in schools, gather lessons from it, and use that information to look toward the future of school culture.

*History is not a burden on the memory
but an illumination of the soul.*

—John Dalberg-Acton

CHAPTER 2

UNDERSTAND THE PAST, PRESENT, AND FUTURE OF ACTIVITIES AND ATHLETICS IN SCHOOL

We've all likely both observed and hopefully attempted to live the George Santayana quote, "those who cannot remember the past are condemned to repeat it" (Santayana, 1905, p. 284). Unfortunately, in the field of education there are far too many instances where, perhaps due to decades-long hypnotic acceptance, we have simply continued to march forward without much adjustment or even consideration for changes that might be possible. This is true about many elements of K–12 education, as well as athletics and activities. The purpose of this chapter is to highlight that, at its most basic level, it's difficult to make progress individually, as a team, or as an organization if you don't understand what came before, what's going on now, and what future trends may emerge. In this chapter, we'll seek to understand the elements of the past that shape us, the opportunities and challenges of the present, and the enticing opportunities we may observe in the future.

The Past

Activities and athletics beyond the school day are nothing new in the educational system. These activities have been implemented in schools throughout the United States and around the world since the 19th century (Burley, 2020). Originally implemented as a way to encourage more organized behavior and supervision for students, they quickly found that the activities brought about characteristics in the participants that were "fundamental to the development of discipline and morality" (Burley, 2020). These activities started to gain traction and flourished in the mid- to late 19th century when schools developed teams and began to play other schools in an organized fashion (Burley, 2020). In the United States, extracurricular activities took two different paths. According to an article by sociology professor and author Hilary L. Friedman (2013), extracurricular activities were dominated by two groups. The majority included students without parental supervision who made up the teams that competed with other schools. The other group included students with more parental supervision and support who participated in the noncompetitive activities, such as dance and music. That changed dramatically after World War II in the mid-20th century when middle- and upper-class students began to dominate the competitive activities.

From the late 1940s through the 1970s, extracurricular activities continued to grow rapidly. Due to fears that competition amongst elementary students would cause harm to the self-esteem of those who weren't as competitive as their peers, policies targeted extracurricular activities for middle and high school students (Baker & Tracey, 2020). Even with these policies in place, extracurriculars catered mostly to male students until the passing of Title IX in 1972. This massive shift in policy opened up opportunities for female students (Baker & Tracey, 2020). Since the 1970s, these activities have continued to become a staple in the educational environment, garnering billions of dollars for companies that have filled a niche for equipment, training, and everything in between, to allow students to become competitive in their chosen activities and sports. According to 2020 Census data, 44 percent of boys and 35 percent of girls participated in a sport, while 37 percent of girls and 27 percent of boys participated in clubs or lessons. These percentages were all up from previous numbers taken in 1998 (Mayol-García, 2022). Even after the COVID-19 pandemic, it seems involvement in these activities has bounced back and continues to grow. The National Federation of State High School Associations (NFHS) participation survey data for the 2023–2024 school year show record-breaking participation with over eight million participants, marking the second straight year of growth and breaking the previous record from 2017–2018 (NFHS, 2024). Extracurricular and cocurricular activities have become an integral part of the educational process as schools open their doors to their communities.

With this brief history in mind, let's examine several trends that continue to have a powerful, historically reverberating impact on your attempt to build strong athletics and activities programs.

Activities and Athletics Were Largely Extracurricular

It wasn't until the second half of the 20th century that educators began to realize the importance of activities and athletics as a complement to what we do in the classroom (Mintz & Rutter, 2016). The notion that these activities were extracurricular was taken much more literally before that time. These activities were seen as high interest and connected to the school, but aligning them with our education programming is still a relatively recent phenomenon.

Post–World War II studies show major connections to extracurricular activities and the educational process and find "activities provide supervision, guidance, and engage youth in enriched learning experiences. By participating in these activities, youth are better able to resist unsafe behaviors such as drug and alcohol use, gang involvement, and criminal activities" (Unterschutz, 2016).

Sports Were Unfairly Prioritized Over Other Activities

As we think about school programming, even the words *activities* and *athletics* are probably used in your own vernacular quite ubiquitously. We have come to associate the two. However, this wasn't always the case. Historically, sports have been seen as the programmatic priority. This concept wasn't even challenged until around the midpoint of the 20th century (Howard, 2023). At that time, we saw the expansion of student activities and the start of leaders suggesting that student activities are just as important as sports programming (Howard, 2023). Before then, they were seen as largely secondary in focus. This is important because sentiments of the past linger much longer than most people assume, and student activities in some schools must continue to fight for the appropriate amount of attention.

Schools and administrators started to see that athletics only served a certain portion of the population while there were many who participated in other activities that could benefit from the character traits and skills developed through competition.

Schools around the United States and Canada started to implement more and more activities into the school day and after school. Activities began to serve those who did not fit the athletic "mold." Walk into schools across North America and you will see teams and competitions developed for band, speech and debate, theater, and a myriad of others. The term *extracurricular* became a term that was all-inclusive. Just ask the esports teams that have emerged in the past few years.

Sometimes, activity programs are referred to as extracurricular; they are, in fact, an extension of the classroom. Through athletics and performing arts, students learn essential life skills such as teamwork, self-discipline, self-confidence, hard work, and fair play (Howard, 2023).

Gender Discrimination Affected Recruitment and Practices

Before we began to more thoughtfully reflect on contemporary images of schooling in the late 20th century, much of our educational focus on sports and activities revolved around activities that featured male students (Horn & Smith, 2019). Before 1972, it wasn't uncommon to offer boys' basketball without any access whatsoever to a basketball experience for female athletes (Bell, 2008). Title IX was a law brought forth by Congress and signed by President Richard Nixon in 1972 with the goal of rectifying this inequality. This new law would prohibit "sex discrimination in any educational program or activity receiving any type of federal financial aid" (Women's Sports Foundation, n.d.). In July of 1974, the scope was narrowed for educational athletics as sports were specifically targeted as a program that must comply with the equality language of Title IX. A federal directive in 1975 gave high schools and colleges a deadline of July 1978 to comply with the new Title IX language. This directive allowed three years for implementation and began a shift in resources and time for both college and high school programs to best serve not only male activities but also female activities. These changes sparked a shift in participation, watching growth for female athletes of 456 percent from 1972 to 2008 (Sportanddev, 2022).

Due to the increase in participation of women in sports, American women were also able to progress in other aspects of their lives. A study from 2010 finds that participation in sports helps increase employment and education levels in America. Moreover, it has also been noted that Title IX was able to create better access to sports facilities for women.

We hope to see these numbers increase as more schools across the country recognize the benefits of activities and athletics and continue to implement programs that benefit our female students.

Student Activities and Athletics Built Social Networks

Preceding the emergence of omnipresent internet connectivity and social networking, students embraced activities and athletics as mechanisms for building their social network. Assistant professor for sport administration Payton J. Stensland and colleagues (2019) label these connections as *social anchors*. Drawing from a study on the concept of social capital, researchers from the Laboratory for the Study of Sport Management at the University of Kansas, Aaron W. Clopton and Bryan L. Finch (2011), reconceptualize social anchors to include the bonding and bridging form of social capital development. Specifically, these researchers refer to social anchors as "any institution—which can take the form of social, economic, physical, political, legal, etc.— that acts as a support for the development and maintenance of social capital and social networks" (Clopton & Finch, 2011, p. 70).

Athletics and activities provide social anchors for students within the educational space. Educators and parents alike began to see these as useful tools for students. How many times have we heard teams referred to as family and the countless stories of ACTs saving lives by both filling voids and supplementing needs within the social constructs of activities and athletics? Brandon experienced this firsthand as he moved several times with his family to take new coaching positions. Each move found his children engaging in relationships quickly through extracurricular activities. A sampling of thousands of responses regarding their "why" behind activities yielded comments such as, "I participate on my high school team because they're more than just my team, they're my family, and I don't know where I'd be today without them," and "In a large school system, student-athletes have the ability to meet and become friends with more students through extracurricular programs. In addition, school programs can increase school spirit and help students stay plugged into their school and community" (Howard, 2023). These social networks tied students to school and all the benefits that come with it.

The Present

Let's observe some trends that undoubtedly impact your leadership in this important area. By better understanding the evolving landscape, the impact we create will be more focused and dynamic.

Club Sports and Activities Are Prominent and Profitable

Since 2014, club sports or profit-driven sports not run by educational institutions have emerged as a significantly profitable business opportunity for coaches and entrepreneurs alike. A study by the National Association of Sports Commissions finds that the travel industry around club sports brings in $7 billion (Smith, 2014). On top of that, the club sports registered as nonprofits brought in an estimated $5 billion (Smith, 2014). This study recognizes that parents are willing to invest a significant amount of time and financial resources in the development of athletic and activity experiences for their children. According to a 2023 study, parents spend an average of $731 per student on extracurricular activities, and this number shows no signs of letting up (Adedoyin, 2023). With colleges putting less emphasis on standardized testing, students are looking to make their college applications more impressive by engaging in extracurricular activities. Districts that fail to invest in these extracurricular activities allow these external clubs to swoop in and start filling the void. In the worst-case scenarios, this allows profit-seeking coaches to invest heavily in students with otherwise marginal interests and talents in a particular area and persuade them to join their clubs. Profit-driven clubs can potentially take advantage of students because they often do not provide the same care for the student that an educational-based athletic program would. Author Brandon Larson sees this often in his role as an athletic director when students get cut from a tryout, only to have parents come to his office to claim how amazing their student is because their club coach sold them a bill of goods to keep club fees coming in, rather than having an honest conversation with the family on the student's actual skill level. In a conversation with a club soccer coach, Brandon was told that they only keep "B" teams to help pay for the "A" team's needs and keep the club afloat. We recognize that this is not all clubs, but that presents a large difference between education-based activities and profit-driven activities.

While we don't necessarily see club sports and activities as comprehensively negative, we do recognize that their presence has created some challenging dynamics for K–12 education. For example, it's not uncommon for students to forgo their school's athletics or activities programming in the face of an emergent club activity. They may posit that competing on a club golf team may generate better competition than doing so at the state level with the school. This represents for coaches and advisors the challenge of competition that simply has never existed before. This is a compounding problem, as the dynamic causes families to feel like they must have their students specialize at a young age to give them an opportunity to compete at the high school level.

There Is Less School Loyalty

Throughout the 20th century, participation in activities and athletics was driven by collectivism (Amaro, 2020). There was a great sense of working toward the community's good, be it for the pride of the city or the school. While this trend continues, especially for our strong and robust schools, we recognize that the availability of so many educational options has created a little less loyalty to a local environment. Stanford University High School online (https://onlinehighschool.stanford.edu), for example, has emerged as a major player in recruiting high school students throughout the world, and a student in your community may decide to forgo your local middle school or high school for the opportunity to compete internationally in an online environment based in Northern California. An offering like this takes away the ability for students to be tied into the local school or community as their participation in sports or activities would have to be club or private-based, rather than school-based. Prior to the internet, these opportunities did not exist, and the potential to connect to the community was higher. In comparison, Arizona is a school-choice state in which a student may choose any junior high school or senior high school they want if the school could enroll them.

This open enrollment culture has caused schools to become magnets for certain types of programs, sports, or activities. A premier musician may choose a school that develops their musical talents, while an athlete may decide on a school that has sent several players to major colleges in their sport. Students choosing to leave their community schools has forced the state to look at how they structure their schools to be attractive to as many students as possible. These options, coupled with technology that can make the world around us meet our own settings and standards (rather than asking us to adapt to the world around us), have made the learning experience far more personalized. This dilemma makes it challenging for coaches and advisors to teach the concept of teamwork.

Students Are Less Reliant on Activities and Athletics to Build Community

While previous generations needed a chessboard or a playing field to find playmates and connect, students in the early 2000s learned at an early age that the click of a mouse would introduce them to playmates engaged in a variety of activities. This shift to socializing mostly on the web has led to several challenging and concerning social factors and some negative outcomes for students and parents alike (Kolhar, Kazi, & Alameen, 2021). The truth is, as school practitioners, we must recognize that we are competing with incalculable amounts of web-driven distractions and access points that represent a challenge to participation in activities and athletics (The Social Institute, 2023).

While this may be a frustrating dynamic, it is a permanent change to the social landscape, and advisors and coaches alike must simply recognize this challenge and commit to capturing and keeping the attention of students. Put another way, the ACTs recruiting in the 2020s have far more distractions than most of us can ever conceive, and it will take extra effort to recruit them. We must be willing to observe the fact that recruitment and retention structures and expectations of participation and engagement are going to be driven by a new standard that will need to be considered when implementing strategies to create commitment. The reduction in participation in school activities has been linked to increased feelings of isolation and decreased community cohesion among students (Furda & Shuleski, 2019).

Additionally, the lack of participation in school activities has been associated with reduced opportunities for students to build social networks and make friends, which are crucial for their emotional and social development (Tafesse, 2022). This trend has also been linked to lower levels of school engagement and academic performance (Tafesse, 2022).

The Desired Future

We are incurably optimistic about the future in K–12 education, athletics, and activities. That said, we will only continue being optimistic if leaders keep an eye on the future and build programming and possibilities that serve students, parents, and communities alike. Here are some observations and anticipatory plans for the future that we think will make a difference.

Active Recruitment Will Be Necessary

Coaches and advisors are going to have to work harder than ever to market their programming options. They can't just assume that being in the community is enough. Trends are already emerging in schools wherein coaches and club leaders must actively recruit and campaign to help compete and maintain relevance in the school community. The ease of access to information, the increased role of social media, and the idea of school choice gaining popularity in parts of the country are changing the future. For example, to get enough student participants to have a large marching band or a football team with plenty of players, ACTs advertise on social media to get students' attention. Social media has rapidly increased how quickly a school can communicate with its community as well as with anyone in the world. Referencing the previous section on lack of loyalty, parents are more frequently personalizing their child's experience and looking for the best product. This is a massive shift from the turn of the 20th century when students, for the most part, attended the school that their geographical boundary dictated or chose to attend a private school. The increase in number of charter schools created an even greater need for schools to recruit their students. In Arizona, it is common to hear advertisements on the radio or billboards to enroll in a local school or school district based on the programs and offerings of that institution. This will be a major shift to more of a business model for educators rather than traditional models as these ideas begin to expand. Competition and innovation can and will continue to discover new and improved ways to engage learners at a high level.

Equity of Access Will Increase

Our awareness of moving away from programming that emphasized boys' sports was a step toward a world where equitable access is both the law and the practice (Bell, 2008). In the future, we will continue to get better at not only complying with the laws of access but also excelling in our capacity to make every student feel invited to engage. Our strategies will continue to improve and make students feel more welcome than ever to be part of a variety of experiences that shape their growth moving forward.

Additionally, we are beginning to understand at a deep and inextricable level the appropriateness and humanity of equal access and the overarching advantage for everyone involved. Undoubtedly, in the early era of equal access, well-intended educators might have seen the offering of these expanded opportunities as an act of kindness or the right thing to do for the students who may have been previously denied. We have entered an era and will continue to move toward the sensibility that a deeply inculcated commitment to equality simply makes every aspect of our school better for everyone. It makes it more inviting and engaging, while the commitment becomes a ubiquitous element of who we are.

We Will Better Understand the Impact of Activities and Sports on Learning

The more we learn about learning, the more we realize the importance of physical movement. Neurological research suggests that human beings are designed to move between seven and fifteen miles a day in a hunting and gathering posture (Harvard Medical School, 2024). This is one of the reasons why increasing emphasis on walking and movement as a conduit to problem solving has become so popular. It is not uncommon in corporate America to have a senior vice president run a meeting from a walking desk in front of a Zoom camera (Doherty & Forés Miravalles, 2019).

It is crucial to continue to emphasize the health and well-being of students and staff alike, as it acts as a conduit to improving learning. This will bring a slightly different yet accelerated focus to activities and athletics (Xu, n.d.). More programs are beginning to embrace this concept as we've seen bands participating in cardiovascular workouts, theater students participating in yoga, and clubs conducting active gatherings to get their blood pumping (Harvard Medical School, 2024). This is part of the reason why we emphasize the importance of getting everyone involved in activities and athletics as well as academics. A student who is supremely gifted in coding and participates in coding competitions would be well served to engage on the soccer or cross-country teams, if for no other reason than to keep their body moving as a mechanism for expanding their gift (Doherty & Forés Miravalles, 2019). Just because they are differentiated in their performance in computer programming doesn't mean that they aren't holistically benefited by committing to athletics and the gift of movement to further accelerate their talent (Annie E. Casey

Foundation, 2024a). Conversely, a student-athlete can benefit from expanding their abilities off the court or field with the likes of fine arts or clubs. Using the same leadership and problem-solving abilities they learned in their sport could bode well for them in a Model UN competition or competing with the Future Farmers of America (FFA) club (Harvard Medical School, 2024). Student learning benefits from a well-rounded slate of activities.

We Will See More Expectations for Growth and Development Opportunities

Technology is an integrated part of students' lives. They see social spaces and virtual, online connecting points as inextricably connected (Annie E. Casey Foundation, 2024b). While there are many challenging aspects to leading school opportunities with this type of endless access to millions of outside perspectives, they will, in some capacity, forever weigh in on everything we do. If you offer a new activity in your community, it will be compared to long-standing options in other corners of the world. Both the opportunities and potential challenges will be quickly shared and discussed. Not-so-quiet virtual rumblings may occur about a much-needed offering that never crossed school leaders' minds. This could lead to an avalanche of virtual support and drive leaders to consider what is being discussed. An example would be the recent evolution of esports. According to a market analysis from Fortune Business Insights (2024), the esports industry has a global market value of $1.72 billion and is expected to grow to over $9 billion by 2034. The quick advancement of esports led to people in communities pushing for this new opportunity to be evaluated within the schools and governing associations. These communications would ultimately pave the way for state associations to adopt this activity as a sanctioned event, with schools offering esports classes just as they would a band class or basketball class. These changes could lead to potential backlash for schools and administrations that fail to keep up with the wants and needs of their communities.

In other words, if you have a solid plan for anticipating the needs of the future of your activities and athletics program, you're less susceptible to the virtual mob that may come together and simply decide that a new option is required. If you don't have a solid plan for what you're doing, your rationale for avoiding a whiplash response may be less defensible. Social media posts, neighborhood groups, and communication platforms in your community can quickly become toxic and create culture and perception issues that can impact the support for the school or district. Essentially, the internet opens up opportunities for stakeholders to weigh in on decisions that they wouldn't have had previously—all the more reason for the adoption of Rally.

Conclusion

Educators are on a limited timeline to impact the lives of their students. We will continue to evolve and, there will be some challenges along the way that we can't possibly expect. However, there will also be new opportunities. Part of what we hope that you continue to embrace with the Rally model is the development of a set of core principles that will help you to evolve your way of thinking and to keep your programming consistent.

Culture is the heartbeat of a school. It determines the life and success of the educational experience.

— *Steve Gruenert and Todd Whitaker*

CHAPTER 3

DEFINE SCHOOL CULTURE

The goal of this chapter is twofold. First, successful practitioners understand that, in every sense of the word, school culture is the courier for your results (Reason & Reason, 2011). So, we will be providing a simple and quite actionable illustration of school culture and review the process of its construction. More importantly, we will be talking about the role of athletics and activities in constructing that culture and the steps that school leaders can take to allow this important element of school life to improve school culture and enhance access to your best results.

This chapter is devoted to three things. First, we will define school culture, specifically in relation to these activities. Secondly, we will talk about how it is built in a school. Finally, we will conclude with an even stronger case for the relationship between activities and athletics and the ongoing maintenance of this essential element.

What School Culture Is

School culture can be defined as the guiding beliefs and values evident in the way a school operates, encompassing the interactions, behaviors, and shared vision of its community (Bridwell-Mitchell, 2018). This is a phenomenon that can be felt and observed by everyone. If the culture is warm and inviting, a stranger will feel welcomed and eager to engage (Bridwell-Mitchell, 2018).

School culture deeply impacts the learning potential of both staff and students. If a student feels unsafe, physically or psychologically, their learning potential is significantly reduced (Reason & Reason, 2011). Similarly, adults can experience frustration when faced with a big task without excitement or engagement, turning it into drudgery (Reason & Reason, 2011). However, when there is a spark of enthusiasm, even an arduous task can become enjoyable and invigorating (Reason & Reason, 2011). This change in perspective is crucial in a school setting, where students and staff need to feel rigorously challenged and accepted.

Creating a positive school culture involves continuous observation and effort to foster a sense of community and shared purpose. Activities and athletics can contribute to this culture, but the commitment to observing and improving the culture is essential (Bridwell-Mitchell, 2018).

Unfortunately, discussions about school culture can sometimes be vague and mystical. It is important to recognize that culture is shaped by daily collective choices (Bridwell-Mitchell, 2018). By understanding and intentionally working on these choices, a more desirable school culture can emerge (Bridwell-Mitchell, 2018).

The Importance of Daily Actions in Generating and Shaping School Culture

School culture is constructed every moment of every day by everything you do and do not do (Reason, 2015). The idea that every single action taken in your school by staff, students, guests, parents, and community members all contribute to the culture may sound overwhelming, but it is true (Gruenert & Whitaker, 2015). For example, if you have a steady diet of volunteerism, a helpful and engaged student council, and warm and reflective teachers, then your daily collective actions power a palpable feeling of warmth. Conversely, if you have a school with rude and disengaged support staff, disconnected parents, and teachers who are focused on retirement or the weekend happy hour more than their students and their learning, the school culture will reflect that, and everyone, especially the students, will feel it (Bridwell-Mitchell, 2018).

Building a Positive School Culture

Creating a positive school culture involves intentional actions and behaviors that foster a sense of community and shared purpose. Here are six practical steps to build a constructive school culture.

1. **Set clear expectations:** Clearly communicate the values and behaviors expected from everyone in the school community. Reinforce these expectations regularly through meetings, announcements, and visual reminders (Dweck, 2016).

2. **Encourage a growth mindset:** Promote the idea that abilities and intelligence can be developed through effort and perseverance. Celebrate both student and teacher successes and efforts rather than just outcomes (Dweck, 2016).

3. **Foster intrinsic motivation:** Create a learning environment where students and staff are motivated by internal satisfaction rather than external rewards. This can be achieved by providing meaningful and engaging activities that align with individual interests and passions (Ryan & Deci, 2000).

4. **Model positive behavior:** Lead by example. When school leaders and teachers exhibit positive behaviors, such as kindness, respect, and enthusiasm, it sets a standard for the entire school community to follow (Gruenert & Whitaker, 2015).

5. **Build relationships:** Take time to build strong, supportive relationships with students, parents, and colleagues. A sense of belonging and connection can significantly enhance the school culture (Bridwell-Mitchell, 2018).

6. **Recognize and address neglect:** Identify areas where neglect may be impacting the school culture, such as littering, tardiness, or disengagement, and take proactive steps to address these issues (Gruenert & Whitaker, 2015).

Living the Culture in Lincoln

Mrs. Thompson, a dedicated teacher at Lincoln High School, noticed that her students were becoming increasingly disengaged and disinterested in their studies. Determined to change the school culture, she decided to incorporate a growth mindset into her classroom. She began by setting clear expectations and frequently reminding her students that intelligence and abilities could be developed through effort and perseverance (Dweck, 2016). She celebrated not just their successes but also their efforts, encouraging them to view challenges as opportunities for growth. She also modeled positive behaviors by showing kindness and enthusiasm in her interactions, which inspired her students to follow suit (Gruenert & Whitaker, 2015).

Simultaneously, the school's principal, Mr. Rodriguez, implemented a schoolwide initiative to foster intrinsic motivation among students and staff. He introduced various engaging activities, including volunteer programs and extracurricular clubs, that aligned with their interests and passions (Ryan & Deci, 2000). One notable success was the creation of a student council that promoted volunteerism and community service, leading to a palpable feeling of warmth and engagement within the school. Mr. Rodriguez also focused on building strong relationships and regularly meeting with parents, students, and teachers to ensure everyone's voices were heard (Bridwell-Mitchell, 2018). As a result, the school culture transformed into a positive and supportive environment where students felt rigorously challenged and accepted. The daily collective choices of the entire school community created a culture of excellence and belonging, demonstrating the powerful impact of intentional actions on school culture (Bridwell-Mitchell, 2018).

School Culture Develops With or Without Intentional Design

The best school leaders have ideas about what it takes to build school culture. They know that every action they take will build toward some sort of feeling that they have about the school, and that feeling has a rippling impact on academics and behavior (Bridwell-Mitchell, 2018). By having a plan, you can set forth activities that serve to reinforce the plan you have for the culture you hope to build. Sadly, without a plan, the lowest common denominator will often win. Toxic school cultures often grow when leaders do not have much of a design and leave the door open to toxic bullies in the school who see the absence of a plan as an opportunity to exert their own strength and impact the school by promoting fear, disengagement, and the like (Elbot & Fulton, 2007). Without a plan, there are many negative consequences for a school to potentially be stuck with the whimsical will of the moment. With a plan, you can implement, monitor, and adjust. The following case studies show school culture in active practice.

CASE STUDY: INTENTIONAL DESIGN FOR POSITIVE CULTURE

At Lincoln Elementary, Principal Johnson had a clear vision for creating a positive school culture. She began by conducting surveys to understand the current climate and identify areas for improvement. Based on the feedback, she implemented a series of initiatives, including professional development for teachers on collaborative practices, regular team-building activities, and a mentorship program for new teachers. Johnson also established a code of conduct and consistently communicated the school's values to students, staff, and parents. Over time, Lincoln Elementary became known for its supportive and inclusive environment, leading to improved student engagement and academic performance (Elbot & Fulton, 2007).

CASE STUDY: LACK OF PLAN LEADS TO TOXIC CULTURE

In contrast, at Jefferson Middle School, there was no plan for building school culture. The principal, Mr. Smith, focused primarily on administrative tasks and left the development of school culture to chance. As a result, a few influential students began to dominate the social environment, promoting negative behaviors and bullying. Teachers felt unsupported and isolated, leading to high turnover rates. The lack of a cohesive plan allowed toxic elements to take root, resulting in a decline in student morale and academic performance (Elbot & Fulton, 2007).

How Culture Is Built

If you don't take action and build a school culture that's consistent with the design you have for the students and community that you serve, the opportunity to make a thriving school culture happen is diminished, and sadly, the risk of unintentionally promoting a disengaged culture increases at the same time. This section of the chapter will focus on how educators, students, and leaders build school culture through a combination of defining a collective mission, vision, values, and goals and using the "front porch focus" method for activities and athletics.

Embrace the Mission, Vision, Values, and Goals

The best schools are powered by clarity. Everyone in the school community must understand the objectives of the organization, and everyone's roles in meeting those objectives. When we refer to leaders, we're not just talking about the school principal or assistant principal. Teacher leaders at every level, parents, and community members will be a greater asset to the school if they understand the mission, vision, values, and goals of the learning institution (Reason & Reason, 2011). Let's get into the details of each of these terms.

- **Mission:** The mission of a school defines why it exists. Usually, these are big-picture ideas that define the overarching impact of the school (DuFour & Reason, 2015). Here is an example of a school mission: "Our mission is to create a collaborative learning community where every student is empowered to achieve their full potential through high-quality instruction, continuous improvement, and a commitment to excellence."

- **Vision:** The vision is something that we must build each and every day to make our mission come true (DuFour & Reason, 2015). A school may have an overarching mission, but the vision can be observed on a Tuesday at noon. For example, you may believe that critical thinking is important to your mission. The vision for making that happen could involve instituting block scheduling and various interdisciplinary activities that demand critical-thinking application. Your action is the vision, and the mission is the broader objective you are pursuing. Here's an example of a school vision: "Our vision is to build a school environment that prepares students for the world of work, collaborates in every way, and cultivates a nurturing and inclusive educational environment where students are inspired to become lifelong learners, critical thinkers, and compassionate leaders, equipped to thrive in a diverse and dynamic world."

- **Values:** The values of a school are defined by a set of behaviors we must enact and traits we should adopt to make the mission and vision come to fruition (DuFour & Reason, 2015). For example, in a middle school, some useful values to adopt would include respect, responsibility, and perseverance. These values are important not only for the students but also for teachers and staff, as they shape how everyone interacts and works together. The values in your school must define how the people consistently behave toward one another. If respect and responsibility are part of your value orientation in your school, then a lived culture will include opportunities to learn and exemplify these qualities, such as through mentorship programs and student leadership initiatives. This ensures that students and staff alike embody these values in their daily interactions and actions. Here is an example statement of values: "Our values, constructed to live our mission and vision, are respect, responsibility, and perseverance. We will live by them every day!"

- **Goals:** In an era of high levels of academic accountability, it is common for schools to set goals imposed by state departments and other external entities. However, DuFour and colleagues (2015) emphasize the importance of schools setting their own goals that are personalized and aligned with their unique contexts. By doing so, schools can achieve more profound and meaningful outcomes. Goals in education are specific, measurable, attainable, relevant, and time-bound (SMART) objectives that guide the efforts of educators and students toward achieving desired educational outcomes (Drew, 2023). SMART goals provide a direction and framework for continuous improvement and success. SMART goals are characterized as being well-defined, trackable, realistic, aligned with broader educational objectives, and anchored to a timeline (O'Neill, 2000). The following are some examples of SMART goals.

1. **Academic SMART goal:**
   - *Specific*—Improve students' reading comprehension skills.
   - *Measurable*—Increase the average reading comprehension test scores by 10 percent.
   - *Achievable*—Provide additional reading support sessions twice a week.
   - *Relevant*—Enhance overall literacy and academic performance.
   - *Time-bound*—Achieve this goal by the end of the school year (Drew, 2023).

2. **Student activity SMART goal (orchestra):**
   - *Specific*—Improve students' musical performance skills in the school orchestra.

- *Measurable*—Increase the number of students who can perform a piece at an intermediate level.
- *Achievable*—Offer extra practice sessions and individual coaching.
- *Relevant*—Foster students' musical talents and appreciation for the arts.
- *Time-bound*—Achieve this goal by the end of the semester (O'Neill, 2000).

By setting personalized SMART goals, schools can better meet the unique needs of their students and foster a more effective learning environment. Every department within the school should have goals and constantly work toward the realization of the mission and vision while living the values simultaneously. To be more specific, we believe that any healthy organization has a set of goals it is pursuing, and those pursuits should be known to everyone. As this book unfolds, you will see that we look at goal setting in a new way as activities and athletics take on a process-focused approach rather than a results-focused approach. There is a great quote from writer James Clear (2018) in his book, *Atomic Habits: An Easy and Proven Way to Build Good Habits and Break Bad Ones*, which sets this tone perfectly:

> When you fall in love with the process rather than the product, you don't have to wait to give yourself permission to be happy. You can be satisfied anytime your system is running. Goals are good for setting a direction, but systems are best for making progress. All big things come from small beginnings. (p. 27)

To bring this section to fruition, we recommend the following tips and strategies for building your own intentional school culture.

1. **Every school should have its own mission, vision, values, and goals:** These elements should be known to everyone, including students, staff, parents, and community. The greater clarity everyone has about the mission, vision, values, and goals of an organization, the more likely it is help will emerge when needed.

2. **The promotion of all the activities and athletics programs should be built around the collective assumptions of the school's mission, vision, values, and goals.** We think this is critical in that the public-facing nature of sports gives us a chance to follow through when we decide on how we're going to react to the emergence of a particular athletic and activity program outcome. Is what you are displaying on the practice field, at the marching band competition, or in the hallway with an outrageously competitive speech and debate coach consistent with the mission, vision, and values of your school? Simply put, you can't let the public presence of various ACTs undermine the direction of the school. Instead, they need to be exemplars and living examples of what they commit to in these important school documents.

3. **It is imperative to take strategic action for bringing a specific culture to life:** What's key for this level of culture construction is the identification of specific actions. What are your systems? What goals or actions do you need to implement to allow the system to engage? For example, if a school wants to promote honest, competitive, and forthright student-athletes and artists, then what specific programmatic actions can be taken to teach these specific elements? In upcoming chapters (beginning in part 2, page 61), we will give you some specific tools to help in this area. In the meantime, start thinking about the overall vision and plan of the program and what success looks like for your programs.

CASE STUDY: SPRINGFIELD'S AMAZING MARCHING BAND

To help illustrate these points, let's take a look at a case study featuring the marching band program in Springfield. Angela has taken over the K–12 chair duties and has worked with her team, her students, and her community to create mission, vision, and values statements for the program. By working together, building the goals has already begun. Here is what they've generated together.

- **Mission statement:** Our mission is to inspire a lifelong appreciation for music, foster artistic growth, and cultivate a sense of community through a comprehensive K–12 band program that nurtures talent, creativity, and discipline in every student.

- **Vision statement:** We envision a vibrant and inclusive band program where every student, from elementary through high school, discovers their musical potential and develops the skills and confidence to perform at their highest level. Through dedication, collaboration, and a commitment to excellence, we aim to enrich the cultural life of our school and community.

- **Values:**
  + *Inclusivity*—Ensure that every student, regardless of background or ability, has the opportunity to participate and succeed in the band program.
  + *Excellence*—Strive for the highest standards in musical performance and personal development.
  + *Community*—Build a supportive and collaborative environment that fosters strong relationships and teamwork.
  + *Growth*—Encourage continuous improvement and lifelong learning in music and beyond.
  + *Passion*—Instill a deep love and appreciation for music in all students.

Here are the SMART goals the team created for the Springfield marching band program.

- **Goal – Elementary level (grades 3–5):** Increase student participation in the introductory music program.
  + *Specific*—Increase the number of third- to fifth-graders participating in the music program.

- *Measurable*—Achieve a 20 percent increase in participation by the end of the school year.
- *Achievable*—Launch a music awareness campaign, including demonstrations and instrument "petting zoos," to generate interest.
- *Relevant*—Foster early musical engagement, and build a foundation for future band participation.
- *Time-bound*—Achieve this goal by the end of the current school year.

- **Goal – Middle school level (grades 7–8):** Increase enrollment in after-school band classes and summer band programs.
  - *Specific*—Increase the number of seventh and eighth graders enrolling in after-school band classes and summer programs.
  - *Measurable*—Achieve a 25 percent increase in enrollment for after-school band classes and a 15 percent increase in summer program participation.
  - *Achievable*—Offer diverse musical activities, including ensemble performances and workshops, and provide transportation for after-school and summer sessions.
  - *Relevant*—Enhance musical skills and foster a deeper commitment to the band program.
  - *Time-bound*—Achieve this goal by the end of the next school year.

- **Goal – High school level (grades 9–12):** Increase participation in the high school marching band.
  - *Specific*—Increase the number of students participating in the high school marching band.
  - *Measurable*—Achieve a 30 percent increase in participation over the next two academic years.
  - *Achievable*—Implement mentorship programs where high school band members mentor

> middle school students and organize community performances to showcase the band's talents.
> + *Relevant*—Strengthen the marching band's presence and reputation within the school and the broader community.
> + *Time-bound*—Achieve this goal within the next two academic years.

Use the "Front Porch Focus" of Activities and Athletics

There are many reasons why activities and athletics play such a big role in the construction of school culture. These school-based initiatives are sometimes the only thing the public ever sees; hence, they sit on the "front porch" of the school's programs. They serve as a visceral and immediate reminder of what is important for the school. For example, perhaps you have a high school of a thousand students who are beating expectations academically and continuing to ascend to new levels of career and college readiness. You may have great attendance rates and few behavioral problems. Yet, if the football team gets into a physical altercation on the field on a Friday night and it makes the news for unsportsmanlike behavior, the entire school could be saddled with a negative reputation. Activities and athletics need to directly and precisely illustrate what the school culture is all about, and it shouldn't be measured by wins and losses.

Furthermore, leaders at all levels, including ACTs, teacher leaders, and community members alike, need to rally together to authentically observe and celebrate front porch examples of behaviors that drive home the mission, vision, values, and goals of the school. If you have a student-athlete; a supremely commited ACT; or a strong, supportive fan base that exemplifies the actions that reinforce your school culture, as a leader, you need to directly call attention to those wonderful attributes and celebrate them publicly and often. The school environment should be well aware of these positive exemplars. When fair-minded, kind, yet rigorous coaches are doing the right things, they need to be rewarded and celebrated. When students demonstrate the kinds of commitment that are essential on the practice field, in competition, and when preparing for a final exam, those committed behaviors need to be shared and exemplified so they can be replicated and become an integral part of the daily school culture. If you make this commitment, it makes the job of schooling that much easier because everyone realizes what's expected and what's celebrated, and for the most part, you will get a lot more help in building the culture every day.

RALLY IN ACTION

On an October night in 2019, Brandon was at a self-checkout register at his local supermarket. While scanning his items, he received a call from his wife, who was in the car waiting for him. When he answered the phone, a scared and worried voice said, "We need to go now . . . Bohdie was just in an accident."

Brandon quickly finished his transaction and went to the car. His wife received a call from their oldest daughter that a police officer showed up at their home. He was trying to get in contact with us to let us know that Bohdie was being transported to the hospital, and they needed us to head that way. He had also told Belle that the paramedics transporting him had his phone and to give them a call to get updated on his status. Brandon called the paramedics, who filled them in on how Bohdie was physically. The message was simply that Bohdie was doing OK but was beaten up pretty badly, but more than anything, he was annoyed with them poking and prodding him. The EMT told Brandon to take their time and meet them at Banner Desert Hospital.

After a twenty-minute drive, Brandon and his wife pulled into the hospital and parked in the lot. Brandon's wife asked him a question that he had not thought of the entire way there. "Why did they bring him to Banner Desert?"

Banner Desert was not the closest hospital. They passed two hospitals during the twenty-mile drive. The answer hit him like a ton of bricks, and he knew something wasn't right. He remembered that Banner Desert was the Level I trauma unit for the East Valley where they lived. This was not good. A weird feeling settled over him as they approached the entrance.

The couple hurriedly entered the trauma center and headed to the check-in area. After a quick verification of identification to determine who their son was, an officer led them back to the room. You could see on the faces of the hospital workers and the police officer that something was not good. The information came rolling in like a freight train. They were first approached by another officer who identified himself as one of the first officers on the scene. He began to explain that toward the latter part of the transfer to the hospital, Bohdie had started to have issues breathing and eventually went unresponsive, and they had to intubate him. He was currently getting some sort of scan to see why he wasn't breathing, and he would be rolled back to the room in a moment. A minute later, without even a second to see their son, the bed was swooped into the room, and the curtain shut behind him. It became what could only be described as a scene from Grey's Anatomy. Several voices could be heard, all shouting information. At one point, the head doctor shouted for everyone to be quiet so she could start giving instructions. Glimpses of words could be heard: "If he's having a stroke, I want to know," "Get me four more pints of blood." Such statements would strike fear into the hearts of any parents hearing these words about their child. The surgeon came out to address Brandon and his wife. She began to tell them that his lung had collapsed and that he was taking on the fluid in his chest cavity faster than it could be suctioned out. They were trying to find out what was going on but would need to move him to emergency surgery. They were able to see their son for a few precious moments, and Bohdie's mother grabbed his hand and told him to fight, fight as hard as he could. The two parents were taken to the operating floor waiting room, where the next ninety minutes were the longest of their lives.

After what felt like an eternity, the nurse came. She said that they had wheeled Bohdie up to the room, but the doctor would like to talk to them prior to seeing their son. The room was small with a conference table surrounded by some plastic chairs. Brandon had since been joined by his wife's brother, who had rushed to be with them. Brandon, his wife, and his brother-in-law all sat down on one side of the table while the surgeon came and sat across from them. Brandon could see the tears swelling up in the surgeon's eyes.

"I am so sorry to have to tell you this, but your son passed away in surgery. When we went in, he had a major tear in his aorta, and . . ." Brandon didn't hear anything after that. That statement took about

two seconds to process before he felt a crushing weight on his chest and burst into tears. He hugged his wife while her brother comforted her on the other side. She began to sob and just said, "Not my boy, not my boy, not my precious boy." Their lives had just been crushed. They had lost their oldest son at the age of sixteen.

This story is tragic, but what came from this tragedy was something that transformed them in more ways than they thought possible. Please understand, Brandon misses his son every single day, and there is nothing he wouldn't give, even his own life, to just spend another hour with him, but the lessons they learned began to define him as a family and as a school community. The word rally took on a whole new meaning.

For weeks, his community rallied around him and his family. At first, the support came from all angles. School leaders visited his house and brought meals, supplies, and love to help ease the pain as much as they could. Teams and programs from the school where Brandon served as the athletic director, as well as the school Bohdie attended, created posters for the family and tied light blue ribbons around the school and community in a show of support for the family. As a community, a fundraiser was done for Brandon's family that relieved the financial burdens from this tragic accident. The list continued. One of the most special moments for Brandon was to stand up at the celebration of life and see a giant church with standing room only coming to support the family, of which many were from relationships that had been built with students, staff, and parents of the schools the family worked with. For months after the loss of their son, they saw programs continuing to support the family in little ways. On the anniversary of Bohdie's death, the family held a "balls and dolls" toy drive that raised money to help families that had been in similar situations of loss and to help families in need during the holidays so they could enjoy their families instead of worrying if their students would be receiving presents. The family saw not only sports teams but also clubs, activities, and many other factions of the school community come together to help. The drive was so successful that it has become an annual tradition at the school every October.

This love shared by so many helped the family get through what was the hardest moment of their lives. Brandon once said that had this happened during his time at other schools, they would have not received the level of support that they did at his current school. When he assessed why, this was what Brandon came back to.

> - *He had spent the time setting a standard at his school that people matter.*
> - *He had spent the time to make sure that all programs in the school were valued.*
> - *He spent time developing the leadership skills of coaches, advisors, and students.*
> - *He celebrated all.*
>
> *When the time came to help, nothing had to be said. Students and adults alike reacted and rallied around one of their own who was hurting in such a deep way. This culture of family and collaboration and its people saved his family. Without them, he doesn't know where he would have been. He knew that his life's goal now was finding out how to replicate this community's culture. Every student and every adult should be entitled to have a school culture that values them as individuals and will rally around them during the good, but more importantly, the hard.*
>
> *In the years since, Brandon has observed his school and others accomplish milestones that have shown with a focus on activities and athletics as the main support for academics, miraculous things are possible. Working with Casey and his extensive experience as a successful district and campus administrator, as well as a prolific builder of leaders, the two were able to develop the why behind how school culture drives success and trace it back to simple yet effective skills and tools that every school should have in place. Laid out in an impactful, five-concept plan, the concept of Rally will allow schools to leave a long-lasting impact on their campus. We encourage the principals, assistant principals, athletic directors, coaches, advisors, directors, and anyone else willing to dive into shaping their school culture to do one thing after reading this book . . . Rally!*

Conclusion

Every choice you make as an educator or coach contributes to the creation of school culture. We encourage you to be clear about your school's mission, vision, values, and goals. Activities and athletics programs exist to support students. They directly and viscerally live as examples and opportunities for deep application for all of the aforementioned. Furthermore, there should be specific, strategically selected activities in place that you can point to that give observers and participants direct access to practice that will make them better in these areas we aspire to demonstrate. Sportsmanship, resiliency, and passionate yet respectful competition represent behaviors and outcomes that can and should be taught. The best school environments teach these skills thoughtfully and directly. In part 2 of this book, we get busy and put into action your plan for implementing the Rally model.

PART 2

STAGE THE RALLY

In this part, you will take this important foundational information that we've shared so far and apply it to the steps of the Rally model. These chapters are designed to help you develop and ultimately replicate the essential steps you will need for strong activities and athletics programs in your school. Each of the following chapters corresponds to a letter in the word Rally:

- Raise the standard
- Align
- Learning communities for ACTs
- Lead through students
- You're never done celebrating

Excellence is never an accident. It is always the result of high intention, sincere effort, and intelligent execution; it represents the wise choice of many alternatives—choice, not chance, determines your destiny.

—Aristotle

CHAPTER 4

RAISE THE STANDARD

Individually or collectively, things don't get better unless we elevate our standards. Impactful school leaders expect increasingly successful outcomes and drive those expectations with effort and formative, ongoing influence. Put another way, impactful leaders understand that you can't just stumble into what's better. You must expect it and employ more sophisticated approaches that make better results possible. The purpose of this chapter is to illustrate the *R* from the Rally model, which stands for "raise the standard." We examine and adjust the steps school leaders can take to illuminate this standard of committing to improvement and allow it to happen through implementing outstanding athletics and activities. This chapter highlights how raising standards in athletics and activities contributes to a school culture that promotes greater effort and better outcomes in all areas. When you raise the standard in quality athletics and activities, you have a better chance of raising the standards academically. Throughout this chapter, imagine continuously keeping track of the number of program offerings you maintain, the number of participants in each program, and the percentage of students throughout the school who engage in the student activity. Consider also tracking how many staff members working in the school each day are involved in an after-school activity. When you track these key performance indicators, you can do a better job of keeping a formative scorecard for the standards you are establishing and aiming to raise.

Specifically, in this chapter, we provide you with Rally practices around the definition of program offerings, program participation, and setting expectations for important elements like sportsmanship, community involvement, program retention, and how we engage in winning and losing. Set the standard, then build on the standard, and the Rally will begin!

Identifying Challenges of Raising the Standard

It is a challenge to maintain high standards in school programming. Raising, or improving on the established standard, is yet another challenge. After a standard has been set, through encouraging leadership and a commitment to progress, you can continuously revisit and raise that standard of work. This chapter will explore this dynamic and help you develop a system of monitoring and evaluation that will allow you to both set and raise the standard. However, to do so, you must understand the level of resistance you may face or new struggles that may arise when implementing changes. To illuminate these challenges, consider the following scenario.

CASE STUDY: THE FORGOTTEN FIELDS OF DRIFTWOOD

This case study explores the significant challenges faced by Driftwood School District in its athletics and extracurricular activities. It highlights the struggles with poor fan support, minimal student participation, and a lack of community investment. It illustrates the impact these deficits have on the overall school culture. Through compelling characters and specific examples, the study that follows provides insights into the obstacles and potential solutions for raising the standard and revitalizing the school's programs.

- **Overview:** Driftwood School District, a K–12 educational institution, is facing significant challenges with its athletics and extracurricular activities. The district's programs are suffering from poor fan support, minimal student participation, and a lack of community investment. This case study explores the various deficits that have led to this decline and introduces some key characters who represent the struggles and potential solutions within the district.

- **Key Characters:**
  + *Principal Sarah Greene*—The dedicated but overwhelmed principal of Driftwood High School, striving to find ways to improve the school's extracurricular programs.
  + *Coach Mark Thompson*—The passionate yet frustrated head coach of the Driftwood Dragons football team, who is struggling to motivate his players and garner community support.
  + *Ella Martinez*—A talented student-athlete who feels disheartened by the lack of enthusiasm and support for the school's athletic programs.
  + *Tom Baker*—A local business owner and former Driftwood athlete who has lost faith in the school's ability to foster a strong athletic culture.

- **Deficits and Their Impacts:**
  + *Lack of engagement*—The stands at sporting events are often empty, with only a handful of parents and students showing up to cheer on the teams. Those who do attend are generally unenthusiastic and disengaged, contributing to a lackluster atmosphere.
  + *Low morale*—The lack of fan support has a direct impact on the athletes' morale. Coach Thompson frequently notices his players' diminished enthusiasm and motivation during games as

they struggle to perform without the energy of a supportive crowd.

+ *Limited offerings*—The school offers only a handful of extracurricular activities, leaving students with few options to explore their interests and talents. The band program, for instance, has only a few members, and the drama club has not staged a production in years.

+ *Lack of interest*—Without a variety of activities to choose from, students like Ella Martinez feel disconnected and uninspired. Ella, who excels in track and field, often contemplates quitting due to the lack of encouragement and camaraderie within the program.

+ *Financial and voluntary support*—Local businesses and community members rarely invest in the school's programs, either financially or through acts of service. Tom Baker, who once dreamed of seeing his alma mater thrive, has stopped sponsoring the annual sports banquet due to declining interest and support.

+ *Absence of role models*—The absence of strong community involvement means students lack role models who can inspire and mentor them. This further diminishes their engagement and commitment to the programs.

+ *Aging infrastructure*—The school's sports facilities are outdated and in disrepair. The football field is poorly maintained, and the gymnasium lacks modern equipment, making it difficult for students to train effectively.

+ *Limited funding*—With minimal financial support from the community and local government, the school struggles to provide the necessary resources to improve its programs and facilities.

We've painted a pretty grim picture here. But sadly, these issues that affected the Driftwood School District are all too common. Let's check in with some of the challenges and Rally strategies to learn how to raise the standard.

Low Levels of Participation

Some athletics and activity programs have a difficult time being successful in communities where these activities aren't commonplace, or there is a lack of accessibility. For example, living in a part of the United States that has limited access to pools may hurt your capacity to recruit a strong swimming team, or the cost of renting or purchasing instruments may reduce the number of eligible students for a band or orchestra. The same is potentially true with cold weather and ice hockey or low SES areas and dance. Statistician in the Census Bureau's Fertility and Family Statistics Branch Yerís H. Mayol-García (2022) explains that poverty influences extracurricular involvement for activities requiring more parental time, financial resources, transportation, and equipment. That same study shows that 14 percent of students ages 6–17 who live below the poverty line participate in extracurricular activities (Mayol-García, 2022). However, those logistics and challenges notwithstanding, a school that remains perpetually challenged in terms of overall levels of participation in activities and athletics is often a sign that expectations are low. Students, for example, may not believe that they can compete academically and thus won't engage in activities that may stimulate them in this way. In other cases, bullying or toxic cultures have created an environment where students are simply discouraged from putting themselves out there and trying something new. There are many potential symptoms of an environment that discourages participation in activities and athletics.

Minimal Offerings

We recognize that determining the exact number of offerings for your athletics and activity programming isn't easy. For example, small school districts in states with lower population levels may not have as many competition opportunities as their larger, more diverse counterparts. However, perhaps a good indicator would be the number of requests for offerings a school district receives about what they can accommodate. No school can offer everything that is requested. How often are students and parents making requests that are denied? How many community members leave the school for opportunities offered somewhere else? Observing that trend could help examine this particular factor. Schools that are highly successful, optimistic, and deeply engaged will always be pushing the envelope and adding more options.

Poor Fan and Parent Support

In an environment where there are low expectations, there are often examples of low fan attendance at the activities and minimal parent support when those calls for engagement are made. We often refer to "fair-weather fans" as those who show up only when things are going right or teams are winning. Attendance levels based on performance could be a sign of a program in need of improvement. An interesting study was done by two researchers, Massimiliano Ferraresi and Gianluca Gucciardi (2020), on how the COVID-19 pandemic crowds impacted performance on soccer teams. The study finds strong evidence that teams are more likely to perform better in front of a supportive audience (Ferraresi & Gucciardi, 2020). Another way of determining the presence of fan and parental support is to look at the degree to which any past parents, participants, or students come back and continue to support the activity. For example, it's not uncommon for speech and debate parents whose students graduated to be willing to come back and judge occasionally because they enjoy the activity. Or, athletic participants will come back year after year and at least see one game. This is a sign of engagement and the desire to maintain a high standard for the activity, even after the opportunity to participate has gone by.

Little Ability to Change or Pivot

We believe that a robust school with a positive, optimistic school culture will live through some ups and downs with its program offerings. For example, the speech and debate team may be wildly successful for a few years, slow down a bit, and then re-engage a few years later with an influx of new ideas. Simply put, robust activities and athletics programs are always looking for opportunities to pivot, grow, and further engage. An example of this may be a band director whose choice of music and formation demonstrates an antiquated perspective that fits the director's comfort zone, ultimately keeping members from joining. Another example could be the basketball coach who has the personal philosophy that yelling at student-athletes is the best way to coach. Research shows us that negative training can have the potential to decrease motivation, enjoyment, and focus in activities (Stirling & Kerr, 2012). Failure to evolve could prove the need to raise expectations.

No Commitment to a Vision

The most unsuccessful schools that are lacking in the capacity to raise expectations often demonstrate this lack of commitment. They fail to make any progress whatsoever toward a shared vision. This would be the type of school that would essentially have "banners on the wall," but there is no valid evidence throughout the campus of the teams or programs exhibiting behaviors toward that vision. Some schools preach integrity yet recruit illegally. Other schools may have a vision of all students driving to success but only allocate resources to certain programs. High-level athletics and activities programs will live the standards that they present to their community. These five examples of challenges a school may face will give the school a good barometer when it comes to how to raise the standard but also *where* to raise the standard.

We will leave you with some questions at the end of each section of the Rally challenges to help you take a pulse of where your school may be at with these challenges. These questions can be used to assess both qualitatively and quantitatively where your school's athletic and activity programs are, allowing you to go into the Responding to These Challenges With Rally Practices section knowing where some of those challenges may lie.

WHERE ARE WE NOW?

1. How many students are participating in extracurricular activities? List them by both the number of students and the percentage of students.
2. How many extracurricular activities are offered at your school? List them out by activities and athletics.
3. What are your current attendance levels for your athletic events for the last three years? How many parent volunteers do you field in a school year?
4. When was the last time leaders conducted an assessment of the number of and types of activities offered on your campus?
5. Does your athletic and activity program have a published vision statement?

Responding to These Challenges With Rally Practices

In this next section, we will provide several Rally practices that we know are essential to your ability to set and then raise the standard. You can certainly set standards in several ways, but we would recommend deep and sustained consideration of setting quality standards in the following areas: participation expectations, program offerings, activity commitment, hiring ACTs, program evaluation, sportsmanship, and community and parent support.

In this section, we want to help you make an accurate assessment of how well your school is meeting each standard. As you look at these tools, remember they are just that, tools. These are used as guides to help establish a process. The process goal of setting a standard for participation will take the information just discussed to identify the initial value (What is the current percentage of participation compared to the school's population?), end-of-year target benchmark (What do we want that number to be at the end of the year?), and midyear check-in (Where are we at as of winter break?). At the end of the year, establish what your actual participation percentage is and compare it to your desired benchmark. Were you ahead of your benchmark, behind it, or on target? Evaluating these numbers can then help you develop a new benchmark moving forward. Remember that these numbers don't define your school. They are simply a standard to aspire to. The process will be the focus, the benchmark is simply a tool to help you measure the standard.

Rally Practice 1.1: Participation Expectations Standard

To meet this standard, a school should establish program participation expectations. We define participation in terms of literally setting the expectation for student engagement with activities and athletics. Although there are several ways of measuring this, we would recommend that a school set a goal for participation around the students instead of the program.

We would hope that every student in the school is involved in at least one athletic endeavor or one student activity endeavor in their elementary, middle, and high school years. To clarify, an athletic endeavor does not necessarily have to be a cut-sport program. Many schools offer noncut sports where students can be on a team as long as they uphold the program standards and complete the requirements of the sport. This may also be a club that has an athletic component to it that isn't sanctioned by the state's athletic governing body, such as pickleball, yoga, or noncompetitive dance. Many students engage much more than this, but setting up some expectations is helpful. We recommend that schools establish a reporting feature where students are listed by the number of activities they participate in. This will help you to more directly observe just how many students are engaged in at least one sport and activity. This observation will also help you to see trends by observing if there are certain populations in your school that seem less compelled to participate. If so, you can indeed begin the work of involving and engaging any group that might be missing.

The makeup and size of student populations differ in every school, so we advise working in percentages when evaluating the participation standard. Evaluate where the school's current numbers are, where they have been historically, and compare these to similar schools in the area. These three categories will give the school a picture of where they are, where they have been, and where they want to move to in the future. Why is this important? First, the school needs to have a solid understanding of its current participation numbers. For a school of over 3,000 students, a participation rate of 35 percent may be high, as there are a finite number of places where students can play in terms of teams and available spots on those teams. Whereas for a school of 500 students, a 35 percent participation rate may have the school scraping by to fill spots on a team. Secondly, understanding where the participation rates have been in the last five or ten years can give you historical data to see if your school is growing, declining, or staying stagnant. Understanding the trends is pivotal when it comes to making plans on how to attack the areas needed for growth. Lastly, evaluating the demographics of similarly sized schools in your area to see what they are doing can give you a barometer of where you stand with your peers and what new or potential goals to consider. Once these three areas are identified, creating benchmarks for the future are now tangible. Figure 4.1 is an easy tool that can be used for not only this practice but other practices moving forward to set those benchmarks.

Metric	Initial Value	EOY Target Benchmark	Midyear Check-In	EOY Check-In	New FY Benchmark
Number of Participants					

FIGURE 4.1: Benchmark goal sheet.

*Visit **go.SolutionTree.com/studentengagement** for a free reproducible version of this figure.*

To summarize this Rally practice: As school leaders, we hope to support the development of future adults who demonstrate high levels of participation. We want them to participate in the voting process. We hope they participate and are engaged in raising their future families. We hope they're highly engaged in their work and their community. Getting in the habit of getting involved is an essential element of sports and student activities. Meeting the following standards will help you to quantitatively set up goals for activities and athletics participation.

- Establish clear participation expectations for students in activities and athletics.

- Focus on setting process goals for student engagement with the programs, aiming for involvement in at least one athletic or one activity endeavor per academic year.

- Implement a reporting feature to track student participation in sports and activities.

- Monitor trends in participation to identify any groups or populations that may be less compelled to participate.

- Evaluate participation rates in percentages relative to the school's population, historical data, and similar schools in the area.

- Set benchmarks for participation rates to measure progress over time.

- Emphasize that participation expectations should align with the school's mission and vision.

Rally Practice 1.2: Program Offerings Standard

Every school that offers competitive and dynamic activities and athletics should have a specific set of defined program offerings. Unfortunately, some school leaders simply inherit the offerings their school has established and give precious little time to thinking about this issue comprehensively. At least once a year, leaders must analyze all the athletic and activity offerings in the school and evaluate the appropriateness of the offerings.

Like the standard of participation, the standard of offerings will be approached in the same way, but using hard numbers rather than percentages. Leaders must evaluate offerings on the campus, what options were offered in the past, and what options are being offered in similar schools in the surrounding areas. This evaluation will give a picture of where the school is in terms of the offerings it provides. A school with fifteen athletic offerings and twenty activity offerings may be small to some perspectives and more than plenty to others. Compare your school to other schools in the area. Take for example, an area that participates in open enrollment or a school of choice, whose offerings could be the difference between a student selecting the local school or the neighboring school. The next part of that will be ensuring your offerings are right for your community. Some offerings would not be possible or practical in certain circumstances. For instance, the Future Farmers of America may not be pushed in a heavily populated urban area where there is no room to house the animals and needs of the program. A tool to help with this is a basic community survey asking a few simple questions.

- What offerings do we currently offer that you feel are valuable?
- What do we not currently offer that you would like to see in our school?
- What offering may have been offered in the past that you would like to see brought back?

These are just a few simple questions to help evaluate the types of offerings within the school. See the template in figure 4.2 for a sample survey you might send out to stakeholders to gather similar information.

School Program Offerings Survey
Name:
Date:
Relationship to school:
Survey:
What offerings do we currently offer that you feel are valuable?
What do we not currently offer that you would like to see in our school?

What offering may have been available in the past that you would like to see brought back?

FIGURE 4.2: Sample school offerings survey.

*Visit **go.SolutionTree.com/studentengagement** for a free reproducible version of this figure.*

Once leadership has the data of current and desired offerings, they are now armed to create benchmarks. Determine the baseline for how many offerings are available and where you want to see those numbers go and check in periodically. Remember to take the data from the community surveys into account. Leaders must ensure that offerings are going to be utilized by the students and not be a burden. An example of this would be a school creating a badminton team, but with only a few students having the desire to play, while more than twenty students are interested in participating in Model UN, but there has been no planning for this activity with the students. Though we must use numbers to quantify offerings, in the end, we need to ensure they are qualitative as well.

To summarize this Rally practice: Think of the kinds of sports and student activities your students deserve. It's easy when cutting programming to see a line item for an activity and simply make it go away. However, these program offerings define the constellation of opportunities students have to participate and engage in your school. We believe that school leaders must take enormous pride in their program offerings and constantly strive towards a better overall set of options. They need to remain doggedly aware of the emerging needs of their students.

- Define a specific set of program offerings for activities and athletics.
- Regularly analyze and evaluate the appropriateness of the offerings.

- Compare the school's offerings to those of similar schools in the area.
- Consider community input through surveys to determine valuable offerings.
- Set benchmarks for the number of program offerings based on community needs and school resources.
- Ensure program offerings are both quantitative and qualitative.
- Align program offerings with the school's demographics and community needs.

Rally Practice 1.3: Program or Activity Commitment Standard

We believe that a school must define specifically what commitment to a program or activity means for students and parents. We realize that this may differ depending on the level and the specific program involved, but having specific parameters for what it means to commit to the program is essential. After all, when a student commits to an activity or a program, they are representing the school, and that commitment must be quantified.

A steadfast commitment to the program in which students are involved is an essential element for growth in activities and athletics. This would involve, but isn't limited to, the amount of practice, participation, and overall engagement. Does your school allow your student to miss three-quarters of the season and then decide to try out for the activity or sport? Is it OK if they miss a certain number of practices? What is the flexibility that you're willing to offer for students who might have family or life obligations? To expand on this further, are your standards the same for starters and for students who are struggling? Students perform better when the common standards for their performance are made clear to them (Dotson, 2016). This is true in both academics and in after-school activities. There is some flexibility required here, but in the end, students need to understand that these programs and activities are important to the school, and a defined program commitment is necessary to stay engaged.

Each program may establish different parameters based on their needs; an example of this could be as simple as establishing the rule that to retain membership in a club, members must attend 80 percent of scheduled meetings or activities. Another example would be a soccer team that sets a rule that being late unexcused to a practice the first time equates to sitting a half during the competition, while a second tardy would result in missing a complete game. This was a policy that a first-year soccer coach enforced at one of Brandon's schools. Seven starters were late to a Saturday breakfast for a playoff game. The coach stood by his policy and sat them for the first half. Fortunately, the team still won the game and advanced, but the next three years he coached there, there was not another student late to a practice.

Beyond what happens during the season, we must also set a standard for what happens outside of the season. Highly engaged student activities and athletics programs have both in-season and out-of-season activities. The degree to which out-of-season participation and preparation are expected should be defined. In this area, we advocate both commitment and flexibility. Athletics and activity programs that attempt to sequester a student's year-round commitment at the cost of other activities and athletics serve ultimately to diminish the student's overall experience at school. We want students who are involved in multiple activities in the school, and they certainly need to prepare year-round for participation. However, we can't make that so rigorous that they cannot enjoy other things. It isn't easy to establish the delicate balance between maintaining rigorous off-season expectations while simultaneously supporting participation in other activities, but this should be the standard. So how do we set a standard that can encapsulate these practices?

First, allowing students to come and go as they please can lead to a lack of commitment, leaving ACTs frustrated and programs lacking resources. A tip for establishing this standard is the idiom, "We finish what we start." Each offering or program will have different time frames for participation. For example, a sport may have a two- to three-month season with specific start and end dates, while a band or a choir may be a yearlong commitment. Clubs can establish standards for participation time frames based on their needs as well. In our experience as educational leaders, having a policy that states that if a student chooses not to finish or is removed before the conclusion of a season or commitment time frame, the student may not begin another activity or join another athletic team until that previous season is completed. Having a policy in place like this communicates to students the importance of finishing what they started and communicates to ACTs that their offering provides value to the school and is worthy of student commitment.

Second, ensure the standard of commitment considers the longevity of the commitment. We recommend that you gather another piece of data that is essential for program development: persistence. Specifically, track the number of students who try out or engage in an activity, and stick with it for multiple seasons or years. We want to examine how many students stay with the program over several years, from the starting point to the ending point. But more importantly, why? To track this, we recommend including it as another benchmark in the metric evaluation (see figure 4.1, page 72).

This is an important data point to track on all levels. It can tell us a bit about school culture and the level of engagement students feel, and it can give us some idea about the overall success of a program. Remember, we can sometimes be misled in particularly large schools when we have programs and just enough students to participate. There may be a lot of students who aren't learning to persist in the programs they chose, and that is certainly a value that schools should emphasize with the students we serve.

To summarize this Rally practice: Just showing up isn't enough. Whether it is at work, supporting a family someday, or being engaged in political, social, or community activities in the future, students need to learn that a commitment standard is necessary to get a commensurate return. Sports and student activities show how there is a return on the investment of a season of engagement. School leaders must be conscious of this and teach the merits of not only involvement but also commitment once the showing up is done. Here are some thoughts on how to make that commitment come to life.

- Establish specific parameters for commitment to programs and activities for students and parents.

- Define expectations for practice attendance, participation, and overall engagement.
- Maintain consistency in standards across all participants, regardless of their role or performance level.
- Encourage commitment within and outside of the season, balancing rigor with flexibility.
- Track persistence by monitoring the number of students participating in multiple seasons or years.
- Communicate the importance of commitment to students and parents to uphold program standards.

Rally Practice 1.4: Standards for Hiring ACTs

Hiring advisors, coaches, and teachers is one of the most essential tasks that a school leader can do. Also, when a new head coach or lead advisor is appointed, they must surround themselves with the right types of educators, providing the best kind of support necessary. We believe that some important demarcations must be adhered to when hiring high-quality ACTs. These suggestions are as follows.

Each school and each program will ultimately have different needs from the hiring of their ACT to lead their program or assist their program. The chess team is not going to need the same requirements as the basketball team. The school must determine what set of values their ACTs must possess that would fall in line with the overall vision of the school. Hiring teams must answer questions like the following to determine the "best fit" for a campus.

- Do we only hire on-campus coaches?
- Do all coaches need to meet certain criteria of experience?
- Are we looking for coaches that value character over winning? What are the character traits that we value as a school in our ACTs?
- What leadership traits are we looking for in a candidate? How will those leadership traits mesh with the culture of the school?

Ultimately, we can't spell out what the perfect ACT would look like because the needs of each school are so vastly different. Cultures, demographics, and budgets can all play roles in hiring practices for a school. Each school may have a different take on this, but in the end, there needs to be consistency in the hiring process to bring together like-minded people toward a common goal.

This can be done through a standard of evaluation when going through the hiring process. Interview questions geared toward values are imperative. You can also get creative with your questions. Brandon has used random questions at times to see if the candidate would fit in culturally with the school and if they can think on their feet. When he asks a question like, "If you could be any type of animal, what would it be?" he looks at body language and the auditory answers. Does the applicant get uncomfortable? Do they enjoy the thought-provoking question? Do they feel it's a waste of time? He evaluates the nonverbal queues to see if the candidate fits with the culture of the school. We believe that hiring an ACT is more than finding the most qualified candidate. It's about finding the candidate who is the best fit for the school's culture as well as the program they will lead.

Tying interview questions to core values can allow leaders to dive deeper into what they expect from an ACT on their campus or their standard for hiring. This can be done in a plethora of ways. Here is an example of utilizing questions based on the core values of a program. Figure 4.3 uses two interview questions that would tie into a core value of "enthusiasm."

Enthusiasm:

Demonstrates a genuine passion for coaching and working with students

Shows excitement about fostering a positive and energetic team environment

1. What strategies do you employ to maintain a high level of enthusiasm and passion when coaching or leading, and how do you ensure it translates to a positive team atmosphere?
2. Can you share an example of a situation where your enthusiasm positively influenced your students, fostering a sense of excitement and motivation within the team or group?

(Maximum Points: 20)

Evident Passion (0–10):
0: Lacks enthusiasm
5: Shows moderate enthusiasm
10: Demonstrates high levels of passion and excitement
Positive Team Environment (0–10):
0: Neglects team morale
5: Maintains a somewhat positive environment
10: Fosters an enthusiastic and positive team atmosphere

FIGURE 4.3: Core value evaluation survey.

*Visit **go.SolutionTree.com/studentengagement** for a free reproducible version of this figure.*

The questions in figure 4.3 can open doors to ensure that the interviewee speaks to their philosophy on that specific core value. As a leader, you can evaluate the answers toward the standards you have established. This style of questioning takes the emotional "swaying" out of interviews and solidifies it to a rubric that is clear-cut. How many times has a hire been made because the candidate knew all the buzzwords, only later to find out they were not a great fit? By establishing a standard for hiring, leaders can be laser-focused on what they are looking for. This may allow some candidates who previously wouldn't have been considered to be a surprisingly good fit.

To summarize this Rally practice: Entertainers and artists will oftentimes establish protocols that they see as on-brand or off-brand. High-functioning companies establish a culture where leadership behaviors or innovation standards are established, and everyone understands that consistent behaviors are expected to deliver emergent outcomes. The same is true in schools when hiring ACTs. Your school has a mission and it serves its students and their families. School leaders must set a standard for how to create consistency in both expectations and the outward behaviors of your ACTs. Here are some tips on how to make that happen.

- Determine the values and qualifications required for hiring coaches, advisors, and teachers that align with the program's vision and mission.

- Establish consistent criteria for evaluating candidates during the hiring process.
- Utilize interview questions aligned with core values and program expectations.
- Assess candidates' fit with the school's culture and vision.
- Ensure transparency and consistency in the hiring process.
- Emphasize the importance of finding candidates who align with the school's mission and program goals.

Rally Practice 1.5: Program Evaluation Standard

Programs tend to grow and change in relationship to three things: (1) where we put our attention, (2) what we evaluate, and (3) what we celebrate. All three of these things are important. Ideally, with a well-organized school, we put our focus on things that matter, and we evaluate and celebrate the things that align with those expectations. When it comes to activities and athletics, we must evaluate the right things if we're going to get a consistent outcome that we can measure and expect, and we can eventually push to accelerate.

Evaluation can be seen as a negative word, depending on the way it is characterized. We, however, believe that evaluation is an opportunity. How many ACTs have stepped into a position where they don't know what is expected of them, yet they get reprimanded or even fired for not holding to those expectations? Setting a standard of evaluation communicates to your staff, community, and students that how we conduct ourselves as ACTs and how we run our programs matter. We believe that when setting a standard for the evaluation of programs, there should be three distinct areas of focus, each building on the previous one: (1) establishing process goals, (2) progress monitoring, and (3) action planning.

ESTABLISH PROCESS GOALS

We start with establishing process goals and benchmarks. As stated in earlier chapters, we believe that the school's focus should be on the process rather than fixating on the results. When results are not obtained, we tend to look at ourselves as failures rather than recognizing that there is still growth within the process. For example, imagine a student whose goal is to ace a mathematics test versus a student who aims to study mathematics for one hour every day. The latter will build strong study habits and a deeper understanding of mathematics over time, while the first student might either achieve their goal or fall short without any established plan for continued learning and improvement. Focusing on the process encourages consistent effort and development, leading to sustainable success in the long run. Leaders must set a standard for what process they want to evaluate while creating benchmarks as check-ins along the way. For example, students are expected to behave during their activities and athletic programs in a manner that is a positive reflection of the school and its community. This would be the standard, while the benchmark would be looked at differently. For a club, it may be how many discipline referrals have been made about club members during a quarter, while athletics could add the number of ejections, technical fouls, or red cards within their competitions. The programs could also look at the positive recall and benchmarks to track how many positive comments, emails, and awards each student has received during the same time frame. Each school and program will have different needs, objectives, and challenges, but there can be specific process goals that span each of those areas to unite those programs and their standards. One final note is that these standards should align with the school's mission or vision. We will discuss aligning and synergizing in a future chapter.

MONITOR PROGRESS

To continue the process, progress monitoring is imperative. Nothing is more frustrating than being given goals and no one ever following up on them. Leaders must make the time to monitor progress after the benchmarks are set. For example, if a benchmark is set to be looked at after a year, then monitoring that progress quarterly would be acceptable to ensure that the ACT and the program are on track. These do not have to be long, drawn-out meetings or even meetings at all. These can be electronic forms of communication, such as surveys or emails. As long as the conversation is ongoing, the mode doesn't play as big of a role. Another suggestion is, as administrators, we know how busy the job can be. Have the ACT present you with the current data, where the benchmark should be, and if they are meeting that benchmark. Then, simply ask the question, why do you think we are at this point? This will allow the ACT to give feedback, either positive or negative, and suggest possible changes. The ACT has the ownership of the process and you can enjoy having delegated the data collecting to the individual with the closest experience to the respective program.

PLAN ACTIONS

Lastly, let's discuss action planning. Process goals have been set, progress has been monitored—now what? Have you ever been in an hour-long meeting where several items were discussed, but nothing was accomplished or moved forward? It is important to always end a meeting with everyone restating what actions they were leaving with. We would recommend the same with your standards of evaluation. After you set goals and monitor the process, create actionable steps for how the process should continue. For example, if a mock trial team was given the standard to be prepared for every competition they face to represent the school with pride, while the progress monitoring was finding that they continued to score low on cross-examination, there must be actionable steps for how to make changes. Evaluating the process they use for their preparation, the ACT can look at ways in which the team can overcome that deficiency moving forward and discuss those with their overseeing administrator. From there, the cycle will continue. New or amended process goals will be established, and the monitoring will begin again.

This process is not anything new, but it is simple and allows leaders to create a standard for evaluation that, no matter what the program is, you know exactly what is expected of you as well as how you will be evaluated as a program.

To summarize this Rally practice: Our true colors as leaders come out when those we lead observe what we reward, what we punish, what we ignore, and what we support. A winning program in sports with unsatisfactory competition behaviors would evaluate the standard for leadership. Does this idea align with the expectations of students, staff, and the community? Knowing what you value, knowing what you will reward, and knowing what you will and won't remain silent about are all standards that you must have as a school leader to be successful. Here is a list of a few things to consider when implementing standards.

- Focus on evaluating the process rather than just the results.
- Set process goals and benchmarks aligned with the school's mission and vision.
- Monitor progress regularly to ensure alignment with established benchmarks.
- Utilize action planning to address areas needing improvement or adjustment.
- Encourage ongoing dialogue and feedback between ACTs and administrators.
- Align evaluation standards with program goals and school values.

Rally Practice 1.6: Community and Parent Support Standard

The leaders and ACTs who frequently share information and updates with the community and parents can usually expect support in return. This support includes the things that they can do to help students participate with success. It also could include things that they can do to help the overall program flourish and grow. Finally, it also can include the things that can be done when watching the sport or activity, and how they can show up in a way that represents the school and the intention of the activity itself. Here are some specific suggestions on how to make that happen.

Schools that thrive in their activities and athletics often have a high level of parental and community involvement. It can be challenging to set a standard for parental support, but there are three major areas in which the school can foster community and parental support: (1) engagement, (2) communication, and (3) collaboration. Fostering engagement can take many forms, such as hosting informational sessions, workshops, and volunteer orientations. These events can educate parents about the programs and ways to contribute. Additionally, encouraging parents to attend games, performances, and competitions helps them feel connected and invested in the students' experiences. Allowing parents to take on specific roles or projects in established committees or task forces fosters a sense of ownership and commitment and recognizes their valuable contributions. These examples are ways that schools can cultivate strong engagement with parent groups and enrich the overall experience for student-athletes and participants by allowing standards to be communicated with all parties.

To foster communication standards with parent groups in activities and athletics, establish regular meetings, generate recurring newsletters, and take advantage of social media's potential for connectivity. These channels keep parents informed about schedules, events, and opportunities for involvement. Additionally, establishing policies with specific ways in which parents can communicate with ACTs and administrators where parents feel comfortable expressing their concerns or suggestions can enhance communication. Creating dedicated online platforms or social media groups can facilitate ongoing dialogue and engagement. (The use of social media will be more closely addressed in chapter 8, page 175.) Schools must actively seek input, address concerns promptly, and transparently share information. Through this, schools can cultivate a strong sense of partnership and collaboration with parent groups, enhancing their support for activities and athletics.

When setting the standard for support, parents and communities will be more willing and able to garner support for the school's programs when they feel heard and appreciated.

To summarize this Rally practice: Joseph de Maistre (1811), a Savoyard philosopher, said, "Every nation gets the government it deserves" (p. 15). His profound and provocative statement speaks to the need for leadership accountability, the demand for engagement, the power of empowering others, and the need for thoughtful cultural reflection. All these years later, the same is true for us. The parent and community support that emerges at our schools is a reflection of everything we do, everything we fail to do, and the cumulative action or inaction. This means that you will need to build the community and parent standard for support of your activities and athletics based on what you're committed to building, supporting, managing, and developing. Here are a few steps to help you get there.

- Foster engagement, communication, and collaboration with parents and the community.
- Host informational sessions, workshops, and volunteer orientations to educate and involve parents.
- Utilize regular meetings, newsletters, and social media for communication.
- Establish policies for parent communication and feedback.
- Recognize and value parent contributions to activities and athletics.
- Cultivate strong partnerships between parents, ACTs, and administrators.

Rally Practice 1.7: Sportsmanship and Integrity Standard

A lot of people talk about sportsmanship, but few put it into action. To help establish the standard, we must first define what sportsmanship is. According to the Merriam-Webster online dictionary, the definition of *sportsmanship* (n.d.) is "conduct (such as fairness, respect for one's opponent, and graciousness in winning or losing) becoming to one participating in a sport." Though the definition includes the word *sport*, this definition can be tied to any competition. Sportsmanship is essentially conducting ourselves in a way that is respectful to our opponent as well as our institution. This concept presents as integrity in noncompeting activities. How one conducts oneself in a club, meeting, or student council summit must also have that same level of respect for peers within the activity.

Students, parents, and community members must have a fully realized idea about what a school expects in terms of student behavior in activities and athletics, and how we respond, regardless of positive or negative outcomes. The schools that don't set this standard may see behaviors exhibited that have nothing to do with the mission, vision, and values of the school. Conversely, when a school is open and direct about its mission, vision, and values and has a clear idea of what they mean by sportsmanship, and how they are going to act when they win or lose, there is far greater alignment.

In figure 4.4, you will see an example of a sportsmanship and integrity standard as sample rules for respect.

> **Respect 5!:**
> - Respect the competition—rules are in place for a reason.
> - Respect your teammates—you all play for the same team; lift each other up.
> - Respect your opponents—people are bigger than the game; give maximum effort but they are not your enemies.
> - Respect the officials—without officials, we can't play the game; remember they're not perfect.
> - Respect yourself—your value is not determined by the outcomes of the competition; stay positive in all that you do.

FIGURE 4.4: Sample rules for respect.

Figure 4.4 features five easy standards of sportsmanship that could be referenced, regardless of sport, activity, or club. Both ACTs and students could reference these to hold each other accountable to the standard. What you choose to use is not as important as the consistency in which they are both referenced and implemented by students, ACTs, and community members.

It is just as imperative to address the sportsmanship standard and how a program handles the results of a competition, win or lose. Participants and communities must learn the school's expectations for how they need to react when winning or losing. First, celebrating a win is absolutely appropriate. It's an in-the-moment victory when hard work and concentration in competition have come to fruition, and players and ACTs deserve the opportunity to actively and rigorously celebrate. We recommend that students emphasize celebration together. Nothing can ruin a win more than students or ACTs celebrating by putting others down or attempting to bring attention to themselves. Individual celebrations that don't involve each other are less preferred versus celebrations that engage fellow participants or teammates. Secondly, that participation should never be obscene, vulgar, or simulate violence. It must instead simply be an opportunity to actively experience the exhilaration of experiencing a successful conclusion, perhaps including but not limited to winning. Finally, another important element of winning is showing grace, respect, kindness, and dignity toward the losing team or participant. All participants must show appreciation for their competition and be generous in their support for the losing team or individual.

In losing, we must also have a standard for how we respond. This response should not include demonstrations of anger, frustration with any judges or referees, or anger toward fans or community members. Disappointment is a legitimate emotional feeling after trying hard to win but doing so in a graceful way is essential. Congratulate the other team on a competition well played. Afterward, positive event interactions and positive social media posts are all examples of programs with high levels of respect for their opponent. Setting this standard is essential for it can brighten or dim your front porch in a hurry.

To summarize this Rally practice: When Margaret Wolfe Hungerford (1878) wrote, "beauty is in the eye of the beholder," she was gracefully referencing art's rich subjectivity and its embrace of diverse interpretations. While this is a beautiful standard perhaps for appreciating art and literature, the authors of this book realize that we can sometimes provide a bit too much lush subjectivity in defining what healthy sportsmanship is like. Allowing participants, team and activity leaders, and even parents and community members to define sportsmanship with situational fluidity can create significant problems for schools and school leaders. When trying to create the consistency that's required, consider the following.

- Define sportsmanship expectations for students, parents, and community members.
- Emphasize fairness, respect, and graciousness in winning or losing.
- Celebrate wins with teamwork and respect for opponents.
- Ensure participation is respectful, avoiding obscenity or vulgarity.
- Show grace and kindness toward opponents in victory and defeat.

- Set standards for appropriate behavior during competitions and post-event interactions.
- Align sportsmanship standards with the school's mission, vision, and values.

RALLY IN ACTION

Several years ago, Jeff took over as an athletic director in a school that had little success in the previous decade with academics, athletics, and activities. The school, once the pride of the city, resided in an area that had been a victim of suburban growth just outside of its boundaries, leading to a mass exodus of students over time. Once there were 3,000 students, but now the school had 1,000. Jeff went into the school with the intent of not allowing recent failures to define the future of the students there. Over the next two years, Jeff intentionally utilized the Rally strategies to raise the standards at his school. He helped establish a specific vision for the program. Students and ACTs frequently discussed improvements. They changed the language about standards and helped coaching expectations meet those standards. They learned how to win and to lose with grace, although losing happened more often than not. Action plans were enacted to address behaviors and strategies that could be implemented immediately, while every effort was made to engage the community in the school's plans and invite them to participate.

The school did not become an overnight success. What the school administrators and educators observed was better behaviors from students in the classroom, better grades, and more competitive activities. For example, behavior referrals became almost nonexistent for athletes as compared to prior years when athletes accounted for most of the referrals on campus. Attendance at games increased by over 20 percent over the course of two years. The school moved to a weekly grade-check policy that held athletes accountable. The results were a drastic reduction in ineligible athletes. Soccer was a prime example where the varsity team averaged five to seven players being ineligible at the end of a semester, to eventually having the weekly grade checks result in only one varsity player being ineligible during Jeff's last year at the school. All of this led to excitement around some of the programs that hadn't experienced enthusiasm in a long time. Little wins around the campus allowed for better conver-

sations with students at risk about the importance of education. As efforts continued to build a better school culture, it was evidenced by the students' behavior on campus. More students engaged with each other and adults than ever before. Coaches noticed the shift and continually made comments about the change and its impact on their ability to do their jobs in a positive way. When Jeff left the school, the effects were quickly noticed as the new leaders came in but did not uphold the new standards. The school quickly reverted to its old ways with eligibility issues, behavior issues, and ultimately a toxic culture.

It's amazing how some of the smallest actions and expectations can lead to big change. Casey recalls a high school basketball coach who changed him forever. Bruce Brown was a successful basketball coach in the state of Ohio. He was known for his fiery, red face and his perpetual chatterbox input to his players from the sidelines. One year, the team was said to be a bit down because several skilled players had graduated and the team didn't seem ready to compete. To combat this, Coach Brown tried to teach the student body and the fans that their enthusiastic cheering for the right things would make a difference. During a pep rally, he came into the gym in a leather jacket, riding a Harley-Davidson motorcycle, roaring with a vengeance as it rolled up to the center of the gymnasium floor with the screaming student body peering down.

After dismounting his Harley, he grabbed a microphone and began to loudly address the audience. He told them that when they came to a game, he didn't care if they cheered for a scored basket or a win, but he wanted to see them cheer for the demonstration of unbelievable effort, particularly on defense. To demonstrate this, he screamed to the audience that if they saw "this" happen, they should indeed go ballistic. With that, he threw the microphone to one of his players and ran out to stand underneath the basket. From the bench, the largest and heaviest player on the team grabbed the ball and began dribbling toward his coach. This player was 6'3" and 230 lb. His coach was probably about 5'8" and 160 lb. Not to be denied, his coach stood in perfect defensive form while the high school player drove down the lane and smashed into his coach. His coach went flying back and hit the floor. He took the charge, meaning that the basket didn't count and the defender won. The crowd went crazy as they watched the coach fly across the gym floor and land on his back in a heroic effort to sacrifice his body for his team. This painful yet full-throated commitment by his coach to show his players and his

> *community what mattered to him created an unbelievable commitment on the part of his team to do the things that they could control and be rewarded for process over products instead of wins and losses.*
>
> *Several months later, when playing in the district finals, the team's best defender got into foul trouble in the first half and a junior, Casey Reason, went into the game and was guarding the leading scorer in the region. Down by ten, Casey's team made a dynamic comeback. In overtime, Casey found himself on the wing, guarding a determined leading scorer. With seconds left, his opponent drove baseline and Casey stepped out and stood ready to take the charge, just like his coach had shown him during the pep rally a few months earlier. The leading scorer hit Casey's chest, knocking him down, and the referee's whistle blew. The fans erupted in complete adulation as the underdog had risen. In this case, the win was driven by a focus on the one thing you can control. A commitment to, and a consistent celebration of process.*
>
> *These examples are snippets of how standards can change an entire culture. By being intentional and raising the standards in a school, the leaders are simply increasing the odds that their programs will function at a high level. Don't be afraid to set the bar high. Nothing good ever came from lowering our standards.*

Conclusion

In this chapter, you have learned a lot about identifying those strategic tipping point standards that make a difference for your school. Schools are all about setting the right standards, adhering to them, and then pursuing adherence for optimal results. Picking the right things to focus on is paramount. School leaders need to prioritize standards and focus on their students' success in activities and athletics. Once standards have been set, you will be in a much better position to continue to accelerate progress.

Alignment is the secret to achieving great results. When everyone in an organization aligns their efforts towards the same vision, the collective power becomes unstoppable.

— Peter Drucker

CHAPTER 5

ALIGN

In the Rally model, *A* stands for "align." What does it mean to be aligned? If your car needs realignment, you're probably veering to the left or the right and risking going off the road. When your efforts are not in alignment, you take action and the synergy of those actions doesn't pay any positive dividends toward bigger goals and objectives.

The purpose of this chapter is to help you learn to build an athletic and activity program that creates aligned forces with other efforts you extend in school to synergistically come together and make it more likely to achieve better results. The authors of this book understand that the dedication and discipline that students learn when participating in athletics and activities help them to then extend that discipline when learning trigonometry. Furthermore, when teachers see the relationship between athletics and activities, they understand that the discipline it takes to consistently do your homework aligns perfectly with understanding the discipline it must take to strengthen your body to prepare for the next season kind of competition. When students and staff come together and see the power of this alignment, the school makes much further progress down the road, just like your car after realignment.

In addition to the horizontal alignment within a school that we see as deeply beneficial for school leaders, this chapter will also illuminate the vertical, K–12 alignment that is necessary for athletics and activities to build strong, deeply impactful programming. You know the importance of developing early elementary, upper elementary, middle school, and high school skills and performance expectations. This same goal of alignment in athletics and activities pays dividends and provides reciprocal, mutually beneficial support.

Identifying Challenges of Aligning

When evaluating your athletic and activity programs, here are four signs that alignment and synergy are lacking in a program. If these challenges are present, don't despair. We have Rally practices to help you!

Your Community Doesn't Know the Mission and Vision of the Program

It could be evident that your community doesn't know the mission and vision of the program. For example, a competitive, new assistant on the swim team may declare statements to parents about the importance of winning state or division championships while the head ACT espouses the mission of contributing to the lifelong health and well-being of students and teaching qualities like sportsmanship. Schools that lack alignment create a lot of confusion for students and parents alike. ACTs at different levels have different perspectives on the mission and vision of the program.

If parents don't understand the mission and vision of the program, they can't support it and even begin to understand the merits of what their students are experiencing. In a highly interconnected world where we are bombarded with social media, parents can get mistaken ideas about what the program could or should be. This is further distorted by club sports programs which are likely to have a different set of goals and expectations. If ACTs aren't clear about the mission and vision for their program, it will be left to interpretation and potential misunderstanding.

At the most basic level, if students who participate in the program don't know what successful engagement and participation means, they aren't as likely to achieve desired expectations.

ACTs at Different Levels Have Different Visions of the Program

The aforementioned example of misalignment between a head ACT and an assistant can also happen where there are overall disconnects from different grade levels, such as misalignment emerging from a sixth- or seventh-grade program advisor through high school. See the following case study for an illustration of the potential misalignment.

CASE STUDY: THE DISJOINTED JOURNEY OF RIVERTON'S MUSIC PROGRAM

Imagine a high school with a thriving and inclusive music program, where students of all skill levels are encouraged to join the band or orchestra and participate in various performances and competitions. The high school music teachers are passionate about fostering a love for music in every student and providing ample opportunities for practice, growth, and performance.

However, at the middle school level, the music program is run by a teacher who is very selective and only focuses on students who already demonstrate a high level of musical talent. This teacher discourages students who are new to playing an instrument or who struggle to keep up with their peers, suggesting that they might be better suited for other activities. As a result, many students who might have developed a passion for music are turned away or discouraged early on.

This misalignment creates a significant challenge for the high school music program. By the time students reach high school, many of those who could have become enthusiastic members of the band or orchestra have already given up on music. The high school music teachers are left with a smaller pool of students to work with and must spend additional time and effort trying to rekindle interest in those who were previously discouraged. Here are the impacts of misalignment.

1. **Reduced participation:** The high school music program sees a decline in student participation due to early discouragement at the middle school level.
2. **Lower morale:** Students who were turned away or discouraged may feel less confident in their abilities and less willing to take risks in other areas of their education.
3. **Missed opportunities:** Talented students who might have flourished with the right support are lost, and the overall quality of the music program suffers.
4. **Cultural disconnect:** A disconnect in the values and approaches between the middle school and high school programs undermines the efforts to create a cohesive and supportive music community.

Recognizing and addressing such misalignments is crucial to maintaining a strong and inclusive program across all grade levels, ensuring that students can explore their talents and passions fully. Disconnects in this area could be disastrous.

WHERE ARE WE NOW?

1. What percentage of your ACTs know the vision of the athletic and activity program?
2. What processes are in place to communicate the overall program vision to lower-level and feeder programs?
3. What practices are established to communicate program vision to parents of students? What percentage of parents could repeat the program vision?
4. What practices are established to communicate program vision to students? What percentage of students could repeat the program vision?

Responding to These Challenges With Rally Practices

When considering how to realign teams and bring synergy back to the organization, consider the following solutions to the challenges we introduced in the previous section.

Rally Practice 2.1: Align Programs From the Top Down

In visualizing and aligning programs in activities and athletics, a very simple and important question to ask is how you want the experiences for your students to culminate. If you are hoping to develop a soccer program where students are prepared to compete for a league or state championship by the time they are juniors and seniors, what sort of introduction should be established in early elementary and middle school? What specific things need to be done to establish that end-game mentality? The late Stephen Covey's wisdom here is still sage. We should "begin with the end in mind" (Covey, 1989). This is a prime example of that wisdom.

One way to look at top-down alignment is to go "upstream" (Heath, 2020). Going upstream is essentially going to the top and evaluating what is in place and what results are happening with the current processes. From there you can determine what the vision of the athletic and activity programs needs to be. It allows you to create plans of action for change, starting from the top and moving down to the bottom. To ensure a top-down alignment, everyone in the downline must understand two things: First, what is the overarching vision of the program? Second, how does their role connect to that vision? Communication of these two items is imperative to having a healthy synergy throughout the school, the community, feeder schools, and programs as well.

A band or orchestra learning a new song is the perfect example of top-to-bottom work. The director chooses the song they feel the group can perform at a high level. Once the decision is made, the individual pieces of the band are given their own piece of music. Each group has benchmarks, and understanding the vision of the conductor, they work toward perfecting their piece to fit into the song to be played by the entire group. Eventually, the groups will come together as a whole and bring all the pieces together to make a beautiful song. The director will give feedback, and the groups will go back and work on the parts that will make the whole better. At the end of the process, you have a sweet piece of art that is performed at the concert or competition. We strive to build that same process into our programs as the overarching vision is disseminated and embraced from top to bottom. Consider this case study as an example of a successful top-down alignment.

CASE STUDY: THE SUCCESS STORY OF PINEWOOD HIGH'S THEATER PROGRAM

Pinewood High School is home to one of the most successful theater programs in the state. The program is renowned for its high-quality productions, passionate student involvement, and the professional development it provides to young thespians. The theater program's success has not only elevated the school's reputation but also set a standard for other grade levels to aspire to and build upon. The vision of Pinewood High's theater program is to develop students' artistic talents and foster a lifelong appreciation for the performing arts. This vision is communicated clearly to all students, faculty, and community members, ensuring that everyone understands their role in achieving this goal. The high school's theater program serves as the pinnacle of achievement, and this high school aspiration sets the mark for the rest of the grade levels. Here's how they ensure alignment.

- **Elementary school (grades K–5)**
    + *Introduction to theater*—Students are introduced to basic theater concepts and activities, such as storytelling, improvisation, and simple performances. Teachers emphasize the joy and creativity that theater can bring, fostering early interest.

+ *After-school programs*—Optional after-school theater clubs offer young students more opportunities to engage in theater activities, laying the foundation for future involvement.

- **Middle school (grades 6–8)**
    + *Building skills*—Middle school theater classes focus on developing acting skills, stage presence, and an understanding of theater production. Students participate in school plays, gaining valuable performance experience.
    + *Workshops and camps*—Summer theater workshops and camps provide additional training and exposure, helping students refine their talents and build confidence.
- **High school (grades 9–12)**
    + *Advanced training*—High school students engage in advanced theater courses that cover acting, directing, playwriting, and technical theater. They participate in multiple productions each year, showcasing their skills.
    + *Mentorship programs*—Experienced high school students mentor middle schoolers, providing guidance and support, and creating a cohesive community of young actors.
    + *Professional development*—The theater program collaborates with local theaters and professionals to offer masterclasses, internships, and networking opportunities.

The culmination of these efforts is a high school theater program that consistently wins accolades at state competitions and festivals. Pinewood High's productions are known for their high production values, outstanding performances, and innovative staging. The program's success is a testament to the top-down alignment strategy, ensuring that students receive consistent, high-quality theater education from their first exposure in elementary school through

> to their final performances in high school. By beginning with the end in mind and ensuring top-down alignment, Pinewood High's theater program has created a pathway for success that inspires and engages students at every grade level. This case study illustrates the importance of a clear vision, consistent communication, and a structured approach to developing a thriving extracurricular program.

To summarize this Rally practice: We must remember that sports and student activities are oftentimes offered at various points throughout a student's K–12 career. This means that a student in early or upper elementary may likely continue to participate in an activity through middle school, high school, and hopefully beyond. School leaders need to focus on creating the kinds of alignment initiatives that will indeed make programming successful and create a coherent experience for the students we serve. The following is a list of some steps you can take as a school leader to help ensure this top-down alignment. Top-down alignment starts from the apex or the culminating activities, which will likely be in high school, and then works through each grade level from the top to the bottom.

- Align programs by visualizing desired student experiences from top-level goals.
- Ask how early introductions in elementary and middle schools can affect later outcomes.
- Establish an end-game mentality through specific actions to align from the top down.
- Go "upstream" to evaluate existing processes and align them with the program's overall vision.
- Ensure everyone understands the program's overarching vision and their role in achieving it.
- Communicate the program's vision to foster synergy within the school, feeder schools, and the community.

Rally Practice 2.2: Align Programs From the Bottom Up

As a companion to the first recommended Rally practice in this section, we recommend a deep and sustained investment in the early stages of introduction for the desired activities and athletics. What we suggest is that to change the destiny of an athletic or activity program, a long-term view is needed. For example, if an ACT is interested in creating a more dynamic student government program, then we must invest in skill building, practice habit formation, and examine overall commitment patterns as early as possible, in terms of experience levels. In other words, for the program at the high school to look different over time, the ACT must work with feeder schools to develop programs that will begin to yield a different result as the students continue to move through the program, practicing and habituating what's desired and hopefully demonstrating what's expected (Thompson & Thompson, 2018).

Creating a bottom-up alignment relies on a heavy investment in the programs that feed into the high school. For some, this may be middle and elementary schools, while for others it may be organizations outside of the school, such as clubs or private programs. This step is often overlooked because the time and effort needed will not result for several years. In some cases, these "feeder" programs may not exist and need to be created but in other cases, the programs are already in place and may just need some direction (Huck & Zhang, 2021). Either way, there must be a concerted effort to introduce students at a young age to new activities as well as develop the skills they need in the future. We have seen this done successfully in both activities and athletics. Consider the following case study to understand bottom-up alignment.

CASE STUDY: STRUMMING UP SUCCESS WITH RIVERVIEW'S ORCHESTRA PROGRAM

Riverview School District, nestled in a small, picturesque town, decided to take a bottom-up approach to build a robust and successful orchestra program. The vision was to introduce students to string instruments in early elementary school, provide continuous skill development through middle school, and eventually create a large, accomplished high school orchestra. The goal was to ensure that students not only developed a love for music but also acquired the technical skills needed to excel in the high school orchestra.

- **Elementary school (grades K–5)**
  + *Introduction to strings*—Starting in third grade, students are introduced to string instruments, such as the violin, viola, cello, and double bass. This is done through a fun and engaging curriculum that includes hands-on lessons, demonstrations, and interactive performances.
  + *After-school clubs*—To foster early interest, Riverview offers after-school string clubs where students can explore different instruments, participate in group lessons, and perform small recitals for their peers and parents.
  + *Community events*—The elementary students participate in community events and school assemblies to showcase their growing talents. This not only builds their confidence but also generates excitement and support from the community.
  + *Workshops*—The school hosts workshops led by high school orchestra members and local musicians, providing young students with exposure to skilled players and role models.
- **Middle school (grades 6–8)**
  + *Building skills*—Middle school students receive more structured and advanced training. They are enrolled in orchestra classes where they learn music theory, ensemble playing, and advanced techniques on their chosen instruments.
  + *Performance opportunities*—Students participate in school concerts, local competitions, and joint performances with the high school

orchestra, providing them with ample opportunities to showcase their skills and gain performance experience.

+ *Summer camps*—Riverview offers summer music camps where middle school students can immerse themselves in intensive training and collaborate with peers from other schools.

+ *Mentorship program*—High school orchestra members mentor middle school students, offering guidance, support, and encouragement. This helps create a sense of continuity and community within the program.

- **High school (grades 9–12)**

  + *Advanced training*—High school students engage in rigorous training and participate in multiple ensembles, including chamber groups and full orchestra. They work on challenging repertoires and prepare for state and national competitions.

  + *Professional development*—The program collaborates with local colleges, professional musicians, and orchestras to offer masterclasses, workshops, and performance opportunities beyond the school setting.

  + *State competitions*—The high school orchestra consistently participates in and wins accolades at state competitions, showcasing the culmination of years of dedicated training and practice.

  + *Community engagement*—The orchestra performs at local events, charity functions, and school celebrations, reinforcing their connection to the community and inspiring younger students.

By adopting a bottom-up approach, Riverview's orchestra program has created a pathway for success that engages and nurtures students from a young age. This comprehensive strategy ensures that students develop a love for music, acquire technical skills, and contribute to a thriving high school orchestra. The success of the program is a tes-

> tament to the importance of early investment, continuous skill development, and community engagement.

To summarize this Rally practice: With this vision of building alignment in mind, we also see some benefits to visualizing this alignment from the bottom up. In other words, starting from the beginning and offering programs to students allows them to build a set of experiences from K–12. Whether it's a top-down or bottom-up alignment process, a fully aligned and well-articulated program needs to work both ways. This list will give you a perspective on how to see the program development from the bottom up.

- Invest in early-stage programs to change the destiny of athletic and activity programs.
- Focus on long-term investment in skill-building and commitment patterns. Standards of your program should not be new when they are introduced to your campus.
- Invest in feeder programs to introduce and develop students in all activities.
- Establish community events and workshops to expose young students to all activities.
- Focus on skill building and character development from a young age to yield long-term results.

Rally Practice 2.3: Practice Loose-Tight Leadership With Continuous Review

Successful leaders at all levels understand that they must communicate to their constituents their loose and tight expectations. Historically, *loose-tight leadership* refers to the leader's ability to directly identify those elements of the program that must be strictly controlled and executed in a consistent, or *tight* way. Conversely, these leaders are also aware of the structures within the system that are *loose*, allowing leaders of other levels to self-organize and define in their own way (DuFour et al., 2024; Sagie et al., 2002).

This type of clarity and leadership has helped get individuals in the organization to understand where autonomy is allowed and expected and where adherence to a specific action orientation or series of steps is the ask. For our application with Rally, ACTs must be provided clarity about the things that are important. Furthermore, they should be told about the things that are less important in the program and can afford flexibility. An example would be a large high school that has a chronically underrepresented and small marching band. A new marching band director may discover that at the middle school and elementary level, the directors were instituting nearly impossible practice standards that resulted in numerous defections before ever reaching high school. To change the district's goal for increasing the size of marching bands, the leadership would need to be tight about encouraging participation while maybe being loose about other elements of the elementary and middle school program that wouldn't relate as much to program retention and persistence.

As a leader, you must familiarize yourself with the fact that loose-tight leadership stems from the standards that were outlined in the previous chapter (page 63). The standard will always be the standard, but how we approach it may differ at times. There are many ways to do this. In the next section, we highlight four tips that we highly encourage to ensure that all parties are aligned with the standard.

REFLECTING INDIVIDUALLY AS ACTS

It may sound obvious, but for ACTs to be successful, they must be directed and indeed encouraged to review their progress toward the vision continuously on their own. At a minimum weekly, or perhaps in some cases daily, successful ACTs remind themselves where they're attempting to go and the steps they are taking to progress. It is important to understand that growth is a journey, not a destination. We don't simply "get there" but are on a never-ending journey to see how far we can go. This continuous reflection and review sets a direct intentionality about their actions that will undoubtedly help them to recognize opportunities and move optimistically toward the things that matter. It also helps them stay observant of what might be an emerging resource or an opportunity to grow.

ACTs should be able to share with school leaders exactly what the vision of the program is and how the school vision aligns with those process goals. For example, if a coach or advisor is committed to increasing participation in their program, and the administration does not know it, it makes it difficult for any progress in that program to happen. Additionally, if the vision of the school focuses on character and culture, while the ACT is focused on performance, the actions taken by the ACT could come in direct conflict with the bigger picture.

REVIEWING WITH ASSISTANTS AND ACTS AT OTHER LEVELS

No matter the level at which an ACT is working, they should take direct steps to communicate with ACTs at other levels to ensure there is indeed alignment about expectations, standards, and anticipated steps moving forward. Things are happening at one level should support the expectations at another level. For example, what can an ACT working with third graders do to prepare for the student experience in ninth and tenth grade? By sharing these expectations with assistants and ACTs at other levels, there's a fighting chance for alignment and synergistic growth. An example of this would be a football program that consistently meets with their coaches at all levels and goes over a scaffolding of what they want to implement. The head coach may communicate to the youth program that he wants to have them begin using certain terminology while teaching basic techniques. The aforementioned levels could be implemented more and more as they move up the ranks. The ability for the leader to communicate what this looks like for an end product and how they want it installed while allowing for some autonomy of how that gets done would exemplify loose-tight leadership.

SHARING WITH THE COMMUNITY AND PARENTS

Unfortunately, some ACTs are reluctant to share their vision with the community and parents for one simple reason. They are afraid if they don't uphold those standards, they'll be made to look like they are ineffective. However, we would argue that without their support, your chances of meeting your expectations are diminished.

You need community members and parents to team with you in helping those expectations you have come to fruition. Clarity and transparency will serve in two important ways. First, parents and community members can help you create progress toward your vision. Secondly, your outward-facing commitment will serve to redouble your efforts and those of the students you serve. When the students know that the community, parents, and other members of their own school community are all observing their attempt to grow in a specific way, accountability alone can lead to the opportunity for accelerated outcomes (Garfin, Silver, & Holman, 2020; Terada, Merrill, & Gonser, 2021). Here are three steps you can take to establish more effective community-sharing practices.

1. **Public presentations:** Host public meetings and presentations to share the vision and strategic plans for the extracurricular programs. This includes outlining the goals, expected outcomes, and the steps the school is taking to achieve these objectives.
2. **Regular updates:** Send regular newsletters and updates to parents and community members. This can include progress reports, upcoming events, and ways they can get involved or support the program.
3. **Community advisory boards:** Establish advisory boards that include parents, local business leaders, and community members. These boards can provide feedback, support fundraising efforts, and help ensure the programs meet the community's needs.

By constantly communicating the vision from top-to-bottom and bottom-to-top programs, while focusing on leading from a loose-tight lens and aligning the programs, the synergy of all stakeholders can be solidified. This will also allow leaders to focus on what is important and that is the standards set.

To summarize this Rally practice: The brilliance of loose-tight leadership is that we can provide support in various ways depending on the situation and the constituents involved. A newer coach or advisor might need more oversight. A more senior, experienced, and fully realized advisor may need you to work diligently at remaining loose, and simply keeping obstacles out of their way. At times, it is beneficial for a coach or advisor to struggle through some problems and learn from mistakes. Running in to rescue them doesn't generally lead to the kind of growth that coaches or advisors need. Here are a few more tips on how to achieve that loose-tight sensibility.

- Set expectations while allowing flexibility within the program.
- Identify elements that must be strictly controlled (tight) and those that allow flexibility (loose).
- Encourage individual reflection among ACTs to review progress toward the overall vision.
- Ensure school leadership understands the vision and aligns school goals with program objectives.
- Foster communication and alignment among ACTs at different levels.
- Share the program's vision with the community and parents to garner support and accountability.

Rally Practice 2.4: Be Intentional With Other Programs

In the multifaceted environment of K–12 education, collaboration and mutual understanding among coaches and advisors are crucial for the holistic development of students. When educators are aware of the needs and demands of fellow coaches and advisors in other programs, it creates a supportive and flexible environment that benefits everyone involved, particularly the students. This collaboration can significantly impact students who participate in multiple activities, easing the family demands and fostering a balanced approach to extracurricular involvement.

UNDERSTAND FAMILY DEMANDS

Students who participate in multiple activities often face significant family demands. Balancing schoolwork, extracurricular activities, and family responsibilities can be challenging and stressful. Coaches and advisors must be intentional in observing what parents and students might be experiencing. This awareness helps in understanding the pressures on the household and allows for more empathetic and supportive interactions. For example, if a student is involved in both the marching band and a sports team, the time commitment required for practices, performances, and games can be substantial (Miller, 2024).

CREATE SCHOOLWIDE AWARENESS

It's essential for coaches and advisors to be aware of, at least on a basic level, the work demands and expectations of other programs. This schoolwide awareness helps in creating a more cooperative environment where the needs of students can be met more effectively. For instance, if a basketball coach understands the time and effort required for a student's participation in the marching band, they can adjust their expectations and provide the necessary flexibility. This cooperation ensures that students do not have to choose between multiple activities or athletic interests and can excel in several areas (Thompson & Thompson, 2018).

COOPERATE TO SEE BENEFITS

When coaches and advisors work together and communicate effectively, it leads to several benefits.

- **Reduced stress:** Students experience less stress when their schedules are coordinated, and their commitments are understood by all involved parties.

- **Enhanced participation:** More students are likely to participate in multiple activities if they feel supported and their efforts are recognized.

- **Stronger community:** Collaboration fosters a sense of community among coaches, advisors, students, and parents, which leads to a more supportive and inclusive school environment.

Consider the following case study to better understand what we mean by cooperation.

CASE STUDY: HARMONIZING THE RHYTHM BETWEEN MR. BLACK AND MR. BROWN

Mr. Black, the marching band instructor, and Mr. Brown, the basketball coach at Central High School, both recognize the importance of their programs in the students' lives. However, they face a challenge: Several basketball players are also enthusiastic members of the marching band. The overlap in activities requires careful coordination and cooperation to ensure that students can participate fully in both programs without undue stress or conflict.

During the fall marching season, Mr. Black and Mr. Brown hold a meeting to discuss their schedules and the demands of their respective programs. They understand that while the basketball season is not in full swing, conditioning and training sessions are still ongoing. Similarly, the marching band has several performances and practices that require the students' full attention. Here is how the two teachers established a relationship that prioritized collaboration, cooperation, and flexibility.

- **Schedule coordination:** Mr. Black provides Mr. Brown with the marching band schedule, including practice times and performance dates. Mr. Brown does the same for basketball training sessions. They identify potential conflicts and work together to adjust practice times, ensuring that students do not have to miss important sessions in either activity.

- **Shared support:** Mr. Brown encourages his basketball players to communicate openly about their commitments to the marching band. This openness allows for better planning and reduces last-minute scheduling issues. Mr. Black, understanding the physical demands of basketball, ensures that band practices are structured in a way that does not overly fatigue the student-athletes.

- **Joint meetings:** Mr. Black and Mr. Brown hold periodic joint meetings with the students involved in both programs. These meetings serve as a platform to discuss any concerns and provide mutual support and encouragement.

The cooperation between Mr. Black and Mr. Brown results in a harmonious balance that allows students to thrive in both the marching band and basketball. The students feel supported and less stressed, leading to better performance in both activities. The collaboration sets a positive example for other coaches and advisors, highlighting the benefits of working together and being aware of each other's programmatic needs.

This case study exemplifies the importance of cooperation and flexibility among coaches and advisors in K–12 education. By understanding and accommodating the needs of students and fellow educators, schools can create a more supportive environment that fosters student success and well-being.

To summarize this Rally practice: Remain aware of the goals and intentions of other programs, and make sure that while coaches and advisors pursue the goals and objectives for their season with enthusiasm, they are aware of how their efforts, expectations, and activities may influence the goals and aspirations of other programs. Without this awareness, competition between programs can emerge, and in fact, that's not what we are looking for in a well-led series of student athletics and activities.

- Create intentional connections and collaborations among ACTs to drive program improvement.
- Avoid operating in silos and collaborate with other programs.
- Share ideas, help one another, and work toward a common goal.
- Establish learning communities or meetings to facilitate knowledge sharing and collaboration.

- Foster a culture of collaboration and shared learning among ACTs.
- Recognize the value of collective efforts in improving programs and serving students better.

RALLY IN ACTION

Most people have seen the movie, read the book, or have heard the statement, "Friday Night Lights." This phrase, though dubbed for football games, encompasses so much more than just the game on the field, and few do it better than the state of Texas. Andrew had the opportunity of being around educational athletics for over twenty years. It wasn't until he moved to Texas that he understood the magnitude of that phrase, "Friday Night Lights," and what went into it. This experience began to show Andrew the gold-standard example of how synergy and alignment came together in almost a beautiful entanglement involving the entire school. He would learn exactly how alignment worked both vertically and horizontally, and the term "guns up" still holds a dear place in his heart.

Andrew moved into a community in central Texas with his family several years into his career as a football coach. This quaint suburban city was a large district with several schools, in which his family was zoned for one of their five high schools. Having been new to Texas, he asked neighbors about how to get his children involved in youth sports and activities, which traditionally had been run through community programs in the state he came from. What he found was community programs in Texas were an extension of the schools. His oldest son got involved with football while his oldest daughter wanted to be in band. What happened that season was like nothing their family had seen before. Both teams kicked off the season with parent meetings, which to Andrew's astonishment were led by the head coaches and directors of both the high school programs. The meeting went over expectations of the students and parents being involved in the program moving forward, which would match the vision and goals of the varsity programs. Andrew was blown away. His son was only a fifth grader, and his daughter was a third grader. As the season progressed, the uniforms were the same colors—the mascots, the music, and even the playbook were the same. Even the phrase "guns up," implemented after their mascot the Raiders, was brandished throughout all the communications. The students were invited to participate in a youth night during the opening game, running out with the team, playing with the varsity band pregame, and having a special section to sit during the game to watch. The family had resided in the area for less than two months and the alignment already hooked them in the community.

As time went on, he was even more impressed with the connection to the high school as they received a big brother and a big sister from the school. These big "siblings" wrote letters to his children each week with words of encouragement for the upcoming week in their activity as well as their academics. The students also wrote letters back to the players and bandmates with similar sentiments. When the coaches and directors stated that this was a family, that vision was not lost and it was known throughout the community. What was amazing was as Andrew became more involved in the community, it didn't stop with football or band. Almost every sport and activity that the school could get out into the community, they did! In later seasons, Andrew's children were able to participate in soccer, choir, National Honor Society . . . all connected to the school and their vision of "guns up." One of Andrew's children even ventured out to try chess at a school-sponsored chess clinic. At a school picnic, Andrew saw that the principal was in attendance and engaged in a conversation with him about the community. Andrew simply asked how she had gotten the community all on the same page with everything they did. Her story was quite remarkable:

"As a kid, I grew up in a small town in Georgia. Everything we did in that town revolved around events that were put on by the school. It seemed to be the connection between every class of people. No matter what kind of money you made, what your last name was, or how good or bad you were at something, the community always came together for school events. When I went to college to be a teacher and eventually wanted to be a principal, I told myself I wanted to make sure I created that connection for my school. When I got this job, we were one of five high schools in the city, so the task was going to be a little tougher. I started by inviting leaders within the school to meet to help me create a vision. What we came up with was 'guns up!' It stood for grit, unity, no fear, and selflessness. We decided that we were in a battle each day to be better. Teachers, students, staff . . . everyone was in the fight. As we pushed this out to the community, we knew that activities and athletics would be the key. We had each team and group implement the new vision with fidelity and tasked them with pushing it out to the feeder programs. I asked them

> *if they could commit to doing this within two years. They agreed and the result was that everyone tried to align the school's vision from the top to the bottom. If you ask anyone on campus what our vision is, you should hear 'guns up!'"*
>
> *The principal beamed with pride as she divulged her story of aligning her vision for the community. As Andrew experienced this, he thought that maybe he was lucky to land in this community. But it wasn't luck. Andrew was a football coach at a school in Pflugerville at the same time and the standard was not any different. He was expected to visit junior high and elementary schools, work camps, and teach coaches the systems at the lower levels. There were a few more obstacles, but the standard was still the same. In Texas, a majority of the communities operate similarly. Vertical and horizontal alignment and synergy are ingrained in the fabric of their education system, as communities place high values on activities and athletics. For those of you who think we're just talking about football, tell that to Allen High School and their 1,000-member band who take over twenty buses to get to a game. Friday Night Lights align an entire community from a football team to band, cheer, pom, drill team, student council, and ultimately the student body and the community members within their specific and important roles. As 15,000 people come together, it's more than just a game. It's a culture. It's an event. It's Friday Night Lights!*

Conclusion

Riding a bike with crooked tires makes for a very bumpy ride. Episodic efforts at one level that aren't replicated earlier or later in the career of a student defeat the purpose. This creates an uneven experience and, as illustrated, a bumpy ride, Alignment is essential. Your school administration needs a predictable, symmetrical pathway for your activities and athletics programs. Specific steps taken to make consistent those important things that matter will create an opportunity for the program to move students through with success, have a more even and predictable experience for parents and community members, and ultimately accelerate performance and outcomes as old standards are met and new opportunities are unleashed.

*The PLC process has helped to redefine the
role of educators from isolated individuals
in isolated classrooms to collective
teams of colleagues working collectively
to solve problems.*

—Casey Reason & Richard DuFour

CHAPTER 6

LEARNING COMMUNITIES FOR ACTS

The first "L" in the Rally model is for learning communities for ACTs. We are raving fans of the professional learning communities (PLC) concept. We have lived the model as practitioners. Furthermore, Casey wrote a book on the concept with PLC architect, Richard DuFour (DuFour & Reason, 2016). Rick would have smiled at that reference. The purpose of this chapter is to build a sustained and aligned culture that lasts. In this chapter, we take a deep dive into the role of quality collaboration and the construction of learning communities as a mechanism for improving schools as well as the design and delivery of athletic and activity programming. You will see that we have taken some of the key elements of what it means to conceptualize and deliver the PLC model and utilize those same commitments when it comes to athletics and activities.

Establishing a Collaborative Learning Culture

The PLC structure is a specific, school improvement design endeavor that requires strict adherence to the well-formulated, implementation model (Dougherty & Reason, 2019). While we are giving you actionable guidance to create a more general collaborative team structure, the working elements of the PLC model can inform the construction of a highly effective learning community structure for ACTs. Here are a few elements we can implement to ensure we're creating a sense of community.

Shared Mission, Vision, Values, and Goals

Establishing programmatic K–12 missions, visions, values, and goals are essential for creating a cohesive and effective educational environment. A unified mission provides a clear purpose, guiding all stakeholders toward common objectives (Gurley, Peters, Collins, & Fifolt, 2015). Vision statements inspire and direct long-term aspirations, while values foster a shared culture and ethical framework. Goals, both overarching and leveled, ensure that each educational stage is aligned with the overall mission while addressing the specific developmental needs of students at each level (Hwa, Kaffenberger, & Silberstein, 2020). This approach not only promotes consistency and coherence across the K–12 spectrum but also allows for tailored strategies that cater to the unique requirements of elementary, middle, and high school students, ultimately supporting the holistic development of every learner (Dekker, Schippers, & Van Schooten, 2023). Consider the following case study, which will help illuminate this dynamic.

CASE STUDY: THE UNIFIED VISION OF RIVERTOWN'S GIRLS SOCCER PROGRAM

In Rivertown School District, a comprehensive approach has been implemented to develop a thriving girls soccer program. This case study explores the overarching mission, vision, values, and goals for the entire K–12 program and demonstrates how these align with specific goals at the elementary and middle school levels.

K–12 Girls Soccer Program

- **Mission:** To inspire and empower young athletes through soccer, fostering teamwork, discipline, and a lifelong love of the game across all grade levels

- **Vision:** To create a cohesive and inclusive soccer program that nurtures talent from elementary through high school, preparing students to compete at high levels while developing strong character and leadership skills
- **Values:**
  + *Inclusivity*—Ensure every student has the opportunity to participate and succeed in the soccer program.
  + *Excellence*—Strive for the highest standards in both athletic performance and personal development.
  + *Teamwork*—Promote collaboration, communication, and mutual support among players, coaches, and the community.
  + *Growth*—Encourage continuous improvement and lifelong learning on and off the field.
  + *Passion*—Instill a deep love and appreciation for soccer in all participants.
- **Goals:**
  + *K–12 goal*—Develop a pipeline of talented and passionate soccer players who demonstrate sportsmanship, leadership, and academic excellence.
  + *High school goal*—Achieve consistent performance in state-level competitions and foster college recruitment opportunities.
  + *Middle school goal*—Increase participation rates and enhance skill development through structured training and competitive play.
  + *Elementary school goal*—Introduce soccer fundamentals and cultivate a love for the sport through fun and engaging activities.

Elementary School Girls Soccer Program

- **Mission:** To introduce young students to the joy of soccer, fostering basic skills and a love for the game in a fun and supportive environment

- **Vision:** To create a foundation for lifelong participation in soccer by providing engaging and accessible opportunities for all elementary students
- **Values:**
  + *Fun*—Emphasize enjoyment and enthusiasm in all soccer activities.
  + *Learning*—Focus on teaching basic soccer skills and rules in a supportive atmosphere.
  + *Inclusion*—Ensure every student has the chance to participate, regardless of skill level.
  + *Team spirit*—Foster a sense of belonging and teamwork among young players.
- **Goals:**
  + *Participation*—Increase the number of elementary students participating in soccer activities by 20 percent each school year.
  + *Skill development*—Introduce fundamental soccer skills, such as dribbling, passing, and shooting, through age-appropriate drills and games.
  + *Community engagement*—Organize family-friendly soccer events to build community support and involvement.

Middle School Girls Soccer Program

- **Mission:** To build on the foundations established in elementary school, providing a structured and competitive environment that promotes skill development and teamwork
- **Vision:** To prepare middle school athletes for high school soccer by offering advanced training, competitive opportunities, and leadership development
- **Values:**
  + *Development*—Focus on enhancing individual skills and understanding of the game.

- + *Commitment*—Encourage dedication to training and team success.
- + *Respect*—Promote sportsmanship and respect for teammates, coaches, and opponents.
- + *Leadership*—Develop leadership qualities in each player to prepare them for high school and beyond.
- **Goals:**
  - + *Skill enhancement*—Increase the proficiency of technical skills and tactical understanding among middle school players.
  - + *Competitive success*—Improve team performance in district and regional competitions.
  - + *Retention*—Ensure that at least 80 percent of middle school players transition to the high school soccer program.

Rivertown School District's girls soccer program exemplifies how a unified vision, mission, and set of values can be effectively aligned across K–12 education levels. By establishing specific goals tailored to each developmental stage, the program ensures a cohesive and supportive environment that nurtures young athletes from their first introduction to soccer through high school graduation. This comprehensive approach not only enhances athletic performance but also fosters personal growth, teamwork, and community spirit.

Collective Inquiry

Collective inquiry is a structured process where members of a group, such as collaborative teams within a PLC, come together to systematically examine their practices, ask questions, develop theories of action, determine action steps, and gather and analyze evidence to assess the impact of their actions (Donohoo, 2015). This process is rooted in collaboration and shared knowledge-building, aiming to improve educational outcomes and foster continuous improvement (DuFour et al., 2024).

Collective inquiry in academics encourages teachers to work collaboratively to identify and address common challenges, share best practices, and develop innovative solutions (Donohoo, 2015). This collaborative approach leads to improved teaching strategies, enhanced student engagement, and higher academic achievement (Gillies, 2023). By fostering a culture of continuous inquiry and reflection, teachers can create a more dynamic and responsive learning environment (Donohoo, 2015).

In the context of athletics and activities, collective inquiry helps teams and groups develop a shared understanding of their goals, strategies, and performance metrics (Zumeta, Oriol, Telletxea, Amutio, & Basabe, 2016). This process promotes a sense of unity and collective efficacy, where team members believe in their collective ability to achieve success (Bandura, 1997). By engaging in collective inquiry, teams can identify areas for improvement, implement effective training methods, and enhance overall performance (Zumeta et al., 2016). The following are examples of collective inquiry operating in various settings.

- **Academic setting:** In an academic setting, a group of teachers might engage in collective inquiry to address a common issue, such as improving reading comprehension among students. The teachers would first identify the problem and gather relevant data, such as student test scores and reading assessments. They would then collaboratively develop a theory of action, hypothesizing that implementing a new reading program could improve comprehension. The teachers would design and implement the program, collect data on its effectiveness, and analyze the results. Based on their findings, they would make necessary adjustments and continue the cycle of inquiry to ensure continuous improvement (Donohoo, 2015).

- **Athletic or student activity setting:** In an athletic setting, a soccer team might use collective inquiry to enhance their defensive strategies. The team would start by identifying weaknesses in their current defense through game footage analysis and player feedback. They would then develop a theory of action, hypothesizing that a new defensive drill could improve their performance. The team would implement the drill during practice sessions, monitor its impact on their defensive performance in games, and gather feedback from players and coaches. Based on their analysis, they would refine the drill and continue the cycle of inquiry to achieve better results (Zumeta et al., 2016).

QUESTIONS DRIVE INNOVATION AND CREATIVITY

Questions are powerful tools for driving innovation and creativity. They encourage curiosity, challenge assumptions, and open up new possibilities (Shuck, 2023). By asking the right questions, individuals and organizations can explore uncharted territories, uncover hidden opportunities, and foster a culture of continuous improvement (Shuck, 2023). Questions serve as catalysts for brainstorming sessions, prompting diverse perspectives and pushing teams beyond conventional boundaries (Shuck, 2023).

In an academic setting, teachers can use powerful questions to inspire students to think critically and creatively. For example, instead of simply asking students to memorize facts, teachers might pose questions like, "What if we could travel back in time to witness this historical event? How would it change our understanding?" This approach encourages students to engage deeply with the material, explore different viewpoints, and develop innovative solutions to complex problems.

In a student activity setting, coaches and activity leaders can use questions to enhance team performance and foster a growth mindset. For instance, a soccer coach might ask, "What if we tried a new formation in our next game? How could it improve our defense?" These questions prompt players to think strategically, experiment with new tactics, and collaborate to find the best approach. By encouraging questions, coaches can create an environment where students feel empowered to take risks, learn from their experiences, and continuously improve.

COLLABORATIVE TEAMS ENCOURAGE INTERCONNECTION

Collaborative teams harness the power of interconnection, working together towards common goals with a level of synergy that detached groups often lack. Research highlights that while groups consist of individuals working independently, teams are characterized by high interdependence and collaboration. This interconnectedness fosters a sense of shared purpose and mutual accountability, driving collective success (Dunn, 2025). These six factors are integral to the formation of collaborative teams.

1. **Focus on the right work:** Highly effective teams carefully select the right goals and objectives, ensuring alignment with the organization's mission, vision, and values. This strategic focus is crucial for meaningful collaboration (Dunn, 2025).

2. **Learning and growth:** A hallmark of effective teams is their commitment to continuous learning and growth. Cooperative learning environments promote personal and team development, enhancing overall performance (Johnson & Johnson, 2008).

3. **Scheduled collaboration time:** Consistently setting time aside for collaboration is essential. Teams that commit to regular meetings and collaborative efforts create a structured environment for idea exchange and problem solving (Gillies, 2023).

4. **Reciprocal accountability:** Every team member is expected to come prepared and contribute significantly to the team's objectives. This reciprocal accountability fosters trust and ensures that all members are equally invested in the team's success (DuFour & Eaker, 1998).

5. **Agreed on work rules:** Establishing work rules, such as punctuality, preparedness, and respectful disagreement, helps maintain a productive and harmonious team environment. These rules ensure that the team operates smoothly and continuously (Dunn, 2025).

6. **Ongoing learning and improvement:** A commitment to ongoing learning and never-ending improvement is vital. Teams that embrace this principle take ownership of their results and strive for continuous evolution, fostering a culture of excellence (DuFour et al., 2024).

Through the power of collaboration, interconnected teams create an environment that fosters innovation, shared accountability, and continuous growth, ultimately leading to superior outcomes for all involved.

Action Orientation

Action orientation in the context of PLCs refers to the proactive approach teams take to turn aspirations into action and visions into reality (DuFour et al., 2024). It emphasizes the importance of moving quickly from planning to implementation, ensuring that learning and insights are consistently applied to achieve tangible results (DuFour et al., 2024).

In an academic setting, maintaining an action orientation means that teachers and administrators are constantly seeking ways to improve student learning outcomes. For example, a school might identify a need to enhance reading comprehension among students. Instead of merely discussing potential strategies, the team quickly implements a new reading program, monitors its effectiveness through regular assessments, and makes data-driven adjustments as needed. This continuous cycle of action and reflection ensures that the team is always moving forward and making progress (DuFour et al., 2024).

In athletics and activities, an action orientation involves regularly evaluating and refining training methods and strategies. For instance, a high school basketball team might notice that their defense is weak. The coach and the team quickly develop and implement new defensive drills. They then assess the impact of these drills during practice games and make necessary adjustments based on performance data. This proactive approach helps the team continuously improve and achieve better results (Reason, 2017).

Imagine that a middle school mathematics department notices that students are struggling with algebraic concepts. The team decides to implement a new teaching method that incorporates more hands-on activities and real-world problem solving. They quickly develop lesson plans, train teachers on the new method, and start using it in the classroom. After a few weeks, they analyze student performance data and find that student understanding has improved. The team then refines the method based on feedback and continues to monitor progress, ensuring that the new approach is effective (DuFour et al., 2024).

Consider another example where a high school soccer team identifies a lack of coordination among players during set pieces. The coach organizes a special training session focused on improving communication and positioning. The team practices these skills in various game scenarios and evaluates their effectiveness during scrimmages. Based on the outcomes, the coach adjusts the training plan and continues to work with the team to enhance their performance. This ongoing cycle of action and evaluation helps the team develop stronger strategies and achieve better results (Reason, 2017).

Commitment to Continuous Improvement

Continuous improvement in PLCs refers to the ongoing process of evaluating and enhancing educational practices to achieve better outcomes for students (DuFour et al., 2024). This concept involves a deep commitment to regularly assessing teaching methods, student performance, and overall school operations to identify areas for growth and implement effective changes (Gillies, 2023).

In an academic setting, continuous improvement might involve a collaborative team of mathematics teachers who regularly analyze student test scores to identify common areas of difficulty (Gillies, 2023). The team collaborates to develop new instructional strategies, such as incorporating more hands-on activities or integrating technology into lessons. They implement these strategies, monitor their impact through ongoing assessments, and make necessary adjustments based on student performance data. This iterative process ensures that teaching practices are constantly evolving to meet the needs of students (DuFour et al., 2024).

In the context of athletics and activities, continuous improvement could be seen in a high school soccer team's efforts to enhance their performance (Gillies, 2023). The coaching staff and players might regularly review game footage to identify weaknesses in their play. Then, they work together to develop new training drills and strategies to address these issues. By consistently evaluating their progress and making data-driven decisions, the team can continuously improve their skills and achieve better results on the field (Gillies, 2023).

A Results Orientation

A results orientation in PLCs refers to the unwavering focus on achieving measurable outcomes that demonstrate student growth and success (DuFour et al., 2024). This concept emphasizes the importance of setting goals, monitoring progress, and making data-driven decisions to ensure continuous improvement in educational practices (DuFour & Fullan, 2013).

In an academic setting, an English language arts collaborative team might focus on improving student literacy rates. The team sets specific, measurable goals for reading and writing proficiency and regularly reviews student assessment data to track progress. They identify effective teaching strategies and implement them across the school. By consistently analyzing data and making necessary adjustments, the team ensures that their efforts lead to tangible improvements in student outcomes (DuFour & Fullan, 2013).

In the context of athletics and activities, a results-oriented approach might involve a high school basketball team aiming to increase their win rate. The coaching staff collaborates to develop a training plan that targets specific skills and strategies. They track the team's performance in games and practices, using this data to refine their approach. By focusing on results, the team can identify areas for improvement and implement changes that lead to better performance on the court (DuFour & Fullan, 2013).

Shared Knowledge

Shared knowledge within PLCs refers to the collective understanding and information that team members accumulate over time through collaboration and shared experiences (Capone, 2020). This concept encompasses the competencies, skills, and insights that educators or team members develop as they work together, creating a rich repository of knowledge that benefits the entire group.

Shared knowledge is the constellation of abilities and insights team members develop through ongoing collaboration. It involves the exchange of best practices, innovative strategies, and effective teaching methods that enhance the overall performance and outcomes of the team (Serviss, 2022). This collective intelligence is crucial for continuous improvement and achieving common goals.

In an academic setting, shared knowledge within a PLC might involve teams from across the PLC collaborating to improve student reading outcomes (Capone, 2020). For instance, a team of educators might share effective reading strategies, assessment tools, and intervention techniques that have worked well in their classrooms. By pooling their knowledge and experiences, they can develop a comprehensive approach to address reading challenges and support student success (Serviss, 2022).

In the context of athletics and activities, shared knowledge can be seen in a high school basketball team working together to improve their performance (Serviss, 2022). Coaches and players might share insights on effective training drills, game strategies, and mental preparation techniques. Through regular practice and communication, the team develops a shared understanding of what works best, leading to improved performance on the court (Capone, 2020).

Identifying Challenges of Learning Communities

The first attempt to bring leaders from activities and athletics together for a common goal for any school will always come with challenges. For many, the two entities are completely separate, but we feel that they are much closer aligned than most leaders understand. The tools needed to be a successful athlete are usually similarly needed in activities. Take endurance for instance. A Model UN student may not need to have the lung capacity to run a four-minute mile but may need the mental stamina to endure through high-intensity competition just the same. It's no different than a tennis player who will need to have a cerebral approach to their match that would include some of the same skills an esports student may have. Learning to thrive in any situation is something all students can learn as it will lead to success in any field. Beginning to identify potential roadblocks to bringing leaders together is the first step to this newer, out-of-the-box thinking. We have identified a few major challenges you may face as a leader in this area.

Unresolved Competition Between Programs

In every school striving to continuously improve in their athletic and activities programs, there is going to be competition for student time and attention both in-season and off-season. When Casey served as a football coach and a speech and debate coach at his high school, some of his players followed him from the offensive and defensive line right into extemporaneous speaking and Lincoln Douglas debate in the winter. This kept them from joining the wrestling team, and in some cases prevented them from participating in some of the winter workouts with football. Invariably, ACTs must have the ability to be respectful of each other's attempts to grow the program, and be careful not to put students and their families in the middle of this attempt to grow.

Bullying and Fighting

In the most toxic and unhealthy school cultures, we have observed that this competition for participants, and confrontation between programs, can manifest into ugly forms of bullying and conflict. For example, in some of the worst examples we've seen, students who want to play in the marching band and simultaneously compete on the football team or other fall sports activity might be ridiculed by teammates or even ACTs for their proclivity to participate. If this is going on in abundance in your school, it is indeed a sign of lack of communication and trouble.

WHERE ARE WE NOW?

1. What practices do we have in place to provide consistency amongst ACTs on vision, values, and goals?
2. Do we have any programs that have historically competed for students? If so, how have those been approached by leadership both in the program and from a school level?
3. Is there a program that has been intentionally or unintentionally positioned above other programs in the school? If so, what has been the outcome of the overall school culture?
4. If put into a room, how many of your ACTs could greet by name every other ACT in the room?

Responding to These Challenges With Rally Practices

In this next challenge section, we share strategies for responding to some of the more difficult implementation hindrances you are likely to observe.

Rally Practice 3.1: Establish What an ACT Community in the School Really Is

In the Rally model, the ACT community of practice is a deeply interconnected group of advisors, coaches, and teachers who are committed to meaningful and sustained collaboration with the sole effort of trying to create a sense of interdependence within the group, raising the quality of the experience for all the students in the school.

Establish with the ACTs why this process is essential. The coordination of this type of group is essential because if there is going to be consistency in expectations, such as sportsmanship, requirements for participation, and commands for fan and parent support, all activities must indeed be in agreement. ACTs can begin to understand that if all ACTs are on the same page with expectations, no matter what students come their way, they will all eventually understand the standard doesn't change from one activity to the other.

We recommended an initial meeting with the ACTs to establish these expectations and begin to elicit their support and ideas. Ask them what they think will be the challenges of this process. What results do they want to see from this process? What commitments are they willing to begin with? As a leader, once you understand the thoughts and concerns of your ACTs and what challenges they foresee, you can begin a process that can accomplish the goals of the learning community while at the same time addressing the concerns of the ACTs. The more you can get the ACTs involved with the implementation, the better chance the learning community has for success. We would invite you not to get discouraged, as we have seen thirty-year veterans who were resistant to the process at first have a complete change of heart. They understood this was all to make their experience and the experience of the students more enjoyable and ultimately easier. Students who understand and adhere to expectations are more likely to experience fewer discipline issues and increased competitiveness (Posselt & Lipson, 2016). Research indicates that expectations and consistent enforcement of rules create a structured environment that promotes student self-discipline and academic success (Posselt & Lipson, 2016).

Resistance to collaboration within teams is a common challenge that PLCs face. This resistance can stem from various factors, including individual reluctance to change, fear of the unknown, and institutional barriers. Preparing to address and overcome this resistance is crucial for the successful implementation and sustainability of PLCs (Maag, 2009; Provini, 2013).

Resistance to collaboration in PLCs refers to the opposition or reluctance of individuals or groups to engage in collective efforts and shared decision-making processes. This resistance can manifest as skepticism, lack of participation, or outright refusal to cooperate. Understanding and addressing this resistance involves recognizing the underlying causes and implementing strategies to foster a culture of openness and mutual support (Maag, 2009; Provini, 2013).

In an academic setting, resistance to collaboration within PLCs might involve teachers who are accustomed to working independently and are hesitant to share their practices or seek input from colleagues.

To address this, school leaders can provide professional development opportunities focused on the benefits of collaboration and create structured time for team meetings. For example, a school might implement regular "collaboration days" where teachers work together to develop common assessments, share effective teaching strategies, and analyze student data (Provini, 2013).

In the context of athletics and activities, resistance to collaboration can occur when coaches or team members are resistant to new training methods or strategies proposed by their peers. To overcome this, coaches can lead with curiosity, listen to their team's concerns, and present ideas clearly and concisely. For instance, a high school basketball coach might introduce a new defensive drill and explain the rationale behind it, while also being open to feedback and adjustments based on the team's input (TrueSport, 2024). Scholars Sneha Tharayil, Maura Borrego, and colleagues from the University of Texas at Austin, Texas recommend the following general strategies for dealing with resistance in extracurricular activities (Tharayil et al., 2018).

1. **Clear communication:** Explaining the purpose and benefits of the activity can help reduce resistance. When participants understand the value and goals, they are more likely to engage.

2. **Inclusive decision making:** Involving team members in the decision-making process can foster a sense of ownership and commitment. This approach can reduce resistance by making participants feel valued and heard.

3. **Incremental changes:** Introducing new ideas or methods gradually can help ease participants into change. Small, manageable steps can prevent overwhelming resistance and allow for gradual adaptation.

4. **Positive reinforcement:** Recognizing and rewarding positive behavior and participation can encourage continued engagement. Positive reinforcement can build a supportive environment that reduces resistance.

5. **Open dialogue:** Encouraging open and honest communication allows participants to express their concerns and suggestions. Addressing these concerns directly can help mitigate resistance and build trust.

To summarize this Rally practice: Simply calling another meeting won't be met with much support unless the expectation is that you're building a learning community that is designed to solve problems and build an entire set of program offerings for everyone. Here are some tips on how to define and establish your ACT community.

- The ACT community of practice is a collaborative group comprising advisors, coaches, and teachers committed to improving the student experience.
- Expect resistance from long-standing ACTs but emphasize the benefits of collaboration and shared goals.
- Tips for success include establishing why the process is essential, holding initial meetings to elicit support and ideas, and involving ACTs in the implementation process.
- Continuous engagement and communication are crucial for success, even with initial resistance from some members.

Rally Practice 3.2: Implement the Elements of an Effective ACT Learning Community

Implementing proven collaborative practices becomes imperative to the success of the learning community. Much like any well-oiled machine, a missing part can have devastating consequences. It's similar to an old song by Johnny Cash called "One Piece at a Time" in which he builds a car by taking one piece at a time from several factory lines. When he comes home to build the car, he finds that pieces don't fit, headlamps don't match, and ultimately it takes him years to build the car. In the end, it works, but it's not pretty. Building the ACT learning community, when done right, can be like a Bentley coming off the factory floor: beautiful, sleek, and custom-made for the owner. Ultimately, each school will have some differing needs, but following these tips can help establish some non-negotiable elements.

- **Head coach and advisor representatives:** First, we believe that the head coach or advisor of any competitive program or activity on campus is the representative for this collaborative community. With heavy caution, the leader could assign a representative, but this must only be done in times of emergency in which the ACT has no other choice but to delegate. However, this representative must have the authority to make decisions regarding the program, and the head coach or advisor has to live with that. We would encourage ACTs as the learning community becomes more established to invite assistant coaches and advisors to attend as well. Done correctly, these will not be inconsequential discussions.

- **Meeting times:** The ACT community of practice must meet at least quarterly throughout the year to continue to reinforce their work but is recommended to be held monthly. A time must be set up that is most available given the season and other variables. It is also important to set up a meeting time that allows for the greatest amount of participation as possible. In some cases, we have seen school leaders make this a part of in-service days and other times when everyone is available and ready for attendance and engagement. Consistency is a key as most ACTs are busy beyond those of their peers, and anything that can be done to ensure this doesn't end up in the "useless meeting" bucket will lead to a higher chance of success.

- **Collaboration on the selection criteria of ACTs:** In addition to having aspirations and an activities or athletics vision, the most important element of an outstanding program is clarity on the selection of outstanding ACTs, as we alluded to earlier in the book. Therefore, ACT selection needs to be an ongoing discussion. Here are a few examples of selection challenges to solve: how to ensure the school can hire new on-campus ACTs, how to ensure ACTs have personal philosophies that align with the vision of the activities and athletics programs, and how

ACTs can appropriately articulate how they have, or will, demonstrate collaboration with other programs. At times, as leaders, we need to know the expectations of a group so we know the types of leaders we want to bring into the group. For many leaders, this can be a challenge because we often let our egos affect our hiring practices. We have seen groups that have used this process begin to hire coaches that stay on longer at the school and contribute more to the group once onboarded.

- **Preparation and support of ACTs:** When looking at ACT preparation, there should be ongoing training elements that are consistently implemented. This goes beyond safety measures like CPR and how to handle bloodborne pathogens. Indeed, when referencing the earlier section on the agreement of standards for athletic and activity participation, all new ACTs should be trained in these key areas and should be able to demonstrate a competent understanding of the expectations of the organization. In the most effective ACT learning communities, these expectations are not just dictated by leaders but are developed and established by the learning community itself. If your ACT community expects sportsmanship, celebration after the game, commitment to the activity, and relations with competitors or the community, those details must be collaborated on and committed to by the ACT community.

  With a deep and sustained commitment, all ACTs should work on consistently helping each other to remain aware of the aspired standards of practice and to maintain high levels of alignment and goal attainment. In some of the most successful schools, there are support mechanisms for new ACTs. For example, a new ACT in one activity could be assigned a partner ACT, who has been an assistant in another activity, just as an ongoing guide or mentor partner. By having a support mechanism, we're far more likely to improve the performance of certain ACTs and help them elevate, if that is indeed their desire, within the school. This can help build trust amongst the ACTs, leading to increased morale, self-esteem, and self-worth, all factors of improved performance within social networks (Bukko, Liu, & Johnson, 2021)

- **Local teacher engagement:** Finally, a continuous effort at the ACT community of practice level must be made in trying to get teachers to consistently support and be involved in ACT efforts in the school. We believe that even if a teacher isn't as experienced in a particular activity, there is great value in getting their engagement with students and working within the activity. We have known some football coaches who made it their mission to hire assistants who were teachers in the school, even if they didn't have as much football knowledge as someone from the outside who wanted to coach. Their presence in the school and the ability to be more observant of the students on an ongoing basis and their overall engagement to the institution made their engagement much more valuable. This should be an ongoing effort, and the ACT community should consistently try to reflect on ways in which they can create inviting opportunities for teachers to be more holistically involved with activities and athletics.

To summarize this Rally practice: The details matter when maintaining a healthy ACT community based on your goals and principles. The following suggestions will help you simplify the creation of these learning communities and maximize their effectiveness.

- Head coach or advisor representatives should lead the collaborative effort, with assistant coaches and advisors encouraged to attend.
- Regular meetings are essential, ideally monthly, to reinforce collaboration and goal alignment.
- Collaboration on ACT selection criteria ensures alignment with program vision and goals.

- Preparation and ongoing support for ACTs are crucial, with consistent training and mentorship opportunities provided.
- Engagement of local teachers is necessary to support and participate in ACT efforts, even if they're not directly involved in the activity.

Rally Practice 3.3: Establish the Norms of the ACT Learning Community

We have heard the term *norms* a thousand times in the educational setting when it comes to meetings, PLCs, and other professional environments. There is a reason they are there. Setting established norms allows the members of the learning community to understand what is expected of them so there are no misunderstandings or surprises (DuFour et al., 2024). The ACT learning community is no different. If you were to attend the ACT learning community at Brandon's high school, you would see laughter, tears, discussion, vision, and more. The school has had this learning community for eight years now, and even the most hardened veteran will bare their soul because the learning community is a safe, inviting, and purposeful space. This community did not get there overnight. It took an amazing leader to come in and work diligently to show these coaches that the students were worth the investment in becoming better. Here are the norms that we would recommend as you establish the learning community.

- **Civility:** Setting a civility standard makes sense. If these disparate ACTs have never been asked to work together, it will be important to lay out the expectation that everyone will be civil and will grow together and improve.
- **Vulnerability:** ACTs will be asked to open themselves to new ideas and ways of operating that may challenge core beliefs or systemic practices. It is imperative that ACTs are willing and able to be vulnerable in both receiving and sharing.
- **Timeliness:** Despite the demands of schedules, all ACTs will be expected to be at these events on time and participate with enthusiastic and robust thinking

and commentary. Leaders need to keep these meetings around forty-five to sixty minutes and have objectives laid out before the meeting to respect the time of all parties.

- **Improvement:** The goal of attendance at the ACT community of practice isn't to improve the future of any one specific activity. The goal is that all programs get better because of everyone's engagement.

- **Diligence:** Do the work! It will not be enough to just talk in these meetings. Action items that are drawn from the meeting must be acted on and reflected on outside the meeting to ensure the work is getting done.

To summarize this Rally practice: One of the things that is missing in so many communities and schools is the lack of well-established group norms. As articulated in the PLC process, with well-established group norms, groups come together with an understanding and expectation for how the meetings will be run, how time will be respected, how members will treat each other, and how the work will be executed (DuFour et al., 2024) With these expectations and the following tips in mind, we are far more likely to reach success.

- Establish norms for civility, vulnerability, timeliness, and focus on improvement across all programs.

- Emphasize the importance of active participation and follow-through on action items outside of meetings.

- Focus on improving all programs collectively, rather than any one specific activity, to ensure overall success.

Rally Practice 3.4: Establish the Agenda Around the Vision

After a school establishes an ACT collaborative team, they must then establish regular topics of discussion. We have found that almost every school will have a vision or core values set up at their site or sometimes their district. If you don't, that's the starting point. Establish the vision and core values with your group.

Once those are established, or are already present, begin the meeting agendas about how the ACTs can incorporate and support that vision within their programs. Starting here can have several positive impacts. First, it allows the ACTs to familiarize themselves with what the standard of the vision is. Secondly, it allows the ACTs to dive deeper into what that looks like for them, their program or team, and for their students. For example, at one school where we worked, there were five core values. Each semester the learning community would choose a book that dealt with one core value and participate in a book study and discussion, which would lead to discussions about how we wanted our programs to look. This last year the group's focus was on the core value of integrity, and the book study was done on *Extreme Ownership* by Jacko Willink and Leif Babin (2017). Each member was asked to read certain chapters prior to the meeting. The members of the PLC would discuss what principles were being taught in each chapter, how that tied into integrity, how it looked within our school, and what systems needed to be implemented or adjusted to incorporate the principle. The discussions that came from those meetings were amazing. Everyone, including the facilitator, would leave enthusiastic about how to move forward with new ideas. You know that some of your best lessons were from peers teaching peers when you were simply a facilitator. An effective ACT learning community will be no different.

To summarize this Rally practice: To avoid the unfortunate notion of meeting just to meet, true learning communities establish an agenda around a vision for a well-articulated program. This most certainly will require some support from a school leader at the beginning, but to make sure the time is in fact used correctly, quality time spent articulating expectations and goals will be key. Some tips for making this happen are as follows.

- Start by establishing or revisiting the school's vision and core values with input from the ACT learning community.

- Use the vision and core values as the foundation for meeting agendas and discussions on how ACTs can support and incorporate them into their programs.

- Encourage deeper exploration of the vision's implications for individual programs and students, fostering enthusiasm and innovation.
- Consider bringing in a third party to facilitate vision workshops to ensure unbiased facilitation and consensus building.

RALLY IN ACTION

This last year, the Highland ACT learning community entered its eighth year of existence. Though it had started with only athletics, it had since built into both activities and athletics and became a high-functioning group that met monthly. Within those forty-five minutes, there was intentional and innovative work being done. Brandon was starting to receive calls about how his school had sustained the success it had over the last couple of years. When speaking with schools, Brandon communicated the high need for an ACT learning community. In the second semester of 2023, two administrators from a neighboring school requested to see an ACT learning community in action. Brandon was more than happy to allow them to attend since he wanted to see more schools approach activities and athletics with the same zeal. Todd and Yvonne were able to sit in on the next meeting. Here was their experience.

Sitting in the lecture hall having just experienced the plan "on paper" for the meeting, Yvonne and Todd were on the edges of their seats waiting for the learning community to start. They sat in what was called the Lecture Hall, a large stadium-style seating classroom. As the bell rang, they could hear students in the hallways. Brandon propped open the door to the lecture hall, smiled at the two, and simply said, "Let's do it!"

Brandon stood at the door as ACTs came in. It was an amazing sight to see; the ACTs, as they came in, were generally excited to be there. They came in with smiles on their faces and a ready-to-go energy. Each ACT greeted Brandon, then conversed with others. The minute they noticed Yvonne and Todd in the corner, they immediately headed their way and introduced themselves. It was like being at church and everyone saw the new guy walk in. The ACTs were very friendly, asking the two where they were from, what they did, and so on. The meeting hadn't even started and the two were already feeling the impact of the room. Then, Randy entered the room. Randy was the character coach Brandon hired to run the learning community meetings. Even though Brandon was fully capable of running the meetings, he loved being in the learning process with the ACTs. He enjoyed the exchange of thoughts about the programs as a whole. With a smile that could light up a room, Randy said in a booming voice, "Yvonne! Todd! Brandon told me all about you guys coming today! We're so blessed to have you here! One thing, though—you aren't just observers today, you're participants. Come up here to the front and sit."

Randy invited Yvonne and Todd into the two seats front and center. The two were starting to wonder what they got themselves into. As they moved to the front, the last of the ACTs rolled in, and the learning community was ready to begin.

Randy started the meeting off by having the coaches talk about celebrations they have had since the last time they met. Coaches took turns rattling off celebrations from a huge win against a cross-town rival, to the robotics team who finally figured out how to program a certain move they needed to give them an edge with their design. Not only did they celebrate their programs, but they gave celebrations about things they noticed in other people's programs as well. This took about the first ten minutes of the forty-five minutes scheduled for the learning community. After that, Randy dove into the topic for the day. The topic was how to celebrate with humility. Brandon had told Yvonne and Todd before the meeting that the ACTs spent the last session discussing challenges they were seeing throughout the programs. One of the most common issues they noticed was that after a team saw some success, they would inevitably lose a competition they should have easily won. One of the ACTs expanded that they see the same thing in the classroom when a student gets a concept, they go into cruise control and don't give the same effort moving forward. The group ended up deciding that they needed to talk about, as a school, how to celebrate success but in a manner that was humble and still promoted effort from the students.

Randy guided them for the next thirty-five minutes on the topic of celebrating with humility. There were discussions about why entitlement creeps in. There was an activity with breakout groups on solutions that other schools and entities have installed to attack the issue. There was a whole-group discussion on which solutions they wanted to address with their student leadership and what may work for their programs. The collaboration was intense. Yvonne and Todd were expected to jump in with both feet, participate, and stay engaged as if they were part of the school the whole time. Brandon was even involved as a participant, allowing Randy to run the learning community and facilitate the conversations. At the end, each ACT committed to one strategy they were going to take back to the program and address with their student leadership. Randy ended with some homework for the ACTs as they were going to need to come back and share some data regarding what they implemented and how it worked or didn't work. The next session would center around fine-tuning what they implemented after this meeting. As Randy broke the meeting, the ACTs didn't immediately leave. Most of them stayed around for another fifteen to thirty minutes just chatting with each other and the two guests. Yvonne was amazed at the relationships that had been built between all of these staff members. You could see genuine friendships and love for one another. Eventually, the room emptied. Yvonne and Todd walked with Brandon back to his office. Randy gave them both one final goodbye and gave them the name of a character coach in their area who could help them with their learning community process if needed.

Back in Brandon's office, the three leaders began to debrief. It hit Yvonne and Todd that they had overthought the ACT learning community process at their school. After talking and observing, they boiled down the ACT learning community process to the following.

- Spend the time to build relationships with the ACTs because nothing can move forward until they trust one another.
- Identify the needs of the programs that the learning community feels they want to address.
- Attempt to identify the cause of the issue as well as potential solutions.
- Implement the solutions and collect data on the process and results.
- Bring data to the learning community and discuss successes, challenges, and implement any changes from these data discussions.
- Reflect on the results of the solutions and determine if we move forward, change, or stop the practice.
- Identify the next issue, and then do it all over again.

As Yvonne and Todd finished up their conversation with Brandon, they thanked him for letting them experience the learning community process. What they learned was amazing, and they now had a

> *better understanding of how they wanted to move forward at their own school. Brandon thanked them also. Yvonne and Todd walked away with a notebook full of notes on what they had just learned and began the implementation of their own learning community shortly after. The two have stayed in contact with Brandon and reported that their own implementation has already yielded positive results. They see ACTs who would normally have had no reason to interact begin to form relationships on campus. The two schools continue to collaborate. Brandon helps them not only with learning communities for ACTs, but all the elements of the Rally model.*

Conclusion

So far in this text we've learned to set standards for our programs, get them aligned, and now we've introduced the all-important idea of learning together for ultimate growth. This notion of getting clear on what we want, aligning our efforts, and working hard as a team is at the heart of just about every successful endeavor that human beings embark on. This is at the heart of how a good business is run, how PLCs engage, and how outstanding individual teams come together. We want you to use the power of highly engaged collaboration to power your Rally model. As you have no doubt seen throughout your life, when people come together and are committed, amazing things are always possible.

To become a great leader, you must first understand the elements that constitute great leadership. Without this clarity, growth and improvement become impossible.

—John Maxwell

CHAPTER 7

LEAD THROUGH STUDENTS

In this chapter, we will be providing eight leadership competencies that provide a framework for leadership expectations in athletics and activities. We provide these suggested competencies because we recognize that we can't make progress in developing excellent leadership at the student level in athletics and activities unless we're really clear about what it means to be a good leader. At times, leadership training and advice can be quite fuzzy and esoteric. It can feel good in its observation, but we lack the practicality about what to do on a Monday morning when leadership is needed. This chapter clarifies what this means for leaders and gives practitioners some specific direction about how to apply this model, and the expected benefits and outcomes. Furthermore, as has been the case with every element of the Rally model, a commitment in this area to athletics and activities will have cascading benefits throughout the school, helping develop student leaders understand the call to leadership during the school day and after.

Identifying Challenges of Leading Through Students

Starting a student leadership group on a high school campus for activities and athletics can address various challenges and provide opportunities for students to develop essential skills. Here are four signs that you may have challenges on your campus that could necessitate the formation of such a group.

Lack of Student Engagement and Involvement

Many middle and high schools face the challenge of disengaged students who may feel disconnected from school activities and initiatives. Recognizing the potential for greater student engagement and involvement, the formation of a student leadership group presents an opportunity for students to actively participate in shaping their school experience. This sign suggests a desire for students to be more involved in extracurricular activities and other campus events to create that connection to the school that is lacking.

Research indicates that participation in extracurricular activities is positively correlated with increased academic engagement and performance. For example, students involved in these activities often show improved grades, higher educational aspirations, increased college enrollment, and reduced absenteeism (Christison, 2013; Furda & Shuleski, 2019). By fostering a sense of belonging and providing opportunities for students to develop leadership skills, schools can enhance both academic outcomes and overall student well-being (Afalla, 2020).

Incorporating extracurricular activities into the school culture can also help address issues of disengagement and dropout rates. When students feel connected to their school community through activities such as sports, arts, and clubs, they are more likely to stay engaged and motivated in their academic pursuits (Fujita, 2006). This holistic approach to education emphasizes the importance of balancing academic rigor with opportunities for personal growth and social development (Honor Society, 2023).

Lack of Leadership Opportunities for Students

The desire to provide students with meaningful leadership opportunities suggests a recognition of their potential and a commitment to their personal and academic growth. Based on our experience, for many schools, the challenge is that student leadership is nonexistent. With everything teachers and administrators manage already, many choose not to take on additional work. By forming a student leadership group, schools signal their intent to empower students to develop essential leadership skills to foster a culture of collaboration, innovation, and positive impact within the school community. Activities and athletics are the front porch of the school. Receiving students' feedback and teaching them how to be leaders could have a tremendous impact on a school's culture.

WHERE ARE WE NOW?

1. What practices are in place to develop student leadership on your campus?
2. Does the participation percentage in programs mirror the demographics of the school?
3. What practices are in place to evaluate the mental health of your students?
4. What practices are in place to elicit feedback from your students on your programs and/or the school as a whole?

Responding to the Challenge With Rally Practices

Given the previously mentioned challenges, we know that leading through our students is imperative to healthy and high-functioning athletics and activities programs. We want to give you the *what* you need to teach to your student leaders as well as the *how*. The following two Rally practices will teach the eight leadership competencies as well as implementing the Rally model and using it with student leadership programs.

Rally Practice 4.1: Implement the Eight Leadership Competencies

We strongly recommend the adoption and implementation of a well-formulated leadership model. A leadership model for the students who serve will help ACTs, students, and parents work together in better understanding the type of leadership needed to support and develop their activities and athletics. By getting clear and specific about your expectations, you put everyone in a much better position to achieve success. Our recommended practice is a leadership model with eight defined competencies that should be instilled in the students as they become leaders on campus. In the following section, we will define these eight competencies and provide you with examples.

OBSERVE AND CELEBRATE EVIDENCE OF POSITIVE INFLUENCE

When a leader at any level excels, their actions and energy inspire those around them to change their behavior. In a school setting, if a teacher leader demonstrates positive influence, it encourages fellow teachers to strive for more and positively impacts students. Students who exhibit this quality help their teammates and classmates maintain strong academic standing, develop good work habits, practice in the off-season, and compete with grace and dignity. Simply put, student leaders who excel in this area do the right thing and inspire others to follow suit. Influence is crucial, as many leaders have been taught that people don't follow titles. Just because a student is placed in a leadership position doesn't guarantee that others will follow them. The student leadership program should both teach and model this competency, showing students how to become positive and inspiring influences for their peers (DuFour & Fullan, 2013; Gillies, 2023).

Research indicates that students involved in athletics demonstrate higher levels of transformational leadership, particularly in managing self and emotions, which are essential for positive influence (Christison, 2013). For example, a student-athlete who consistently demonstrates sportsmanship and dedication can motivate teammates to adopt similar behaviors, thereby enhancing the overall team dynamics. Another study by the Pew Research Center emphasizes the importance of fostering leadership skills in school settings, highlighting that student leaders who model positive behavior can significantly impact their peers (Braga, Hurst, Greenwood, Zanetti, & Mandapat, 2024). This underscores the importance of incorporating leadership development into student athletics programs, ensuring that students learn to influence others positively.

One practical example of teaching positive influence in student athletics is through structured leadership activities. For instance, coaches can organize sessions where student-athletes discuss the role models they admire and analyze the traits that make these individuals influential. This reflection helps students understand the qualities of effective leaders. Additionally, integrating leadership exercises into regular practice routines can reinforce these traits. For example, student-athletes can be assigned roles when they lead warm-ups, mentor younger teammates, or take charge of specific drills. These experiences allow them to practice leadership in a supportive environment, making them more effective influencers both on and off the field (EY Global, 2020). Such initiatives help build a culture of positive influence, ultimately contributing to students' personal and athletic growth.

SHOW OPTIMISM AND POSITIVE ENERGY

Optimism and positivity are crucial for overcoming fear, negativity, and distraction. To reach a new standard of performance, students in athletics or activities must believe in themselves and their capacity to improve. Such students don't complain about challenges or practice; they overcome difficult points in the season, remain optimistic, and continuously encourage others with energy and purpose.

This competency alone can help turn programs around (Gillies, 2023). Instilling optimism can be challenging, but there are effective tools available. Tim Kight's (2020) formula, Event + Response = Outcome (E + R = O), teaches students that while they may not control events, they can control their responses, leading to positive outcomes. This approach helps students focus on what they can control, fostering a more optimistic mindset (Kight, 2020).

Another valuable resource is John Gordon's *The Energy Bus* (2007), which outlines a ten-step process for maintaining positive energy through various circumstances. The ten steps are summarized here.

1. **You're the driver of your bus:** Emphasizes personal responsibility for your life and career

2. **Desire, vision, and focus move your bus in the right direction:** Stresses the importance of having a clear vision and focus for your life and work, and the drive to pursue it

3. **Fuel your ride with positive energy:** Highlights the necessity of positivity to propel oneself forward and influence others positively as well

4. **Invite people on your bus and share your vision for the road ahead:** Discusses the significance of teamwork and sharing your vision with others to foster a collaborative and supportive environment

5. **Don't waste your energy on those who don't get on your bus:** Advises not to spend effort on trying to win over the skeptics or the disinterested, but rather to focus on those who are supportive and engaged

6. **Post a sign that says, "No energy vampires allowed" on your bus:** Encourages setting boundaries to protect your positive space from negativity and energy drains

7. **Enthusiasm attracts more passengers and energizes them during the ride:** Underlines the power of enthusiasm to attract like-minded individuals and energize your team or community

8. **Love your passengers:** Teaches the importance of showing appreciation, respect, and love for those around you, enhancing mutual respect and affection within a group

9. **Drive with purpose:** Highlights the necessity of having a purpose that fuels your drive and gives your journey meaning

10. **Have fun and enjoy the ride:** Reminds readers to enjoy the journey, not just the destination, and to find joy in the everyday

These tools teach students the importance of optimism, a key leadership competency they need to possess and promote within their programs (Gordon, 2007).

Recent research supports the importance of optimism in leadership. A study published in the Boston University *Journal of Graduate Studies in Education* found that students involved in sports exhibit higher levels of enthusiasm, dedication, and energy, which correlate with strong leadership skills (Christison, 2013). Additionally, research from Ernst & Young highlights that 94 percent of women in the C-suite played sports, indicating that sports participation builds leadership skills that are transferable to professional settings (EY Global, 2020).

BE A SELFLESS SERVANT LEADER

A servant leader is someone who prioritizes the needs of others and focuses on their growth and well-being. This concept, first introduced by Robert Greenleaf in his 1970 essay, "The Servant as Leader," emphasizes that a leader should be a servant first (Purdue University Global, 2020). According to Purdue University Global (2020), servant leadership is a philosophy and set of practices that enriches the lives of individuals, builds better organizations, and creates a more just and caring world (Purdue University Global, 2020).

Ken Blanchard and Renee Broadwell (2018) further elaborate on servant leadership by stating that it involves a combination of mindset and skill set focused on serving others first to develop great relationships, achieve great results, and delight customers. Blanchard and Broadwell (2018) emphasize that effective leadership starts with self-perception and a heart motivated by serving rather than self-interest.

Several programs we have worked with use the concept of love to teach how to be a selfless servant leader. *Love*, defined as selflessness, helps students understand the importance of putting others' needs first. For example, a servant leader who notices a teammate lacking confidence might offer quiet, caring support, while another teammate on the brink of excellence might benefit from enthusiastic, public encouragement (Stewart, 2019). A selfless servant leader focuses on others and personalizes their approach to support their teammates.

This competency can be taught through service projects, which allow students to practice servant leadership and bond over shared experiences. Participating in service projects helps students understand the value of serving others and can translate these experiences to their specific programs (Stewart, 2019).

Student servant leaders in athletics and activities exemplify what it means to lead by serving others. They prioritize the needs of their teammates, coaches, and the overall program, demonstrating selflessness and dedication. These leaders understand that their role goes beyond personal performance; it involves uplifting and supporting those around them to foster a positive and cohesive environment. A student servant leader in athletics and activities shows this commitment in the following five ways.

1. **Empathy and support:** They listen to their teammates' concerns and provide emotional support, helping to build a sense of trust and unity within the team. For example, if a teammate is struggling with a particular skill, the servant leader will offer encouragement and practical advice, spending extra time to help them improve (Stewart, 2019).

2. **Positive role modeling:** Servant leaders lead by example, consistently displaying positive behavior both on and off the field. They show respect for coaches, officials, and opponents, and encourage their teammates to do the same. This behavior sets a standard for others to follow, creating a culture of respect and integrity (Blanchard & Broadwell, 2018).

3. **Encouragement and motivation:** During challenging times, servant leaders keep the team's morale high by staying optimistic and providing motivation. They celebrate their teammates' successes, big or small, and help them see their potential, fostering a culture of continuous improvement (Gordon, 2007).

4. **Collaborative leadership:** They actively involve teammates in decision-making processes, ensuring that everyone feels valued and heard. This inclusive approach helps to build a strong, united team where each member's contributions are recognized and appreciated (Purdue University Global, 2020).

5. **Service projects:** Participating in community service projects as a team can further instill the values of servant leadership. These projects provide students with hands-on experience in serving others, reinforcing the importance of selflessness and community involvement. For example, organizing a charity run or volunteering at a local shelter can help student leaders understand the broader impact of their actions and develop a greater sense of empathy and social responsibility (Stewart, 2019).

Research in K–12 education supports the effectiveness of servant leadership. For instance, a study by Gary J. Stewart (2019), finds that servant leadership in schools leads to a more positive school climate and higher teacher retention. In non-education settings, servant leadership has been shown to improve employee satisfaction and organizational culture. Starbucks and Marriott International are companies that have adopted this leadership style, resulting in stronger work cultures and higher employee engagement (Purdue University Global, 2020).

FOLLOW A TRANSFORMATIONAL VISION COMMITTED TO GROWTH

A student with a transformational vision committed to growth is willing to authentically consider the possibility of outstanding team performance, however that's measured. A student transformational leader in the band dreams of a thirty-member marching band growing to more than a hundred within twenty-four months. While it may never have been possible before, they have the vision of transforming the team they're on and are committed to seeing them perform with outlandish levels of success. Transformational vision requires the aforementioned optimism, with a specific eye on an actual change that matters (Blanchard & Broadwell, 2018).

Instilling a transformational vision in thirteen-to-eighteen-year-olds isn't always easy. Many teenagers just look at what is in front of them and do not have long-term visions. This is due to their cognitive development, as teenagers are still developing the ability to think abstractly and plan for the future (Riddell, 2020). This must be intentional work to open the minds of young students to first establish what their program would look like in a perfect world. Then, they need to understand what they can do to get the program there. From there, the ACT can guide the students through exercises that help them establish how to possess a transformational vision moving forward to accomplish their goals (Purdue University Global, 2020). Here's how these applications can manifest in athletics and activities.

- **Setting ambitious goals:** Encourage student-athletes to set challenging yet achievable goals for themselves and their team. For example, a soccer team might aim to improve their ranking within the conference over the next two seasons. This goal should be supported by actionable steps, such as enhanced training routines, diet adjustments, and team-building exercises (Stewart, 2019).

- **Vision-casting workshops:** Conduct workshops where students envision the future of their team or activity. This could involve brainstorming sessions, creating vision boards, and setting long-term goals. For instance, a school orchestra might create a vision to perform at a national competition in two years and outline the necessary steps to get there (Blanchard & Broadwell, 2018).

- **Peer mentoring:** Implement a peer mentoring system where more experienced students guide newer members. This helps in creating a culture of continuous improvement and shared vision. For example, senior basketball players might mentor freshmen, helping them understand the team's goals and how to contribute effectively (Purdue University Global, 2020).

- **Regular reflection sessions:** Schedule regular team meetings to reflect on progress towards their transformational vision. This allows for adjustments and keeps the team focused. For instance, a debate team could meet monthly to discuss their progress in achieving higher tournament placements and refine their strategies accordingly (Riddell, 2020).

- **Celebrating milestones:** Recognize and celebrate the achievements along the way to keep the team motivated. This can involve awards, public recognition, or team celebrations. For example, a track team might celebrate setting new personal bests and qualifying for regional meets as they work towards their ultimate vision of competing at the state level (Gordon, 2007).

WIN OR LOSE WITH GRACE

Winning or losing with grace is an essential leadership competency for students involved in athletics and activities. This skill involves demonstrating the ability to show grace after a close win, big win, gut-wrenching close loss, or punishing loss in competitive activities. This principle applies to both individual and team performances.

Authentic and enthusiastic celebration of victories is appropriate and encouraged. Students should never apologize for winning; instead, they should celebrate their moments of excellence as they unfold. However, these celebrations should emphasize two key components: (1) the contribution of others and (2) the spirit of collaboration. In team sports, celebrations should involve the entire team, rather than personalized, self-aggrandizing displays. Even in individual sports, students should celebrate with coaches, fellow players, parents, and community members who contributed to their journey. Collaborative celebrations help leaders use these moments to inspire others and encourage shared joy and motivation (Blanchard & Broadwell, 2018).

When facing a loss, leaders should show gracious appreciation for the competition and their competitors. Even if the opponent's celebration is not gracious, the leader must hold their head high, honor the competition, and learn from the experience. This grace in defeat fosters resilience and respect, both crucial qualities in effective leadership (Gordon, 2007). Here's how these applications can manifest in student athletics and activities.

- **Post-game debriefings:** Hold debriefing sessions after games or competitions to discuss what went well and areas for improvement. Encourage students to express gratitude for their teammates' efforts and to reflect on the lessons learned from both wins and losses (Purdue University Global, 2020).

- **Celebratory rituals:** Develop team rituals for celebrating victories that include everyone involved. This could be a team chant, a group huddle, or a shared meal. These rituals reinforce the importance of collective effort and unity (Stewart, 2019).

- **Gracious acknowledgments:** Teach students to acknowledge their opponents respectfully after each game, win or lose. Handshakes, verbal compliments, and sportsmanship awards can reinforce positive interactions and mutual respect (Riddell, 2020).

- **Role-playing scenarios:** Use role-playing exercises to help students practice handling different competitive outcomes. These scenarios can prepare students to respond gracefully and positively in real-life situations, regardless of the result (Blanchard & Broadwell, 2018).

- **Mentorship programs:** Implement mentorship programs where older, more experienced students mentor younger teammates. These mentors can model graceful behavior in both victory and defeat, providing younger students with tangible examples to emulate (Gordon, 2007).

DEMONSTRATE EXCELLENCE IN PRACTICE AND PREPARATION

Leaders who excel in this area understand that they may be performing at a higher level than some of their teammates. However, for everyone to improve, diligent practice with laser-like focus is essential for continuous improvement. These leaders are meticulous in their preparation habits. During the off-season, they show up for early morning workouts and work on refining their performance details. They emphasize the importance of not overlooking any aspect and encourage others to improve daily. This is particularly crucial for the most skilled and advanced leaders in these activities. Watching a gifted musician practice warm-up scales demonstrates the rigor of practice and the importance of sticking to fundamentals, even after reaching advanced levels. This shows those who follow a commitment to the process, which is an essential element discussed throughout this book (Blanchard & Broadwell, 2018).

Recent research in K–12 education highlights the importance of leadership skills developed through sports and other extracurricular activities. A study published in the *Journal of Educational Research* found that students involved in athletics showed higher levels of enthusiasm, dedication, and leadership skills compared to their non-athlete peers (Furda & Shuleski, 2019). These students demonstrated proficiency in communication, strategic planning, and interpersonal relationships, which are key components of effective leadership (Stewart, 2019). Here's how these principles can manifest in athletics and activities.

- **Set clear expectations:** Clearly communicate the importance of practice and preparation to students (Riddell, 2020).
- **Model excellence:** Demonstrate the behaviors and habits you expect from students (Blanchard & Broadwell, 2018).
- **Provide resources:** Ensure students have access to the necessary tools and support for effective practice (Stewart, 2019).
- **Encourage peer learning:** Foster an environment where students can learn from each other and support one another's improvement (Purdue University Global, 2020).
- **Recognize and reward effort:** Acknowledge the hard work and dedication of students, not just their achievements (EY Global, 2020).

TAKE ACTION TO IMPROVE THE PROGRAM

Strong leaders have the wisdom to continuously take action to improve the overall program as a result of their participation. For example, a senior in high school who is leaving the debate program, basketball team, or sand volleyball team could hopefully look back and observe how their influence on the team led to the program improving overall. This should be a goal that is introduced early and often so that it can be maintained and consistently reinforced. ACTs should meet with student leaders and set the intention that they can articulate when their academic career is over, the impact they had on the program, and how they hope it will influence those who follow. This ties in with the transformational vision competency but puts more emphasis on the action part of the leader. It's one thing to talk about what we are going to do; it's another to put those words into action (Blanchard & Broadwell, 2018).

We recommend that within the teaching of this competency, after meetings between ACTs and students, intentional, specific action items be written down and discussed before the end of the meeting. Once these are written down, the understanding will be that when each group meets again, students will report on the progress toward the processes that was recorded. We will again emphasize, as we have throughout the book, that goals should be process oriented and not results focused. In this competency, focus on those processes (Purdue University Global, 2020). Here's how these principles can manifest in athletics and activities.

- **Set process-oriented goals:** Encourage student-athletes to set goals that focus on improving their skills and teamwork rather than just winning games. For example, a basketball player might aim to improve their free throw percentage by 10 percent over the season (Stewart, 2019).
- **Regular feedback sessions:** Hold regular meetings where student leaders can provide and receive feedback on their performance and progress. These sessions should be constructive and focused on continuous improvement (Riddell, 2020).
- **Mentorship programs:** Implement mentorship programs to have senior students mentor junior teammates. This helps foster a culture of learning and development, ensuring that the program continuously evolves and improves (EY Global, 2020).
- **Action plans:** Develop action plans for achieving specific goals. These plans should include detailed steps and

timelines, helping students stay accountable and focused on their objectives (Blanchard & Broadwell, 2018).

- **Celebrate progress:** Recognize and celebrate the progress made towards achieving process-oriented goals. This can include awards, public recognition, and team celebrations to motivate students and reinforce positive behaviors (Gordon, 2007).

LEAD IN THE COMMUNITY

Serving as a leader in the community manifests in several important ways. First, students who represent the school well avoid actions that could embarrass themselves or their program. They maintain a standard of behavior that reflects positively on their school and the activities they participate in. This means being mindful of their actions and understanding that they are representatives of their team and the leadership they provide (Blanchard & Broadwell, 2018).

On a higher level, exemplary student leaders actively engage in the community through volunteering and helping others, demonstrating gratitude for the opportunities they have. These actions go beyond avoiding negative behavior; they involve taking positive steps to make a difference. Student leaders who excel in this competency understand that their involvement in the community is an extension of their leadership role within their school activities (Purdue University Global, 2020).

This competency aligns well with becoming a selfless servant leader. Service is a powerful tool for community involvement, fostering deeper connections and support for school programs. Bringing community members into student leadership meetings can create meaningful dialogues and partnerships. Hearing firsthand from community leaders can forge strong ties and support for student programs, exposing students to diverse perspectives and potential collaborations they might not have encountered otherwise (Stewart, 2019). Here are some practical applications for student leaders in athletics and activities.

- **Community service projects:** Organize regular community service projects that allow students to give back. This could include activities such as cleaning local parks, volunteering at shelters, or running charity events. These projects provide practical experience in leading and serving the community (Gordon, 2007).

- **Engagement with local leaders:** Invite local community leaders to speak at student leadership meetings. This provides students with role models and can inspire them to take similar actions in their own lives. For instance, a local business owner can share insights on community involvement and leadership (Riddell, 2020).

- **Public representation:** Encourage students to represent their school at community events. This could be through participating in parades, town meetings, or other public gatherings. It helps students understand the impact of their behavior on their school's reputation (Blanchard & Broadwell, 2018).

- **Collaborative initiatives:** Partner with local organizations to create joint initiatives that benefit both the school and the community. This can include fundraising events, awareness campaigns, or collaborative service projects. Such partnerships can enhance the visibility and impact of student-led activities (Purdue University Global, 2020).

- **Mentorship programs:** Establish mentorship programs where older students mentor younger students or peers. This helps cultivate a culture of leadership and service within the school and extends the impact of these competencies beyond individual students (EY Global, 2020).

To summarize this Rally practice: The following list of eight leadership competencies will make a big difference when executed. This bulleted list could serve in the establishment of a rubric or something hopefully easy to follow and focus on as you implement.

1. **Generate evidence of positive influence.**
    + Influence others to strive for more and maintain strong academic, work, and athletic habits.

- Teach through activities like discussing influential figures and modeling positive behavior.

2. **Show optimism and positive energy.**
    - Embrace optimism and positivity as crucial traits for overcoming challenges and achieving success.
    - Utilize tools like Tim Kight's (2020) E + R = O formula and John Gordon's (2007) *The Energy Bus* to instill optimism.

3. **Be a selfless servant leader.**
    - Connect with others and personalize their support based on individual needs.
    - Teach through service projects and personalizing approaches to support teammates.

4. **Develop and follow a transformational vision.**
    - Commit to achieving a transformational vision, envisioning outstanding team performance.
    - Guide students through exercises to establish long-term visions and strategies for program improvement.

5. **Win and lose with grace.**
    - Celebrate wins collaboratively, and graciously acknowledge losses, focusing on learning and growth.
    - Emphasize celebrating together and honoring competitors even in defeat.

6. **Demonstrate excellence in practice and preparation.**
    - Prioritize diligent practice and preparation to inspire continuous improvement.
    - Lead by example, emphasizing the importance of fundamentals and consistency.

7. **Take action to improve the program.**
   + Take intentional action to enhance the overall program based on their participation.
   + Establish clear objectives, track progress, and focus on process-oriented goals.
8. **Lead in the community.**
   + Represent the school positively in the community and serve as an exemplary role model.
   + Utilize service projects and community involvement to teach selflessness and gratitude.

Rally Practice 4.2: Use Student Leadership Programs to Teach the Eight Competencies

The hardest egg to crack at the campus level is knowing the *what* but struggling with the *how*. To be clear; this process does not need to be perfect, nor does it need to be implemented all at once. Schools and leadership can determine what works best for them to teach these competencies. With that being said, utilizing the process of a student leadership group on campus has shown to pay large dividends when it comes to teaching student leadership. These student leadership groups can look different to different people, but here are some common threads that we recommend based on our experiences to establish a student leadership group and teach the aforementioned competencies.

SELECT STUDENTS

Many ACTs lean toward selecting the best athlete or top performer from their group as a representative for student leadership groups or to be the team captain. Although these choices sometimes work out, we don't believe that peak performance should be the overarching qualifier for selecting students for opportunities to lead. What we would advise ACTs to do is to look at the leadership criteria and then think about the students in their program and reflect on which of them represents the expectations of the program the best. Sometimes, quiet, dedicated student leaders, who may not necessarily be peak performers, might be in the best position to offer the specific, program-building, and culture-developing qualities that leaders can represent when given the chance. The bottom line is, you should choose student leadership based on the criteria of what it means to lead, not simply by some demonstration within the activity itself.

SELECT THE RIGHT LEADER

Just as students listen to certain students in their programs, they will also listen to certain adults. We recommend setting egos aside and acknowledging who can connect with the students. A school with a large fine arts representation may not connect with the head football coach, whereas maybe there is a counselor on campus whom everyone adores and can connect with students at a high level. If financially feasible, we have seen great success when outside facilitators come to run these groups and teach about leadership. This allows the ACTs to engage in the process as an attendee and build on level relationships with the students. At Brandon's school, they use a combination of both ACTs and outside leadership experts to develop high-level leadership lessons that are based on the core values of the athletic and activity's vision. This outside advisor brings a different perspective and energy than any of the ACTs could provide.

BE CONSISTENT

It is essential that ACTs establish a consistent meeting time and place. After the initial kickoff meeting, it's helpful to establish a calendar of meeting times that don't move and can be consistently implemented. When consistent routines are put in place, students will feel more comfortable and safer in their environment as well as feel in control (Hemmeter, Ostrosky, & Fox, 2006). These practices will help establish an environment where students can have honest and open conversations.

HAVE A PLAN

Like any teacher would do in a classroom, lay out a plan for what your objectives are for each meeting and for the year. Random lessons can still yield positive results, but intentionality when it comes to desired outcomes will produce the best results. These plans do not need to be overthought or overdramatic. A perfect example is a group of students who Brandon works with who simply did a book study each semester that focused on a competency they wanted to work on. One semester they wanted to work on positivity, so they studied Gordon's (2007) *The Energy Bus*. Another semester they wanted to work on finding peace, so they studied the Arbinger Institute's (2020) *Anatomy of Peace*. Each meeting they discussed the section of assigned reading, what the message was, and how they would implement those strategies moving forward. The process was not complex but yielded amazing results in terms of students learning a principle, implementing a principle, and reflecting on how that principle has helped drive the programs forward. Having a plan for the year in place with specific objectives is a key component of a successful student leadership group.

BE INTENTIONAL ABOUT GETTING INFORMATION BACK TO PROGRAMS

It's one thing to have these meetings and disseminate information to the leaders of your programs, but what makes this process effective is how that information gets implemented back into the program. An intentional process should be put in place for how the students and the ACT will work collaboratively to take what strategies are being learned and how those can be implemented with the team or group. The ACT and students can have a post–student leadership meeting and discuss what was learned, how it impacted them, and how they feel it can be implemented in their program. From there, the ACT and students can establish a plan for implementation with a follow-up time to discuss the progress and reflection of that implementation. An example of this would be if the monthly lesson was on competency—establishing a positive influence. The students and the ACT can speak to each other about what the students learned and the importance of having a positive influence and some ideas that they feel would help improve their program. If the students felt like there should be a captain on the team who was responsible for identifying and celebrating positive behavior during practice and games, you could establish how that could be implemented. After several weeks, the students and ACT can discuss the results they have been seeing from the change, if they want to continue the practice, and with what changes.

Those processes can then be reported back to the student leadership group to be discussed if other programs could benefit from it. This is a full circle of communication that allows information to flow freely from top to bottom and back up again.

TRUST THE PROCESS

Changes don't happen overnight or very often. Leadership is a journey, not a destination. Trusting the process is imperative as some leaders will want to quit or abruptly change when they don't see immediate changes. Look for small, positive examples of change within teams. Point to those examples during meetings or in communication. As you seek to find these, you will begin to see small changes over time that can be attributed to the direct instruction of leadership within the school. Think about it like having braces on your teeth. You may not see a huge change from day to day, but when you look back from where you started, you will see that things have straightened out dramatically.

To summarize this Rally practice: The following list will help you articulate a plan to implement the standards and move towards a more comprehensive embrace of these concepts. Remember, when you are on brand as a school and have some expectations of what leadership looks like for the students you serve, you're far more likely to take the steps to reinforce what's needed and to have more leaders in your school that lead the way that everyone in your community would appreciate and expect.

- **Select students:** Choose leaders based on leadership criteria rather than peak performance.
- **Be consistent:** Establish consistent meeting times and routines to create a safe and comfortable environment.
- **Have a plan:** Set clear objectives for each meeting and the year to maximize outcomes.
- **Select the right leader:** Choose leaders and facilitators who can connect with students effectively.

- **Be intentional about getting information back to programs:** Establish a process for implementing leadership lessons within programs and provide feedback.
- **Trust the process:** Leadership development is a journey; celebrate small wins and trust in gradual progress.

RALLY IN ACTION

The following is a story about a leadership session that Brandon had the opportunity to attend recently. The ACTs, whom we will name Mrs. J and Coach L, led an incredible discussion with over fifty student representatives, including one whom he was able to talk with after the meeting, whom we will call Tasha. Since their mascot is a knight, the student leadership group dubbed their council the "Knights of the Round Table."

Tasha was a member of the marching band and one of their two representatives on the council. Tasha was excited when she entered the first meeting and she saw her good friend, Alisha, who is one of the representatives for the esports program. Tasha quickly learned that each program would be asked to provide one senior and one underclassman for the council. Each year, the underclassman would stay, and the program would assign another leader who was an underclassman. This way they never had all of their leaders graduating at the same time. The first couple of meetings were dedicated to establishing what the council was and its purpose. They collaborated on some common commitments on how the meetings would run and how students were expected to interact. Each student committed to taking what they learned and working with their ACT to implement it within their programs and their social groups. Tasha found she had a knack for leadership as she continued to attend these meetings. The conversations were invigorating and started to bring different programs together faster than she could have expected. She found herself excited for this week's meeting as they were going to start planning how to rally support for all programs on campus. This was the conversation Tasha had been waiting for.

Mrs. J and Coach L were going through the ten profile points of the students. After the initial discussions of setting up the logistics and commitments of the council, this was the next step of action. The council evaluated the ten profile points and came up with a list of what they deemed most important for their campus. Each week, they chose a profile point on the list and discussed what it was, how it impacted you as a leader, and how it would ultimately impact the campus. Today was point #9: Celebrate others and the team. Tasha had a lot to say on this as she had spent the week preparing for the discussion with speaking points to try and get her peers to see how important it was to celebrate others. As the conversation got going, Mrs. J started off with an activity for the council. She broke them up into groups of five. The groups were not allowed to have all athletics or all activities in the group. Their task was to list events that they have attended since attending high school outside of their own sport or activity. Then, discuss in groups what they noticed about this list.

Coach L and Mrs. J moved in and out of groups as they began the activity. Tasha was in a group with a baseball rep, basketball rep, a wrestling rep, and a rep from the drama team. Each one of them took a turn listing the events while the drama rep wrote them down on the paper. The five students went around and started to talk, but something was very consistent. They all struggled to add to the list. As Tasha went, she could only muster up a basketball game when she was a sophomore and a play last year in the spring. The other four were similar because each one was only able to muster a few different events that were outside of their sport or activity. This was not exclusive to sports either. The drama rep had one event to add, when she went to a robotics competition. The conversation started to die down in the room quickly as it seemed that most of the groups encountered the same problem. Mrs. J brought all the groups back together for a group discussion.

"So, who here was able to list one event? Raise your hand," instructed Mrs. J. Almost the whole class raised their hands.

"Ok, keep them up. If you have attended three or more, keep your hand up." About half of the class dropped their hands.

"Five or more?" About ten hands remained.

"Ten or more?" Two hands remained raised. One was a rep from student council, and the other was the representative from the yearbook.

Mrs. J and Coach L both chuckled, "So, did you two go to these by choice or by requirement for your activity?"

The students laughed as well. "A little bit of both," the student council rep replied.

"Thanks for your honesty!" Mrs. J said, gratefully. "Let me ask the council this: Why did you go to the event you did then? Tasha, do you mind if I pick on you for a second? Why did you go?"

Tasha chewed on this for a second. "Well, the basketball game was because I had a crush on a JV player, and the play was because my friend was in the play."

The class giggled as Tasha admitted to following a crush to the game. Mrs. J went around the room and asked several more students the same question, receiving almost all the same answers. Students attended events solely based on a connection they had with another student. Football games were the only exception as they tended to be a social event. The discussion turned as Mrs. J posed another question, "If we only attend events that we have a connection to, how do we get to a place where we can support each other and our programs?"

A woman representing softball raised her hand, "I think we start by just going, even if we don't know anyone. Earlier this year, I went to a robotics competition because my brother was competing. I was enthralled! It was one of the coolest things I've seen as these robots were trying to destroy each other. Had my mom not forced me to go support my brother, I would have never known how interesting the event was."

A senior leader from speech and debate began to chime in. "Where I struggle is I feel like people don't even know we exist. I would love to have half the energy from a baseball or softball game. That would excite us to know we felt like we mattered too. With that being said, I agree with her, we need to find ways to commit to showing up."

Mrs. J continued to facilitate the conversation. "I hear that we need to schedule time for teams to go to other events. Does each team need to go to one athletic event and one activity per season?" The class nodded in agreement. "What else?"

Tasha took this opportunity to bring up one of her points. "Mrs. J, I want to come back to what you were talking about earlier. We seem to only attend events where we have personal connections. I think we could look at how we build those connections with each other. It's a start to require us to go to things, but what if we could build relationships with each other to where we want to go to these events, not just because it's a chore. Don't get me wrong, I think the idea of planning these is a great start, but let's get deeper. Let's figure out how to connect us."

Mrs. J and Coach L were amazed by this observation. "Do you all agree with this? Is this something we should focus on?" The students all affirmed with "yes."

A leader from football began to speak saying, "How can we get the school to be better at advertising these events and then celebrating the results? For me, I would love to start connecting with more people, I just have no idea about everything that goes on around this place."

The group began to discuss his idea. As the discussion grew, the council came up with the idea of installing a students' message center in the main hall of the school. Most students pass by that hall at least once a day, if not more. They also talked about using the school's social media more effectively. The council agreed that social media is where they get 90 percent of their information and would help connect the students to school events. They also discussed being active participants on social media. They agreed that if the school does this, they must commit as leaders to spur positive comments on posts and reels that not only deliver information but also help positively reinforce it.

"I have an idea!" the girls volleyball rep said excitedly. "I think this is all great stuff, but it's all on technology. Is there any reason we can't get programs together to interact in person? I'm thinking we could start with a party each season for sports and activities that are active that season. I'd really like the opportunity to interact with the band. Listening to Tasha . . . it was Tasha, right?" The girl looked at Tasha with a smile to make sure she was getting her name right. "Tasha seems like she would be pretty cool to get to know. I'm probably not brave enough to just approach Tasha to start a conversation unless I was in a class or had a safe situation to do so. Given that opportunity, I think that it is easier to build friendships that way. We could even do goofy games or activities to help create conversations. That's just my thought though."

Coach L wrote down all their ideas.

As the meeting came to a close, Mrs. J addressed the student leaders. "I want to thank you all for your participation today. I think we came up with some great ideas of how we can celebrate each other and start to build those relationships between all the programs. As you go through this week, I want you to think about this: What is my responsibility as a leader when it comes to celebrating? I would challenge you to start now. When you see something good someone else is doing, celebrate it. Start within your own team. Leaders don't wait to be told to do things. They do them, and they teach others around them to do so as well. Take the opportunity this week to be that leader. Get your teammates to celebrate something positive that they saw.

> *Then, encourage them to celebrate somebody outside their activity or sport. If we can encourage people as leaders to do this, we can make a huge difference right off the bat. All of the stuff that we just talked about can now support these initial efforts. Thank you for being knights of the round table! Remember, next week we will be talking about inclusivity. Enjoy the rest of your week."*
>
> *And with that the session ended. It's amazing what happened when students we're not only given the opportunity to lead but were taught how. The discussions and outcomes would be felt for many years to come as they continued to lead their students on campus.*

Conclusion

In reflecting on this work, we hope that you indeed embrace a set of leadership expectations for your students. As students go from one activity to another throughout the year, they will recognize that certain leadership competencies and behaviors are expected throughout. They will then be more likely to improve in these key areas and demonstrate growth. Conversely, if you don't have clear ideas in this space, the chance of growth becomes minimal. In an ideal world, students will leave your school with these leadership competencies well-rehearsed and demonstrated. Colleges, employers, family, and community members will begin to recognize that a different type of leadership is emerging with a deep and abiding reinforcement from this model.

*The more you praise and celebrate your
life, the more there is in life to celebrate.*

—Oprah Winfrey

CHAPTER 8

YOU'RE NEVER DONE CELEBRATING

Author Jeremy Jorgensen (2023) says, "When schools take the time to celebrate their achievements, it fosters a sense of accomplishment and unity." The purpose of this chapter is to examine the role of enthusiastic, full-throated celebration and the development and delivery of outstanding athletics and activity programming. Celebration is a powerful tool that can significantly impact team dynamics and organizational performance. This act of recognition not only boosts morale but also motivates individuals to strive for even greater success. According to a study by Socialcast, 69 percent of employees would work harder if they felt their efforts were better appreciated (Leibtag, 2023). This highlights the importance of acknowledging both small and large milestones, as it creates a positive feedback loop of motivation and engagement.

Moreover, celebration helps to build a culture of appreciation and support. When employees feel valued and recognized for their contributions, they are more likely to develop a sense of loyalty and commitment to the organization (Landry & Whillans, 2019). This, in turn, leads to increased productivity and innovation. As noted by the Lean Leadership Center, positive recognition is considerably more powerful than corrective feedback (Jekiel, n.d.).

By celebrating achievements, organizations can create an environment where employees feel encouraged to take risks and share new ideas, ultimately driving better outcomes.

Additionally, celebration plays a crucial role in enhancing team cohesion. Celebrating together allows team members to bond over shared successes, which strengthens their relationships and improves collaboration. This sense of camaraderie is essential for overcoming challenges and achieving common goals. The *Harvard Business Review* emphasizes that celebration is an opportunity to cement the lessons learned on the path to achievement and to strengthen relationships (Johnson, 2022). By fostering a culture of celebration, organizations can create a more resilient and high-performing team.

When students are celebrated for applying great leadership, great practice habits, or even outstanding outcomes as a result of their athletics and activities, the translation into other elements of their lives becomes much more fluid and authentic. We will be exploring the creation of these celebration opportunities as well as their translation to a larger school context in this chapter.

Why We Resist Celebration

We all know it feels good to celebrate. Our lives revolve, in many ways, around working towards anticipated celebrations. Graduation parties. Engagement celebrations. Even in the end, celebrations of life. Despite the known benefits and feelings about the wisdom of celebrating achievements, many schools struggle to adopt this practice. This resistance often stems from deeply ingrained cultural norms and historical management practices that have failed to serve (Reason, 2015). One significant factor is the legacy of Taylorism, or scientific management, which emphasizes efficiency and productivity through strict control and standardization (Taylor, 1911). This approach often leads to a culture of management by exception, where deviations from the norm are met with corrective actions rather than positive reinforcement (Moore & Newsome, 2019). In such environments, celebrating successes can be seen as a distraction from the primary focus on performance metrics and productivity targets.

Additionally, organizational change theories suggest that resistance to celebration can be attributed to factors such as mistrust, fear of failure, and existing cultural norms (Olmstead, 2022). Employees may fear that celebrating achievements could lead to complacency or unrealistic expectations, which could ultimately result in disappointment and decreased motivation. This resistance is further compounded by the lack of training and support for implementing celebratory practices (Olmstead, 2022).

In the context of schools, this resistance can be particularly challenging. Educators and administrators may feel pressured to prioritize standardized test scores and other quantifiable outcomes over the more intangible benefits of celebrating student and teacher achievements. Also, unlike corporate counterparts who lavishly celebrate generous victories, gratuitous celebration in public school settings obviously can create an optics challenge. However, fostering a culture of celebration can lead to increased motivation, improved morale, and stronger community bonds (Jorgensen, 2023). By recognizing and celebrating successes, schools can create a more positive and supportive environment that encourages continuous improvement and innovation.

Finally, we recognize that there is resistance to and need for celebration, and you have a perfect venue with athletics and activities to have both a reason and a venue to celebrate the good things we are hoping for the students we serve. Let celebration warm the hearts and stimulate the creative minds of the students you serve. Let's explore how thoughtful leaders make that happen.

Identifying Challenges of Celebration

When reflecting on the five elements of Rally, one may assume that this element is the easiest to implement. We believe that this is not the case. There are still many challenges that come with celebrating in schools. Ensuring inclusivity, allocating the right resources, balancing academic benefits, and engaging the community are some of the challenges that a school may encounter when trying to celebrate their athletic and activity programs.

Inclusivity

One challenge is ensuring that all students feel included and valued regardless of their athletic or activity involvement. Often, the focus on high-profile sports or activities can inadvertently marginalize students who are not part of those groups. Schools need to create a culture where every student's talents and contributions are recognized and celebrated. This can be a challenge as some campuses can have over fifty programs running at any given time. How does a school ensure everyone is included? What if programs are struggling? There are several challenges that come with ensuring all programs are represented. An example of this was when Brandon took the athletic director and assistant principal position at a school where he worked, one of the first concerns he received from the community was about the inequity in programs and how they were presented to the community. Why was band not featured on social media as much as football? Why did we not celebrate the "We the People" competitors? Why didn't we hang banners for the choir awards they received? The overarching message was we needed to celebrate more programs than just the major sports. As Brandon began to dive into this concern, it was quickly discovered that the challenge was simply not having processes in place that allowed every extracurricular activity to be celebrated. Great things were happening on campus, but nobody knew about them unless they were in the activity. It wasn't because people didn't care. People cared immensely. But this may not be the case in all schools. Some schools may not see the value in less popular sports and activities, and it comes down to a shift in culture. Either way, this is a challenge that needs to be addressed.

Resource Allocation

Another challenge is allocating resources fairly among different athletic teams and activities. Some sports may receive more funding, attention, and facilities than others, leading to disparities in opportunities and experiences for students. This imbalance in resource allocation could cause challenges between programs and the ability to celebrate them. For example, the football team raises over $300,000 a year and can afford to hire a social media manager. This manager posts on social media nonstop and gives the appearance that one program is being valued over another, even though the school has no control over that resource. Additionally, you may have a tech club that has access to software that allows them to create and post graphics that are of substantially higher quality than those of their peers. Each imbalance brings forth its own challenges that a leader will have to plan and execute. Administrators will need to be aware of how those potential imbalances in celebrations can cause rifts or perceived favoritism amongst the activities and athletic programs.

Academic Balance

Balancing academics with athletics and extracurricular activities can be challenging for students. Participating in sports or activities often requires a significant time commitment, which can sometimes detract from academic performance or lead to burnout. Schools need to support students in managing their time effectively and prioritizing their academic responsibilities while still participating in activities they enjoy. How much does a school disrupt the educational environment to celebrate these students? Brandon was at a school one time in which the teachers revolted when he implemented a "walk of champions" at the end of each season for any program (sports or activities) that was recognized at the state or national level, taking merely ten minutes of class time each walk, three times a year. Teachers equated the thirty minutes to lost class time and therefore felt it should have been celebrated in a different way, whereas the students felt supported and seen in front of their peers, thanking the administration for celebrating them in front of the entire school. Administrators will have to decipher within their schools and communities what their staff and stakeholders will support. These challenges must be accounted for in planning the celebrations that will take place.

Community Engagement

Building and maintaining community support for activities and athletics can be difficult, especially in schools where there is competition for resources or where there is a lack of interest or involvement from parents and other community members. Schools must actively engage with their communities to promote school spirit, encourage attendance at games and events, and foster a sense of pride and belonging among students, parents, alumni, and other stakeholders. What do you do when a community member feels slighted? This could be explained by a group of alumni who feel the school doesn't honor successes that have happened in the past and only focuses on current successes. In some communities, those alumni have the potential to drive culture within the school. Whether real or perceived, the community's outlook on a school can have a huge impact. Having practices in place to not only engage the community but also address the needs of all stakeholders in the community can become a daunting challenge along the way.

WHERE ARE WE NOW?

1. What does inclusivity look like on our campus? Do we actively promote it?
2. How does our school communicate positive celebrations with our community?
3. Does our school prioritize athletics over activities, or vice versa, in our communications to both the school and the community?
4. What is our social media presence? Are we reaching our community where they are at?
5. Does our school have a process to honor those past members of the school community who have had a profound impact on the school?

Responding to These Challenges With Rally Practices

Celebrations can come in many different shapes and sizes as you will see in the following practices. When considering who and how to celebrate, take into account that a celebration is not just a celebration. It communicates to the community and the world about what is important within your school. Most people want to be recognized for their accomplishments. It motivates people to do better, no matter their age. Sports and performance psychology outlines three basic psychological needs required for motivation: (1) autonomy, (2) competence, and (3) relatedness (Horn & Smith, 2019). By using celebrations in different forms, leaders can accomplish all three of those needs and ultimately improve their school's performance and culture (Horn & Smith, 2019). When looking to engage with these Rally practices, think about what it means to be valued for what a student brings as an individual to your school, how they contribute to the whole, and how impactful that communication can be for everyone involved. Allow these Rally practices to help guide and plan celebrations of all types and how a school can help use celebrations to drive culture in the school.

Rally Practice 5.1: "Small-c" Celebrations

ACTs need to be particularly sensitive to the importance of small, ongoing, small-c celebrations. What we mean by this is that, in some cases, just a small word in passing that an ACT shares with a student can have a huge, reverberating impact. Ken Blanchard and Spencer Johnson (2001), authors of *The One-Minute Manager*, are famous for advocating the situational leadership priority of giving small, powerful, intimate one-on-one coaching sessions designed to excite and motivate the recipient. In some cases, these small celebrations may include some coaching and even some redirects. As we describe some tips on how to execute these small celebrations, we hope it will give you a perspective on how to use them in impactful ways.

INDIVIDUAL FORMATIVE FEEDBACK IN THE MOMENT

For ongoing small-c celebrations, ACTs can be impactful by quickly and quietly pulling students aside and giving them a twenty-second overview of what the ACT is observing and what they're doing right. These quick, quiet affirmations can keep the momentum going, especially when the ACT notices something good happening in real time. There's nothing more powerful than providing a learning opportunity in the moment. For example, how many times have you seen a basketball coach or a football coach pull an athlete aside and have a one-on-one conversation with them as soon as the play is over? This isn't always just because they think the play is going to happen again in a few minutes. It's because in that moment, the human brain is in the middle of remembering what just happened, and the ACT is trying to associate exactly what they hope the students will do next time with that moment while it's happening. Those in-the-moment conversations happening concurrently with small one-on-one conversations can, in many cases, have a far greater impact than a full-team lecture with a dedicated guest speaker. In a world that is so deeply interconnected, it's highly likely that the ACT is frequently connected to the students and can send them a note or a text or communicate with them one-on-one on some sort of virtual platform. In some cases, a quick note or personal appreciation or a one-on-one in a private setting could mean a lot to students. Taking advantage of these critical tools and using them on an ongoing basis to privately communicate, share observations about their progress, and point out the specific things that the ACT thinks should be complimented will indeed help to bring out even more of what is good.

THE ADVANTAGE OF FORMATIVE ASSESSMENTS

Formative assessments, which provide in-the-moment feedback, are highly effective in promoting learning and skill development. When feedback is given during the learning process, students can immediately apply it to their work, leading to deeper understanding and improvement. This just-in-time feedback helps students identify and correct mistakes, refine their skills, and build confidence in their abilities (Karaman, 2021).

Research supports the notion that formative assessments enhance student learning outcomes. For instance, a meta-analysis by Pinar Karaman (2021) found that formative assessments significantly improve student performance by providing timely and actionable feedback. Additionally, the Education Endowment Foundation reported that high-quality, in-the-moment feedback can help students make up to eight months of additional progress (Collins & Quigley, 2021). By integrating formative assessments into the learning process, educators can create a more responsive and adaptive teaching environment that supports continuous improvement and mastery of the subject matter (Purdue University Global, 2020).

Wondering what to celebrate? The following is a list of things that we believe are certainly worth celebrating if you want better results and a better program overall.

- **Showing up:** This may sound like a small thing, but if a student is a bit unsure about participation but is showing up consistently, a quiet word of encouragement from the ACT could mean a lot and make them want to keep attending the activity, This teaches students the importance of persistence in participating in an athletic or activity commitment.

- **Dealing with struggle:** When an ACT notices a student struggling, and in the middle of dealing with it, giving the student a small, in-the-moment observance of that struggle. Offering encouragement to their dedication and support could have a resounding impact on their ongoing commitment.

- **Working, failing, and adjusting:** Noticing a student who is working hard, perhaps struggling a bit, making an adjustment, and then hoping for better results represents the quiet work that many students do year in and year out as they participate in activities and athletics. It's admirable. When you think about it, young people don't always have a great deal of experience. Many are operating to some degree on faith. They have no way of knowing that if they continue to work on something they will get better. You may tell them, but they haven't lived it for themselves and are taking your word for it or are simply trying it on. When an ACT sees this going on, encouraging it and rewarding the effort and the willingness to adjust and try is something that can help students produce more grit and dedication.

- **Making progress:** Encouraging even the smallest levels of progress tends to create a scenario where more of it is likely to show up. While students might indeed have lofty goals for their eventual progress, making small moves toward their goal deserves even a small, whispered word of encouragement. Telling them that even the smallest step can sometimes make a big difference. Again, these small efforts and quiet one-on-one moments make all the difference to students.

- **Demonstrating team optimism and rigor:** When an ACT sees students demonstrating optimism and bringing the rigor to practice either individually or to the team, this is obviously something to compliment and encourage. It is a key element to overall progress that is worth noting. An ACT may notice that a student isn't even particularly effective at their craft yet but they are optimistic and they are trying hard. That sort of energy and demeanor makes a difference and will ultimately drive the progress of the program and should be recognized.

- **Working together:** Quickly and quietly recognizing and rewarding students who are willing to work together simply creates a scenario where more of it is likely to happen. When you see it, call it out one on one.

- **Encouraging leadership, even from those without the title:** Quality athletic and activities programs are teaming with students who will someday be leaders in whatever they do. They don't even know their capacity to lead yet, but they're beginning to observe the opportunity. When an ACT sees a student display even a small sample of leadership competency, it is so beneficial to acknowledge and explicitly name the quality.

TEAM CELEBRATIONS

In the previous section, we articulated some small-c celebrations that ACTs can execute one on one with students. Arguably some of these elements could be executed in small groups. Many of the previously mentioned topic areas, or things to celebrate, should likewise be celebrated as a team in addition to what we talk in greater detail about in the following section. What's important to recognize is that when using celebration as a tool to build culture, celebrating as a team within the group has a different impact than celebrating one on one.

In other words, the one-on-one celebration can, in some cases, create a certain type of intimacy that may indeed be preferred and valuable. In other instances, the public declaration of appreciation for excellence in service and performance for a team member or an entire team may likewise send a different message that may pay dividends in the moment or within the year or season. We don't have a magic formula for necessarily bifurcating opportunities for individual and team celebrations. Here are some tips for implementation and celebration.

CEREMONIES

Ceremonies can be emotionally and physically draining and can take a lot of time to put together. However, when ACTs take the time to put together impactful ceremonies, the benefits can be exponential. We know that the excitement and energy around ceremonies can make a big difference. Undoubtedly, you might remember something kind that was said at a banquet, assembly, or other gathering. All these years later, those words, the actions, and the kind of celebration matters. ACTs must remember that they have an opportunity to bring this to fruition with everybody they serve.

Specifically, when teams come together or there are overall program celebrations, it's important to call attention to not only the individual things discussed earlier but also to the more team-oriented commitments that can help to improve the program or activity. There are many ways to make small celebrations happen every day. See the following list for some ideas.

- **Demonstrating excellence in practice:** Celebrating an excellent practice altogether is a most beneficial way of demonstrating to the team the importance of putting the time into and investing in preparation. This is a valuable life lesson and taking the time to recognize what excellence in practice looks like is important. If for some reason there isn't a lot of excellence in practice being demonstrated, even a moment of excellence, the ACT should stop, call out what's right, and continue to build on what's going well, engaging those leading instances and building on them until they become habit forming.

- **Committing to the process and the plan:** ACTs must have a process or a plan in store for their activity. They are trying to build in some form or another, and the team or group needs to be aware of that commitment and the moving parts. When progress is made toward the process or plan, those points of progress must be called out and celebrated. In some cases, we have known ACTs who just assume everyone is recognizing that they are making progress. Unfortunately, this isn't the case, and calling attention to the points of progress makes all the difference.

- **Showing up ready to compete or perform:** When a team or group shows up ready to compete or perform, and they don't win or even perform at a world-class level, you should still recognize and celebrate the fact that they showed up and prepared. Getting excited about readiness will be its own reward. Calling attention to readiness will create reward systems in the collective brains of those who compete or perform for them to show up and be ready to be their best.

- **Demonstrating team optimism and rigor:** Optimism and rigor motivate individuals and groups. Keeping the focus on optimism and rigor makes a big difference in the kind of outcomes we hope to achieve. When we see our teams being optimistic, even in the face of a crushing loss or a major setback, that optimism should be rewarded.

- **Working together:** If a team or a group fails to meet its objective, but shows an incredible ability to work hard, work interdependently, and work with great respect and knowledge of one another, their efforts need to be celebrated. We know it's easy to get caught up in wins and losses. However, celebrating working together is its own reward. Rooting for each other represents camaraderie and every team member can intentionally work to build that team culture together.

- **Publicly encouraging leadership, even without the title:** Previously, we discussed the importance of quietly observing the emergence of leadership, even from those who aren't team captains or designated leads. Recognizing demonstrations of that leadership should also be made public to the team whenever possible. Publicly calling out the presence of an outstanding leader on a team can make it more likely that it will be replicated again.

Small-c celebrations are more formative, quickly applied celebrations that allow for momentum building and the reinforcement of what matters. See the suggestions that follow on how to implement this Rally practice.

- Conduct small, ongoing celebrations to make a big impact on students.

- Give quick, verbal affirmations and coaching sessions to motivate and excite students.

- Include providing feedback during teachable moments in your small-c celebrations and use private communication channels to do so.

- Celebrate as a team and include the use of ceremonies and public recognition.

- Decide what to celebrate: showing up consistently, dealing with struggle, working, failing, adjusting, progressing, demonstrating a commitment to the process and plan, showing up ready to compete or perform, demonstrating team optimism and rigor, working together, and displaying leadership.

Rally Practice 5.2: "Big-C" Celebrations

Schoolwide celebrations are important to identifying the true priorities of the school. As we have discussed earlier, historic habits have developed where little attention is spent celebrating one student activity while overwhelming attention is given to another. Thoughtful leaders must give careful consideration to how they will prioritize all of the student activities and athletics that are available throughout the year. Here are some tips for conducting a schoolwide celebration.

WHOLE-SCHOOL ACTIVITY

It is expensive to have all students committed to some sort of assembly or celebration. We use the term *expensive* in reference to time. When we assemble students, we take away from important learning time they have in the classroom. All school celebrations must be taken seriously and be carefully planned, maximizing the design and the impact of the celebration.

Keep whole-school activities moving, engaging, and fun to avoid making them feel like an assembly of announcements. Make sure the program you plan to celebrate is fun and exciting and involves lots of activities to create a sense of energy to encourage other students to want to participate and compete. This would most commonly be referred to as a "pep rally." Pep rallies that include chants, games, celebrations of accomplishments, and teacher engagement are more apt to keep the attention of students rather than just having a team or group in front of the student body. With the increased visibility on social media programs, such as TikTok and Instagram, pep rally activities are going viral with new and creative ways to engage all the students.

If we are pulling together a schoolwide celebration, there are some important priorities that we should celebrate. If in front of the school, it is imperative to specifically call out and celebrate participation, team or group progress, team optimism and rigor, teamwork, and the all-important skill of leadership. Whenever possible, these important elements should be celebrated in front of the entire school because these are indeed the skills that make the greatest difference. High levels of participation require engagement and engagement supports learning. Focusing on progress, being optimistic, and willing to submit to rigor also helps you learn. Being a leader and working together represents a lifelong skill, and again, makes you better in everything that you do.

COMMUNITY CELEBRATIONS

Finally, our last big-C Rally practice revolves around community celebrations. There are times when we need to take our celebrations out into the community to draw attention to the things that matter most. This could include celebrations before an activity or at halftime, such as homecoming celebrations, and other community-engaging moments of connection.

Community celebrations provide an excellent opportunity to highlight the achievements and efforts of student-athletes and participants in various activities. These events foster a sense of pride and unity within the community while emphasizing the importance of student involvement. The following are some examples of largescale community celebrations.

- **Homecoming parades:** Organize a parade featuring all the sports teams and student activity groups. This can serve as a kickoff to the homecoming game and includes floats, banners, and performances by the school band and cheerleaders. This not only celebrates student achievements but also involves the community in school spirit.
- **Pregame festivities:** Host a tailgate party or pregame rally at the school or a local park. Include booths from different student clubs, games, and performances. These events can help build excitement for the game and create an inclusive environment for students, families, and community members.
- **Halftime recognitions:** Use halftime during sports events to recognize the accomplishments of student-athletes, academic achievers, and club participants. Invite local community leaders to present awards or deliver brief speeches to show their support and encourage civic engagement.
- **Volunteer projects:** Combine celebrations with community service. For example, organize a park clean-up day followed by a community barbecue where students, parents, and the community come together to celebrate their collective efforts in improving their surroundings.
- **Engagement with local government:** Arrange for student leaders to attend city council meetings or host a town hall event where students can present their achievements and discuss their contributions to the community.

This helps students understand the importance of civic engagement and builds stronger ties between the school and local government.

By incorporating these community celebrations into student activities and athletics, we can create meaningful connections that celebrate our students' hard work and foster a spirit of unity and pride within the community.

To summarize this Rally practice: As opposed to small-c celebrations, big-C celebrations are celebrations that require more planning, big-picture execution, and usually involve more people. These can make a big impact. Don't overestimate the power of both small-c and big-C efforts. Some of the best compliments or kudos you may have received might have come quite extemporaneously from somebody you cared about in a moment when you simply needed it. You need both, and effort should be extended. See some ideas in the following list for big-C celebrations.

- Recognize the importance of schoolwide celebrations in demonstrating school priorities.
- Make it a whole-school activity, keep it engaging and fun.
- Decide what to celebrate: participation, team or group progress, optimism and rigor, working together, and displaying leadership.
- Take celebrations out into the community to draw attention to important events.
- Review common big-C celebration conventions, like homecoming celebrations and community engagement events.

Rally Practice 5.3: Social Media Shout-Outs

Because students and adults alike are using technology for hours a day, schools must meet people where they are. There is no disputing that students receive massive amounts of information daily from scrolling endlessly through the likes of TikTok, Instagram, and Snapchat. To effectively celebrate students, the celebrations must be visible and interactive. Through our experiences, we have found that this practice has had some of the greatest returns when advertising the accomplishments of the students and ACTs on campus. This process of celebrations on social media requires an understanding of four components.

UNDERSTAND THE REASONING BEHIND SOCIAL MEDIA CELEBRATIONS

As stated in chapter 3 (page 43), activities and athletics are the front porch of your school. Using social media allows cultures to show the community what their front porch looks like. Is it a decrepit scene that looks like it could be from an Alfred Hitchcock movie? Or is it a house with a white picket fence and a wraparound porch that most people would want to enter? Social media celebrations continue to help tell the story that the school wants to be told. We all know that not everything you see on social media is as perfect as it looks, but the mind naturally gravitates toward the positive and glamorous. There's a quote by author Michael Sitrick (2018): "If you don't tell your story, someone else will." Social media can be used to tell your school's story and celebrate accomplishments with the masses.

KNOW WHICH PLATFORMS REACH THE RIGHT AUDIENCES

As a school looks to use social media to celebrate things such as sustained, prideful effort, it needs to know which platform is best suited to reach certain audiences in the community. The following list describes several social media apps and makes recommendations on how to use them as an educator. We understand that technology is always changing, and applications may come about that overtake the current status quo. As applications are presented and described, please take into account the type of information that is being presented on the application, and if future technology replaces it, you can also replace these recommendations with new applications that accomplish the goal of the celebration.

- **Instagram:** From Brandon's experience, as of 2025, 90 percent of social media engagement with students will happen on this platform. Instagram will focus on celebrations that include visuals, such as photos, reels, and videos. Examples of this would be the halftime performance of the marching band, the robotics team receiving a medal for their accomplishments, or a "throwback" picture of the class of 1985 student council. This site will best help the school use visuals to promote the school's culture and community. According to Pew Research Center, 62 percent of teens say they use this platform regularly, up 10 percent from 2015 (Lin, Parker, & Menasce Horowitz, 2024).

- **Facebook:** This site is used as more of an informational platform. This is used more by parents and used to garner community support. Pew Research Center shows regular use of Facebook for teens has dropped from 71 percent in 2015 to 32 percent in 2022 (Vogels, Gelles-Watnick, & Massarat, 2022). Think of Facebook as your secondary tool to reach older generations and to provide information that may not have visual media associated with it.

- **X (formerly known as Twitter):** Business and recruitment live in this space. As of 2025, this platform is used to help students promote themselves to colleges, trades, and other postsecondary opportunities (NCSA College Recruiting, n.d.). This platform also promotes businesses and business relationships that can be developed between schools and districts. Examples of this may include a coach helping a football player connect with a college coach to show highlights for possible recruitment. Another example of this would be a DECA advisor helping a member promote a business product being presented for a project.

- **Native school applications:** This is a newer form of social media access that is bringing all communications into one place. Native school applications are applications exclusively designed for a specific school and its unique needs. The development of a school app allows schools to have a one-stop shop for access to their social media accounts, schedules, websites, and more. This type of technology becomes a one-stop shop for many of the applications listed previously.

- **Risky applications:** Snapchat and TikTok have emerged as apps that schools will want to use with heavy caution. Snapchat brings ethical and safety concerns due to messages "disappearing" after a set amount of time. This means there may not be a trace of potential harmful or bullying behavior. TikTok also brings cybersecurity concerns to schools and districts. A growing number of educational institutions in the United States have banned TikTok from campus networks and devices due to concerns about data privacy and potential foreign surveillance (Congressional Research Service, 2023).

- **Growing applications:** Other applications will always emerge to find niches within the social media world to help celebrate school events and students. With the ever-changing landscape of technology, it is all but guaranteed that a new platform will be developed and gain traction, possibly taking over the current platforms that are most used. As stated in the section on riskier apps, just take caution when engaging in new applications to ensure you are reaching the community you want, as well as keeping the school and the students protected.

KNOW WHAT TOOLS TO USE

There is a viral quote falsely attributed to Bill Gates saying, "I choose a lazy person to do a hard job. Because a lazy person will find an easy way to do it" (as cited in Mandadi, 2022). While there is no factual proof that he said this, the statement itself is an entertaining outlook on the theory of finding more efficient ways of completing tasks. When using social media to celebrate and drive school culture, a lot of schools believe they don't have the time or creativity to be effective. There are several tools that leaders can put in place that will allow for high-level, professional work even with little to no budget, using secondary school time and resources.

- **Remember, graphics are key:** When using social media, visuals will get schools a lot of attention and traffic to help drive users to the ultimate goal of engagement. There are free programs, such as Canva and Gipper, that allow users to create attractive graphics and require no creative abilities. These programs walk the user through uploading a picture, adding words, customizing colors, and more. Creating graphics allows the end user to be visually stimulated and bring pride to the school when advertising the accomplishments of their students.

- **Schedule programs help eliminate the grind:** Many people believe that organizations with high social media presence are on social media nonstop. That couldn't be further from the truth. The truth is most of these organizations are set up on auto-posting software that allows the user to create content at a single time and schedule posts to be published at various times. For example, Brandon uses Hootsuite and Gipper to create graphics for game days all at the start of the season. The game day graphics are scheduled for posting to all three of the major platforms at the beginning of the season, and he never touches the graphics again. The illusion online is that he is posting several times a day, when in fact he spent a couple hours setting up content for the entire season.

- **Use your students:** Don't know how to make graphics very well? Not creative enough or just don't have time? Use some of the best resources available on your campus: students. This can be done by utilizing graphic design programs, using students as student aids for athletic and activity directors, and allowing these students to create content for the school. Students usually have a grasp of what is trending on campus and can incorporate these into your celebrations and increase engagement.

CREATE A CONSISTENT BRAND

We all know of a school in the area where if someone popped up a logo, almost everyone would know their logo and their colors. Is that your school? Schools that attack celebrations with branding allow themselves to create a visual that can be easily recognized by everyone in the community. Keep the color schemes, logos, and fonts consistent. Keep messaging consistent as well. If the school has a great vision or tagline, use those in everything that is put out for celebrations. Find something that allows your school to stand out beyond other schools. This can be anything that sets the school apart—a special mascot, a tagline, colors, and so on. Step out of your comfort zone and brand to engage with your community. Some of the gimmickiest strategies end up being the most impactful in the end.

With the use of these four social media tools, just remember consistency is key. Don't spend time trying to create excitement, and then not deliver on the promise. Social media is an art of storytelling and a game of constant entertainment and those who master the art of social media celebration will find their endeavors are positive ones (Yellowbrick, 2023).

To summarize this Rally practice: A well-crafted plan can make quite a big difference. Here are a few tips on the importance of social media.

- Understand the importance of social media in reaching students and community members.
- Know which platforms reach the right audiences, such as Instagram, Facebook, X, and other apps.
- Use tools like graphics creation tools, scheduling programs, utilizing students, and branding for consistency.
- Acknowledge the importance of consistency in social media engagement and storytelling.

 **RALLY IN ACTION**

Zach, as we will call him, was a local college journalism student who went to visit a principal who led a campus known for how they celebrated their student body. His goal was to write an article that could portray the community culture that he had heard so much about. The two sat down at the table in the corner one day. Zach peered around the office and asked the principal, Mrs. M, if he could set up a camera to record her during their interview.

"Had I known you were going to film me, I would have done my hair!" the principal joked.

The young journalism student laughed nervously, hit record, and started his interview, "So, I have been tasked with finding out what you do on your campus that you feel no one else does or you are the best at in your state. Can you talk to me about what that looks like at your school?"

Mrs. M smiled and asked a question of her own. "That's quite an accent; where are you from?"

"Texas, ma'am."

"I thought so," Mrs. M said, alluding to a hidden reason for the question. "Let me ask you this, why do you have so much pride in your state?"

"I would say we're good at a lot of things."

"And how do you know that?"

Now Zach's interest was piqued. "I guess it's because we talk about it so much."

Mrs. M gave a slight laugh as she agreed with him. "Exactly. You hear about everything they do well. You hear it all day, every day. If you didn't believe Texas was the best at everything, just give it time, eventually you will. You will hear it at every corner of your life—how awesome the state is, and how no other state can hold a candle to what they do. Take BBQ, for example. What if I told you I like Carolina BBQ is better?"

"Well, I would say, that's just crazy!" responded Zach with southern zeal.

"You say this because all you have ever had put in front of you is the message that Texas BBQ reigns supreme. I'm sure if you head over to Tennessee, they may beg to differ. So, you ask what makes Eastside special? We're like the Texas of high schools in the area. We will inundate you with so much positive about our students, our staff, and our school that eventually you'll see how amazing our school is."

"I get it. So, you would say the way you celebrate your school is special."

"I would," Mrs. M said with all the conviction of a preacher. "I believe that not only do we celebrate our staff, students, and school, but we do it in a consistent manner that puts our story out in front of people and doesn't allow others to tell our story. You always hear that for every one negative comment you encounter, it takes ten positive

ones to offset that. We've embraced that philosophy wholeheartedly. There were several of us who worked together to figure out what that looked like on our campus. We asked teachers, coaches, students, and staff what made them feel valued? What that looked like, sounded like, felt like. Once we got this information, we put together a three-pronged approach."

The young student inquired of the principal if she could elaborate on this approach.

For the next thirty minutes, Mrs. M laid out for Zach the three-pronged approach they took to celebrate things that were happening on campus. It started with their athletic and activity accomplishments but soon spread to the entire school. The approach went as follows.

1. **Meet people where they are:** One thing Mrs. M realized was their few celebrations were not reaching the people they wanted to reach. They found that social media was the quickest way to celebrate their successes as almost everybody was on social media. Students had their noses stuck in phones all day, every day. The adults weren't much better. They quickly found that the engagement with their social media posts was fairly high. With a little bit of marketing in the school, they found they had a couple thousand followers in no time. They also found that there were some strategic areas in which most of the school passed multiple times a day. The school made a small investment in some TVs that could scroll through "announcements" throughout the day. They focused these TVs on "celebrations only" and stayed away from the traditional announcements that the other TVs produced. With a few other tweaks, they found that the engagement levels increased with each addition.

2. **Celebrate everyone:** Their next focus was to make sure that they were focusing on celebrating everyone and everything. ACTs were given a Google Form to submit celebrations on a weekly basis. They learned that nothing was too small to celebrate, and every activity and sport had to submit at least one celebration per week. At first, the ACTs struggled because finding celebrations each week felt daunting. During a couple of sessions, the ACT collaborative group devised strategies to help break that barrier and find ways to make those celebrations easier to come by. It eventually got to a point that they not only submitted celebrations for their own but had to create a second form to show celebrations for other programs. The "We See You!" form became more popular than their own team's celebration.

> *These celebrations were then put all over the school, all over social media, student video announcements, parent newsletters, staff newsletters, and every other medium the principal could get her hands on. You found the football team celebrating the chess team. You found the drama program celebrating the mountain bike club. The negative press became almost obsolete overnight.*
>
> 3. ***Adopt an attitude of gratitude:*** *This was just a little bit different than the celebrations. Celebrations pointed out and brought to light the positive things happening around the campus. These were encouraged through electronic means. The attitude of gratitude brought the human touch back to the equation. ACTs and students in their leadership groups committed to a daily show of gratitude to someone on campus, but it had to be in person. This concept had a simple sentence stem to start with. When you wanted to show gratitude to someone, you simply said "[Name], I am grateful for you because you . . ." It was as simple as that. The thought behind this was to have 80 ACTs and more than 500 students do this every day. It would become 580 positive interactions to show people how they are valued daily. On top of that, in a world that lives in digital communication, it brought back a small portion of much-needed human interaction.*

Zach was amazed. The more he listened, the more he realized that this really was a special place. Mrs. M walked Zach out of her office and into one of the hallways during the passing period. Mrs. M challenged him to see for himself. She offered to pull any student he chose, and he could have a quick conversation with them if he wanted.

Zach watched as students passed each other with smiles on their faces, saying hello, and genuinely looking like they cared for each other. He watched as one student stopped to help another student who had dropped something from their bag. He watched as a student stopped another student to comment on their outfit. When he asked the students if they knew each other, they both laughed and said of course. They served on the student leadership council together. Zach continued to interact with the students for the next few minutes as Mrs. M stood by and watched. Each student was as friendly as the next. He asked one student what he enjoyed the most about the school. His response was the attitude of gratitude tradition they have. He moved here last year from a school in a neighboring state. He said there you would get punched for looking at someone wrong. Here, there is genuine care for each other. The passing period came and went. The two headed back to the administrative office.

Mrs. M wrapped up the interview with a nice bow. "So, do you see what sets us apart? People want to feel valued. We deliver that by celebrating their efforts and accomplishments and letting them know how much we appreciate them. This pays off not just in being the "Texas" of high schools, but it also helps with the hard conversations. When it comes time to have the tough conversations, you've put in the work to build that relationship so people will listen. It all fits into the overarching goal of educating our students. We started this with the athletes and students in activities because they are our campus leaders. You get them bought in, and they'll steer your ship for you. Now, a couple of years later, it's a culture."

Mrs. M said her final goodbyes to Zach as she had to attend another meeting in a few minutes. Zach thanked her for her time and asked her if she wanted any final quotes in the article.

She politely declined. She invited him to write about what he saw and give an honest portrayal. Zach grabbed his bag and let her know he would send her a copy before he published. She assured him it would be great!

A week later, Zach submitted his final assignment to his professor. As the professor looked over the article, all he could do was smile with a small tear in his eye. The professor deliberately withheld that he had a connection with the school Zach had just attended.

The professor's son was a junior there and has Down syndrome. This last spring, he had a part in the play. It was small, but he got to sing a few lines. For the next couple of weeks, they played that clip on the celebration TV at the school. Every student in that school, when they would pass his son, would give him a high five and tell him how proud they were. His son came home and told them how much he loved school and was genuinely excited to go each morning. As a father, the greatest blessing he could ask for his child was that the child experience the feeling of acceptance.

Celebrations can bring a school together. At the end of the day, people want to feel valued and want to feel accepted. Celebrations can monumentally capture both and help set a culture in a school that rallies around every student, not just the superstars. Knowing what to celebrate and how to celebrate are the first steps; the next steps are up to you.

Conclusion

Celebrating may be the last component, but we are never done. We believe that celebrating is one of the most important elements of the Rally model. You have to bring the right energy, leadership, and attitude to what you're attempting to execute. You may have all the appropriate training protocols, but if you have a low-energy, poorly engaged ACTs, then students aren't going to be at their best. Develop your skills to become better at celebrating, and you will be amazed at the growth you'll see in your school.

There is always strength in numbers. The more individuals or organizations that you can rally to your cause, the better.

—Mark Shields

EPILOGUE

A Rally of Your Own

There comes a time in everyone's career when a decision must be made. Some people confront this decision early in their careers, while others encounter it later. That decision is simply this: Am I OK with doing things the way they have always been done? Brandon was once told by a mentor that success and comfort cannot coexist. I'm sure that mentor stole that from some great philosopher or coaching legend, but it hit the same, nonetheless. Rally is a challenging process but a proven framework to elevate your school toward excellence. It pushes us out of our comfort zones by encouraging us to embrace differences. We choose to strive for excellence.

When we began to write this book, we went through several drafts, attempting to find the right language, practices, and message that would allow any administrator to improve their activities and athletics on their campus. As Rally started to unfold, it was amazing how much we found, even more than we already knew, which was the tying bond between academics, athletics, and activities. We began to take parts of the Rally framework and talk with people from around the United States. Many of the people we spoke to loved the concepts and wanted to grow but didn't know how. This gave us hope that we were on the right track. We believe in this model because we have seen it work firsthand. These practices are grounded in experience and proven effectiveness, not guesswork. These practices have been observed in our own schools and those we have worked closely with throughout the years. Brandon's school probably is one of the brightest examples of them all.

Brandon became an athletic director in 2016 after leaving a successful football career as a coach. Both schools he has served since were able to accomplish amazing feats. At his current school, Brandon's teams have won twenty-one state championships in the last five years and multiple FFA, mock trial, and fine arts awards. His school is an A+ school of excellence in the state of Arizona. These accomplishments were capped off in receiving the Arizona Interscholastic Association's Director's Cup Award in 2023. This award is given to the high school with the highest overall excellence in activities and athletics in the state. What's even more amazing is that same year the school excelled in many academic areas as well. The school bought into the concept of Rally as a tool to ensure that all students had an opportunity to be successful in whatever path they chose. One of his biggest challenges was managing a student with a playoff tennis match and a year-end choir concert on the same day. Or the football player who missed multiple Saturday practices to show off his goats at the FFA competitions. The practices described in this book and put into practice at this school with fidelity are a shining example of what can be accomplished when we implement the Rally model.

If implemented well, you can see the Rally model in action everywhere you look. Raising the standard can be seen in the vision that the school holds to with "Elite Hawks, Elite Purpose: Enthusiasm, Love, Integrity, Toughness, Everyday." Students and ACTs alike can talk to you in depth about what is expected of them in every facet of the school. Aligning and synergizing can be seen in the way that the students, ACTs, and community members align themselves to this vision. Additionally, this can be seen in the multiple youth programs that pepper the school in both activities and athletics. Students as young as fourth grade are already committed to being Hawks because of this. Teachers are at all the students' events. Teacher appreciation nights litter the calendar while ACTs support teachers when they are in need of help with students. Learning communities for ACTs are held every month on a Wednesday afternoon where vulnerability can be viewed from a mile away; such as a theater teacher talking to a football coach about her experience teaching her students about enthusiasm and what that looks like in rehearsal, or a soccer coach baring her soul to a room full of ACTs about how she feels less than at times because of past relationships and how that impacts the way she coaches. You can see vulnerability in an athletic director shedding tears with his staff after losing his oldest son, only to be uplifted by the shared love in the room. Leading through students is a weekly occurrence—watching our students become effective leaders before our eyes as they communicate ideas and needs that we have never thought of as adults. A student leader shared how he and a band member independently developed an idea for promoting integrity next semester.

And lastly, you really are never done celebrating. When something good comes along why wouldn't you celebrate it? Furthermore, we owe it to our students to celebrate their accomplishments. In a world of social media, where information is passed almost as fast as it happens, the world needs more positivity in it. It's no secret that mental health is a challenge these days. While students could escape high school challenges at home in the 1990s, the constant connectivity we've experienced since then offers no respite. It's relentless. Seeing the school celebrate even the smallest of programs and what they have done has yielded amazing results. Seeing students read to elementary school students, seeing a choir bring joy to our elderly neighbors during the holiday season, and celebrating a community when they Rally after a fire takes the home of a student all bring joy to the soul. They show that we are all human and we all need to see our value. All these elements don't make the school unique, but rather they are a model for what can be. As we mentioned earlier, this is achievable for anyone willing to embrace change. The results will be worth the effort, and isn't that why we all do this, to ensure that our students have the highest chances of success?

The question remains: Are you ready to Rally?

APPENDIX:
Rally Model School Evaluation

These checklists are designed to help schools assess how well they align with the principles of each of the Rally models. In each reproducible, you will find criteria followed by a list of challenges to watch out for, evaluative questions to answer, a rubric to score your school, and a reflection section. At the end, you'll have space to plan your first action items toward implementing that stage of the Rally model.

Raise the Standard

This checklist is designed to help schools assess their alignment with the principles of "Raising the Standard" in the Rally model. Each section includes challenges, reflective prompts, and a rubric to measure performance. Use the freewriting space at the end of each section for deeper reflection.

Participation Expectations
Challenges:
1. Low levels of participation
2. Difficulty recruiting due to logistical challenges
3. Discrepancies in participation among student groups
Evaluative Questions:
1. What percentage of students are currently involved in extracurricular activities?
2. How does participation compare to historical data and similar schools in your area?
3. Are there specific student groups underrepresented? If so, why?

Rubric:

1. The school has less than 25 percent student participation in extracurricular activities and demonstrates minimal or inconsistent efforts to recruit students.
2. The school has 25–49 percent student participation engaged in ongoing recruitment efforts, but these efforts lack a clear strategy.
3. The school has achieved 50–74 percent participation, demonstrates proactive recruitment strategies, and has some level of tracking data trends related to extracurricular involvement.
4. The school has 75 percent or more participation and exhibits clear expectations for extracurricular involvement, utilizes strategic recruitment methods, and consistently analyzes data to inform their efforts.

Reflection:

Freewrite your thoughts about the current state of participation in your school.

Program Offerings
Challenges:
1. Limited number of extracurricular programs
2. Difficulty meeting community demand for new activities
3. Lack of alignment between offerings and community demographics
Evaluative Questions:
1. How many extracurricular programs are currently offered?

2. When was the last assessment of program offerings conducted?

3. Are your offerings comparable to similar schools in the area? |
| **Rubric:** |
| 1. There are fewer than ten programs with no regular evaluations or updates.
2. There are ten to nineteen programs with occasional evaluations, but there is limited alignment with community needs.
3. There are twenty or more programs with regular evaluation and there is partial alignment with target demographics.
4. There are thirty or more programs with frequent evaluations, there is alignment with community needs, and the school has a mix of quantitative and qualitative offerings. |

Reflection:

Freewrite your thoughts about the breadth and relevance of program offerings at your school.

Commitment to Programs
Challenges:
1. Inconsistent standards for student participation and engagement
2. Low persistence rates across multiple seasons or years
Evaluative Questions:
1. Are participation standards clear and communicated to students and parents?
2. How many students participate across multiple seasons or years?
3. Are expectations consistent across programs?
Rubric:
1. There are no clear standards for participation and the school suffers from low persistence rates.
2. Basic standards exist but lack consistent enforcement. The school experiences moderate persistence rates.
3. There are clear and mostly consistent standards, and the school experiences high persistence rates.

4. There are clear and consistently enforced and communicated standards with very high persistence rates.

Reflection:

Freewrite your thoughts about how your school fosters commitment to programs.

Hiring Standards for ACTs

Challenges:
1. Inconsistent hiring criteria
2. Misalignment between hires and school values

Evaluative Questions:
1. Are hiring standards clear and consistently applied?

2. Do interview processes assess alignment with school vision and culture?

3. Are new hires effectively onboarded to embrace program goals?

Rubric:
1. There is no consistent criteria nor are there alignment checks during hiring.
2. There are basic criteria in place but they are inconsistently applied.
3. Clear criteria is applied consistently with some focus on alignment.
4. The rigorous hiring processes are fully aligned with the school's vision and mission.

Reflection:

Freewrite your thoughts about how your school hires and supports ACTs.

Community and Parent Support
Challenges:
1. Low attendance at events
2. Minimal parent engagement or volunteerism
Evaluative Questions:
1. How many parents volunteer annually?
2. What is the average attendance at events over the past three years?
3. How does the school foster parent and community engagement?
Rubric:
1. There is minimal parent support and low attendance at events.
2. There is moderate parent support with occasional volunteer engagement.
3. There is active parent involvement with consistent attendance and volunteer efforts.

4. There is robust parent engagement with widespread support and strong partnerships.

Reflection:

Freewrite your thoughts about parent and community involvement at your school.

_____
_____
_____
_____
_____
_____
_____

Sportsmanship

Challenges:

1. Inconsistent sportsmanship behavior
2. Poor modeling of values by students, parents, or community members

Evaluative Questions:

1. Are sportsmanship standards clearly communicated?

2. How does the school address violations of sportsmanship?

3. Are standards aligned with the school's mission and values?

Rubric:

1. There are no formal sportsmanship standards or consequences for violations.
2. There are basic standards but they are inconsistently enforced.
3. Clear standards are communicated and enforced with some alignment to values.
4. Robust standards are in place and they are fully aligned with values, consistently enforced, and modeled by all stakeholders.

Reflection:

Freewrite your thoughts about the sportsmanship culture at your school.

_____
_____
_____
_____
_____
_____
_____

Overall Score for Raise the Standard (24 Possible):

Greatest Need:

First Action Item:

Align

This checklist is designed to help schools assess how they "Align" within the context of the Rally model. Each section includes challenges, reflective prompts, and a rubric to measure performance. Use the freewriting space at the end of each section for deeper reflection.

Top-Down Program Alignment
Challenges:
1. Misaligned objectives between leadership and program staff
2. Disconnect between school vision and program implementation
Evaluative Questions:
1. Do all program staff understand the overarching vision of the school?
2. How is the program vision communicated across leadership and feeder programs?
3. What specific actions are taken to ensure top-down alignment?

Rubric:

1. The vision is unclear and not communicated to staff or feeder programs.
2. The vision exists but communication and alignment are inconsistent.
3. The vision is clear and communicated to most levels with partial alignment.
4. The vision is well-defined, consistently communicated, and fully aligned across all levels.

Reflection:

Freewrite your thoughts about the top-down alignment of your programs.

Bottom-Up Program Alignment
Challenges:
1. Inadequate investment in feeder programs
2. Lack of foundational skill building and early engagement
Evaluative Questions:
1. Are feeder programs adequately supported and aligned with the main program? _____ _____ _____ _____ _____
2. How does the school invest in early-stage development? _____ _____ _____ _____ _____
3. What events or workshops are in place to introduce younger students to activities? _____ _____ _____ _____ _____ _____
Rubric:
1. There is minimal support or investment in feeder programs.
2. There is basic investment with limited alignment to the main program.
3. There is moderate investment with partial alignment and some skill building.

4. There is strong investment with full alignment and robust early-stage development.

Reflection:

Freewrite your thoughts about bottom-up program alignment and support.

_____
_____
_____
_____
_____
_____
_____
_____

Loose-Tight Leadership
Challenges:
1. Overly rigid or excessively lenient leadership practices
2. Lack of continuous review and communication among ACTs
Evaluative Questions:
1. What elements of your program are "tight" (strictly controlled) versus "loose" (flexible)?

2. How often do ACTs reflect on progress toward the vision?

3. Is leadership actively fostering alignment through communication and accountability? |
| **Rubric:** |
| 1. There is no clear distinction between tight and loose elements, and there are limited review processes.
2. There is a basic understanding of tight and loose elements but inconsistent practices. |

3. There are clear distinctions with regular reviews and partial alignment.
4. There are well-defined elements, consistent reviews, and strong communication.

Reflection:

Freewrite your thoughts about leadership practices and alignment in your school.

_____
_____
_____
_____
_____
_____
_____
_____

Intentional Collaboration With Other Programs
Challenges:
1. Programs operate in silos with minimal collaboration
2. Lack of shared learning and resources among ACTs
Evaluative Questions:
1. How often do ACTs collaborate with one another?
2. What structures are in place to facilitate shared learning?
3. Are there intentional connections with other programs to improve outcomes?
Rubric:
1. Programs operate independently with no collaboration.
2. There is occasional collaboration but there are no structured processes.
3. There is regular collaboration with some shared learning structures.
4. There is a strong culture of collaboration with intentional connections and shared resources.

Reflection:
Freewrite your thoughts about collaboration among programs and ACTs.

Overall Score for Align (16 Possible):
Greatest Need:
First Action Item:

Learning Communities for ACTs

This checklist is designed to assist schools in assessing the effectiveness and alignment of their "Learning Communities for ACTs (advisors, coaches, and teachers)." Each section includes challenges, reflective prompts, and a rubric for evaluation. Freewriting spaces are included for deeper reflection.

Inconsistent Points of Emphasis
Challenges:
1. Miscommunication or lack of connection among ACTs 2. Conflicting priorities between coaches and program levels
Evaluative Questions:
1. Do ACTs at all levels share consistent goals and priorities? 2. How are conflicts in program objectives addressed? 3. Are internal and external audiences receiving a unified message?

Rubric:

1. ACTs have no shared goals or consistent communication.
2. Goals exist but they are inconsistently communicated or prioritized.
3. Goals are communicated and they are partially aligned across levels.
4. Goals are fully aligned and consistently communicated across all levels.

Reflection:

Freewrite your thoughts on consistency in goals and communication among ACTs.

Unresolved Competition Between Programs
Challenges:
1. Competing demands for student time and attention
2. Lack of respect or collaboration between program leaders
Evaluative Questions:
1. How does the school address conflicts between programs?
2. Are students encouraged to participate in multiple activities without pressure?
3. What steps are taken to foster respect and collaboration between program leaders?
Rubric:
1. School programs compete for students with no resolution or collaboration.
2. Some efforts exist to resolve conflicts but they are inconsistent.
3. Collaborative practices are in place with occasional conflicts.
4. There is a strong culture of collaboration with minimal competition.

Reflection:

Freewrite your thoughts on competition and collaboration between programs.

Addressing Bullying and Fighting
Challenges:
1. Toxic culture and lack of respect between programs
2. Bullying or ridicule of students involved in multiple activities
Evaluative Questions:
1. Are there clear policies to address bullying and program conflicts?

2. How does the school foster a culture of respect and inclusivity?

3. Are communication and conflict resolution strategies effective and implemented? |
| **Rubric:** |
| 1. There are no policies in place to establish a culture of respect, and bullying is prevalent.
2. Policies exist to encourage a culture of respect, but they are inconsistently enforced. |

3. Policies are in place and there are active efforts to promote respect and inclusivity.
4. There is a strong culture of respect with effective policies and conflict resolution strategies.

Reflection:

Freewrite your thoughts on addressing bullying and fostering respect between programs.

ACT Learning Community Development
Challenges:
1. Lack of collaboration and shared learning among ACTs 2. Minimal or ineffective community-building efforts
Evaluative Questions:
1. Is there a collaborative community of practice among ACTs?   2. How often do ACTs meet to share ideas and align goals?   3. Are structures in place to support continuous improvement and collaboration?
Rubric:
1. ACTs operate in silos with no collaboration. 2. There is occasional collaboration with limited structure or support. 3. There is regular collaboration with some shared learning structures. 4. There is a strong community with intentional connections and continuous improvement.

Reflection:
Freewrite your thoughts on the development and effectiveness of the ACT learning community.

Overall Score for Learning Communities for ACTs (16 Possible):
Greatest Need:
First Action Item:

Lead Through Students

This checklist is designed to help schools assess their alignment with the principles of "Leading Through Students" in the Rally model. Each section includes challenges, reflective prompts, and a rubric to measure performance. Use the freewriting space at the end of each section for deeper reflection.

Engaging Students and Encouraging Participation
Challenges:
1. Lack of student engagement and involvement
2. Disconnection from school activities and initiatives
Evaluative Questions:
1. Are there structures in place to actively involve students in shaping school activities?
2. How does the school address disengagement among students?
3. What measures are taken to ensure activities resonate with diverse student interests?

Rubric:

1. Students are minimally involved in shaping school activities; there is no clear strategy for engagement.
2. Some structures exist for student involvement but lack consistency and broad appeal.
3. Students are regularly involved in shaping activities with some alignment to their interests.
4. Robust structures ensure student involvement is central to activity planning with diverse participation.

Reflection:

Freewrite your thoughts about student engagement and involvement in your school.

_____
_____
_____
_____
_____
_____
_____

Addressing Inclusivity and Social Dynamics

Challenges:
1. Bullying and discrimination within the school community
2. Lack of inclusive practices to address changing student demographics

Evaluative Questions:
1. What practices are in place to promote inclusivity and respect among students?

   _____
   _____
   _____
   _____
   _____

2. How does the school address bullying and social conflicts?

   _____
   _____
   _____
   _____
   _____

3. Are social dynamics actively monitored and adjusted to reflect a diverse student body?

   _____
   _____
   _____
   _____
   _____

Rubric:
1. There are minimal efforts to address inclusivity or respond to bullying and discrimination.
2. Basic practices are in place but lack a systemic or proactive approach to inclusivity.
3. There is active monitoring of social dynamics with programs addressing inclusivity and respect.

4. There are comprehensive practices fostering an inclusive, respectful, and adaptive school environment.

Reflection:

Freewrite your thoughts about inclusivity and social dynamics in your school.

Prioritizing Student Well-Being
Challenges:
1. High levels of academic pressure and stress
2. Insufficient support for student mental health and well-being
Evaluative Questions:
1. Are mental health resources accessible to all students?   2. What programs are in place to identify and address signs of burnout?   3. How does the school balance academic demands with student well-being?
Rubric:
1. There are no clear practices to address mental health or academic pressure.
2. There are limited resources and sporadic efforts to support mental health.
3. There are consistent mental health resources with some integration into school culture.

4. Proactive strategies ensure mental health and well-being are prioritized alongside academics.

Reflection:

Freewrite your thoughts about student well-being and mental health support in your school.

Providing Leadership Opportunities for Students
Challenges:
1. Limited or nonexistent leadership opportunities for students 2. Competing priorities that undermine leadership development initiatives
Evaluative Questions:
1. What leadership opportunities are available for students, and how are they structured? 2. Do these opportunities empower students to grow personally and academically? 3. How are leadership programs aligned with the school's vision and goals?
Rubric:
1. Leadership opportunities are rare or poorly structured. 2. Some leadership opportunities exist but lack alignment with broader school goals. 3. Leadership opportunities are structured and empower students in meaningful ways. 4. Robust leadership programs are well-aligned with the school's vision and foster student growth.

Reflection:

Freewrite your thoughts about leadership opportunities for students in your school.

Overall Score for Leading Through Students (16 Possible):

Greatest Need:

First Action Item:

You're Never Done Celebrating

This checklist is designed to help schools assess their alignment with the principles of "You're Never Done Celebrating" in the Rally model. Each section includes challenges, reflective prompts, and a rubric to measure performance. Use the freewriting space at the end of each section for deeper reflection.

Inclusivity in Celebrations
Challenges:
1. Ensuring all students feel valued and included 2. Representing over fifty programs fairly and effectively 3. Promoting campuswide inclusivity through celebrations
Evaluative Questions:
1. Are all student talents and contributions recognized and celebrated?
2. How does the school support struggling programs in its celebrations?
3. What strategies are in place to promote inclusivity across diverse student groups?

Rubric:

1. Celebrations are focused on a few high-profile programs with limited inclusivity.
2. Efforts to include more students and programs exist but lack consistency.
3. Most programs are recognized, but some gaps remain in inclusivity.
4. Celebrations ensure all students and programs are equally valued and represented.

Reflection:

Freewrite your thoughts about inclusivity in celebrations at your school.

Resource Allocation in Celebrations
Challenges:
1. Addressing disparities in funding, facilities, and attention 2. Managing perceptions of inequality in resource distribution
Evaluative Questions:
1. Are resources allocated fairly across programs in celebrations?   2. What steps are taken to support programs that may feel underrepresented?   3. How does the school mitigate perceptions of preferential treatment?
Rubric:
1. Significant disparities in resource allocation with no clear mitigation efforts. 2. Some resources are redistributed but perceptions of inequality persist. 3. Resources are allocated equitably with efforts to uplift underfunded programs. 4. Celebrations reflect equitable distribution of resources across all programs.

Reflection:

Freewrite your thoughts about resource allocation in school celebrations.

Academic Balance in Celebrations
Challenges:
1. Supporting students in managing academics alongside activities
2. Gaining teacher support for balancing academic and extracurricular commitments
Evaluative Questions:
1. How does the school ensure celebrations do not disrupt academics?

2. Are teachers actively involved in and supportive of celebrations?

3. How does the school address academic pressures while promoting activities? |
| **Rubric:** |
| 1. Celebrations disrupt academics frequently and lack teacher involvement.
2. Some balance exists, but academic and extracurricular commitments are misaligned.
3. Celebrations are balanced with academics with partial teacher collaboration.
4. Celebrations complement academics with full teacher support and collaboration. |

Rally! © 2025 Solution Tree Press • SolutionTree.com
Visit **go.SolutionTree.com/studentengagement** to download this free reproducible.

Reflection:

Freewrite your thoughts about balancing academics and celebrations.

Community Engagement Through Celebrations
Challenges:
1. Building and maintaining community support for school activities
2. Promoting school spirit and fostering pride among all stakeholders
Evaluative Questions:
1. How does the school engage the community in celebrations?   2. Are community members, including parents and alumni, actively involved?   3. How does the school address feedback and concerns about inclusivity?
Rubric:
1. Community involvement in celebrations is minimal or sporadic.
2. Some community engagement exists but is inconsistent or limited in scope.
3. Community celebrations are inclusive and involve most stakeholders.
4. Comprehensive engagement ensures all community members feel included and valued.

Reflection:

Freewrite your thoughts about community engagement in celebrations.

Small and Big Celebrations
Challenges:
1. Effectively utilizing small, ongoing celebrations
2. Organizing engaging schoolwide celebrations that reflect school values
Evaluative Questions:
1. Are small, consistent celebrations part of the school culture?
2. How are schoolwide celebrations designed to engage all students?
3. What practices are in place to celebrate team and individual achievements?
Rubric:
1. Celebrations are rare and focused on high-profile events.
2. Small celebrations occur but lack consistency and purpose.
3. Both small and large celebrations are present with occasional gaps in execution.
4. Small and big celebrations are seamlessly integrated and consistently reflect school values.

Reflection:

Freewrite your thoughts about small and big celebrations at your school.

Social Media and Storytelling
Challenges:
1. Reaching the right audience through appropriate platforms 2. Ensuring consistency in branding and messaging
Evaluative Questions:
1. How effectively does the school use social media for celebrations? 2. Are the right platforms used to reach various audiences? 3. How does the school ensure consistent and engaging storytelling?
Rubric:
1. Social media presence is minimal and inconsistent. 2. Some platforms are used but lack consistent branding and storytelling. 3. Social media is actively used with minor gaps in audience reach or branding. 4. Comprehensive strategy ensures consistent, engaging storytelling across platforms.

Reflection:
Freewrite your thoughts about social media and storytelling in celebrations.

Overall Score for You're Never Done Celebrating (24 Possible):
Greatest Need:
First Action Item:

REFERENCES & RESOURCES

Adedoyin, O. (2023, August 22). *One thing parents won't cut from budgets: Extracurricular activities.* Accessed at https://www.command education.com/press/one-thing-parents-wont-cut-from-budgets-extracurricular-activities on July 31, 2024.

Afalla, B. (2020). Blending extracurricular activities with academic performance: Pain or gain? *Humanities and Social Sciences Reviews, 8*(4), 222–229.

Amaro, S. (2020, January 22). *Participation in high school athletics has long-lasting benefits.* Accessed at https://www.nfhs.org/articles/participation-in-high-school-athletics-has-long-lasting-benefits on July 31, 2024.

American Academy of Pediatrics. (n.d.). *Supporting students with depression in school.* Accessed at https://www.aap.org/en/patient-care/school-health/mental-health-in-schools/supporting-students-with-depression-in-school/?srsltid=AfmBOor3s5Hd4s6pTV4iM5i juSitTF-B3TSSaSiwJ0ksTM-WNn2w7Dlz on January 5, 2025.

American Civil Liberties Union. (2008, June 6). *What is the school-to-prison pipeline?* Accessed at https://www.aclu.org/documents/what-school-prison-pipeline on January 5, 2025.

Annie E. Casey Foundation. (2024a, June 10). *2024 kids count data book: 2024 state trends in child well-being.* Accessed at https://www.aecf.org/resources/2024-kids-count-data-book?gad_source=1&gclid=CjwKCAiA-Oi7BhA1EiwA2rIu2wyrhMUsaNvRvxDjAWxUWxlNY5S-r0OgWaeyzYrjrUPT5q2N6NqA4RoCrsIQAvD_BwE on January 5, 2025.

Annie E. Casey Foundation. (2024b, October 22). *The impact of social media and technology on gen alpha* [Blog post]. Accessed at https://www.aecf.org/blog/impact-of-social-media-on-gen-alpha on March 3, 2025.

Anyon, Y., Jenson, J. M., Altschul, I., Farrar, J., McQueen, J., Greer, E., et al. (2014). The persistent effect of race and the promise of alternatives to suspension in school discipline outcomes. *Children and Youth Services Review, 44,* 379–386. https://doi.org/10.1016/j.childyouth.2014.06.025

Arbinger Institute. (2020). *The anatomy of peace: Resolving the heart of conflict* (2nd ed.). Oakland, CA: Berrett-Koehler.

Association for Physical Education. (2019, May 17). *Definitions of physical education, school sport & physical activity.* Accessed at https://www.afpe.org.uk/news/624058/Definitions-of-Physical-Education-School-Sport-Physical-Activity.htm on January 5, 2025.

Bacher-Hicks, A., Billings, S. B., & Deming, D. J. (2024). The school-to-prison pipeline: Long-run impacts of school suspensions on adult crime. *American Economic Journal: Economic Policy, 16*(4), 165–193.

Baker, K., & Tracy, J. (2020, May 11). *Special report: Coronavirus puts youth sports on pause.* Accessed at https://www.axios.com/2020/05/11/coronavirus-youth-sports on July 31, 2024.

Bandura, A. (1997). *Self-efficacy: The exercise of control.* New York: W. H. Freeman.

Barge, M. A. (2020, January 14). *What are extracurricular activities and why do you need them?* [Blog post]. Accessed at https://blog.prepscholar.com/what-are-extracurricular-activities-and-why do-you-need-them on July 31, 2024.

Bayar, A., & Karaduman, H. A. (2021). The effects of school culture on students academic achievements. *Shanlax International Journal of Education, 9*(3), 99–109. https://doi.org/10.34293/education.v9i3.3885

Bedard, C., St. John, L., Bremer, E., Graham, J. D., & Cairney, J. (2019). A systematic review and meta-analysis on the effects of physically active classrooms on educational and enjoyment outcomes in school age children. *PLOS ONE, 14*(6), Article e0218633. https://doi.org/10.1371/journal.pone.0218633

Bell, R. C. (2008, March 14). *A history of women in sport prior to Title IX.* Accessed at https://thesportjournal.org/article/a-history-of-women-in-sport-prior-to-title-ix on July 31, 2024.

Best, J., & Dunlap, A. (2014). *Continuous improvement in schools and districts: Policy considerations.* McREL International. Accessed at https://files.eric.ed.gov/fulltext/ED557599.pdf on January 6, 2025.

Blanchard, K., & Broadwell, R. (2018). *Servant leadership in action: How you can achieve great relationships and results.* Oakland, CA: Berrett-Koehler.

Blanchard, K., & Johnson, S. (2001). *The one-minute manager.* New York: HarperCollins.

Boone, G. (2015, July). *Why do former high school athletes earn more than everyone else?* Accessed at https://www.bls.gov/opub/mlr/2015/beyond-bls/why-do-high-school-athletes-earn-more-than-everyone-else.htm on January 21, 2024.

Braga, D., Hurst, K., Greenwood, S., Zanetti, N., & Mandapat, J. C. (2024, April 4). What public K–12 teachers want Americans to know about teaching. *Pew Research Center.* Accessed at https://www.pewresearch.org/social-trends/2024/04/04/what-public-k-12-teachers-want-americans-to-know-about-teaching on March 3, 2025.

BrainyQuote. (n.d.). *Mark Shields quotes.* Accessed at https://quotefancy.com/quote/1412014/Mark-Shields-There-is-always-strength-in-numbers-The-more-individuals-or-organizations on January 7, 2025.

Bukko, D., Liu, K., & Johnson, A. H. (2021). Principal practices that build and sustain trust: Recommendations from teachers in a high-trust school. *Planning and Changing, 5*(1/2), 58–74.

Burley, M. (2020, May 18). *The history of sport in public schools.* Accessed at www.winchestercollege.org/stories/the-history-of-sport-in-public-schools on July 31, 2024.

Burstein, J. (2023, November 29). *Adaptability: The key for thriving in a VUCA world* [Blog post]. Accessed at https://www.l-eaf.org/blog/adaptability-the-key-for-thriving-in-a-vuca-world on July 31, 2024.

Capone, R. (2020, December 16). *What is a professional learning community?* Accessed at https://www.letsgolearn.com/faq-items/what-is-a-plc on January 17, 2025.

Centers for Disease Control and Prevention. (2010, July). *The association between school-based physical activity, including physical education, and academic performance.* Author. Accessed at https://stacks.cdc.gov/view/cdc/25616/cdc_25616_DS1.pdf on January 7, 2025.

Centers for Disease Control and Prevention. (2020, March 6). *Mental health and coping during COVID-19.* Accessed at https://stacks.cdc.gov/view/cdc/85738 on July 31, 2024.

Centers for Disease Control and Prevention. (2024a, July 18). *Out-of-school time.* Accessed at https://www.cdc.gov/healthy-schools/out-of-school-time/index.html on January 5, 2025.

Centers for Disease Control and Prevention. (2024b, December 3). *Promoting mental health and well-being in schools.* Accessed at https://www.cdc.gov/mental-health-action-guide/about/index.html on January 7, 2025.

Centers for Disease Control and Prevention. (2024c, May 15). *About teen pregnancy.* Accessed at https://www.cdc.gov/reproductive-health/teen-pregnancy/index.html on January 7, 2025.

Centers for Disease Control and Prevention. (2024d, July 3). *Physical activity guidelines for school-aged children and adolescents.* Accessed at https://www.cdc.gov/physical-activity-education/guidelines/index.html on January 7, 2025.

Chen, S., Li, X., Yan, J., & Ren, Z. (2021, September 15). To be a sportsman? Sport participation is associated with optimal academic achievement in a nationally representative sample of high school students. *Frontiers in Public Health, 9.* https://doi.org/10.3389/fpubh.2021.730497

Chesney-Lind, M. (2013). How can we prevent girls from joining gangs? In T. R. Simon, N. M. Ritter, and R. R. Mahendra (Eds.), *Changing course: Preventing gang membership* (pp. 121–133). Washington, DC: U.S. Department of Justice and U.S. Department of Health and Human Services. Accessed at https://www.ojp.gov/pdffiles1/nij/239234.pdf on February 20 2025.

Christison, C. (2013). The benefits of participating in extracurricular activities. *BU Journal of Graduate Studies in Education, 5*(2), 17–20. https://files.eric.ed.gov/fulltext/EJ1230758.pdf

Christle, C. A., Jolivette, K., & Nelson, C. M. (2005). Breaking the school to prison pipeline: Identifying school risk and protective factors for youth delinquency. *Exceptionality, 13*(2), 69–88.

Clear, J. (2018). *Atomic habits: An easy and proven way to build good habits and break bad ones.* New York: Avery.

Clopton, A. W., & Finch, B. L. (2011). Re-conceptualizing social anchors in community development: Utilizing social anchor theory to create social capital's third dimension. *Community Development, 42*(1), 70–83.

Collin, J., & Quigley, A. (2021). *Teacher feedback to improve pupil learning.* Education Endowment Foundation. Accessed at https://educationendowmentfoundation.org.uk/education-evidence/guidance-reports/feedback on March 3, 2025.

Collins, N. M., Cromartie, F., Butler, S., & Bae, J. (2017). Effects of early sport participation on self-esteem and happiness. *The Sport Journal.* Accessed at https://thesportjournal.org/article/effects-of-early-sport-participation-on-self-esteem-and-happiness on January 7, 2025.

Committee on Physical Activity and Physical Education in the School Environment, Food and Nutrition Board, & Institute of Medicine. (2013). *Educating the student body: Taking physical activity and physical education to school.* Washington, DC: National Academies Press.

Congressional Research Service. (2023). *TikTok: Recent data privacy and national security concerns.* Accessed at https://crsreports.congress.gov/product/pdf/IN/IN12131 on January 7, 2025.

Coronado, M. C., Kwok, A., & Lee, J. (2022). *The impact of school facilities on student engagement and learning.* Accessed at https://www.researchgate.net/publication/358044352_The_Impact_of_School_Facilities_on_Student_Engagement_and_Learning on February 20, 2025.

Covey, S. R. (1989). *The 7 habits of highly effective people: Restoring the character ethic.* New York: Simon & Schuster.

Crispin, L. M. (2017). Extracurricular participation, "at-risk" status, and the high school dropout decision. *Education Finance and Policy, 12*(2), 166–196. https://doi.org/10.1162/EDFP_a_00212

Dahab, K., Potter, M. N., Provance, A., Albright, J., & Howell, D. R. (2019). Sport specialization, club sport participation, quality of life, and injury history among high school athletes. *Journal of Athletic Training, 54*(10), 1061–1066.

Dalberg-Acton, J. E. E. (1906). *Essays on freedom and power.* New York: Meridian Books.

Dekker, I., Schippers, M., & Van Schooten, E. (2023). Reflective goal-setting improves academic performance in teacher and business education: A large-scale field experiment. *Journal of Research on Educational Effectiveness, 17*(3), 561–589. https://doi.org/10.1080/19345747.2023.2231440

de Maistre, J. (1811). *Lettres et opuscules inedits, volume 1.* Nabu Press.

Denaver, J. (2023, September 15). *Exploring the psychological impacts of participating in sports.* Accessed at https://seattleanxiety.com/psychiatrist/2023/9/15/exploring-the-psychological-impacts-of-participating-in-sports on November 1, 2024.

Depression. (n.d.). *APA Dictionary of Psychology.* Accessed at https://dictionary.apa.org/depression on January 5, 2025.

Doherty, A., & Forés Miravalles, A. (2019). Physical activity and cognition: Inseparable in the classroom. *Frontiers in Education, 4*(105). https://doi.org/10.3389/feduc.2019.00105

Donohoo, J. (2015). *Collaborative inquiry for educators: A facilitator's guide to school improvement.* Thousand Oaks, CA: Corwin Press.

Dotson, R. (2016). Goal setting to increase student academic performance. *Journal of School Administration Research and Development, 1*(1) 44–46.

Dougherty, C., & Reason, C. (2019). *Inside PLCs at work: Your guided tour through one district's successes, challenges, and celebrations.* Bloomington, IN: Solution Tree Press.

Drew, C. (2023, July 27). *SMART goals in education: Importance, benefits, limitations.* Accessed at https://helpfulprofessor.com/smart-goals-in-education on January 4, 2025.

DuFour, R., DuFour, R., & Eaker, R., Many, T. W., & Mattos, M. (2016). *Learning by doing: A handbook for professional learning communities at work* (3rd ed.). Bloomington, IN: Solution Tree Press.

DuFour, R., DuFour, R., Eaker, R., Many, T. W., Mattos, M., & Muhammad, A. (2024). *Learning by doing: A handbook for professional learning communities at work* (4th ed.). Bloomington, IN: Solution Tree Press.

DuFour, R., & Eaker, R. (1998). *Professional learning communities at work: Best practices for enhancing student achievement.* Bloomington, IN: Solution Tree Press.

DuFour, R., & Fullan, M. (2013). *Cultures built to last: Systemic PLCs at Work.* Bloomington, IN: Solution Tree Press.

DuFour, R., & Reason, C. (2015). *Professional learning communities at work and high-reliability schools: Cultures of continuous learning.* Bloomington, IN: Solution Tree Press.

DuFour, R., & Reason, C. (2016). *Professional learning communities at work and virtual collaboration: On the tipping point of transformation.* Bloomington, IN: Solution Tree Press.

Dunn, A. (2025, February 13). *How mutual accountability drives team success.* Accessed at https://www.deliberatedirections.com /mutual-accountability-the-backbone-of-high-performing-teams on March 5, 2025.

Dweck, C. (2016). What having a "growth mindset" actually means. *Harvard Business Review.* Accesssed at https://hbr.org/2016/01/what-having-a-growth-mindset-actually-means on January 5, 2025.

Eather, N., Wade, L., Pankowiak, A., & Eime, R. (2023). The impact of sports participation on mental health and social outcomes in adults: A systematic review and the "mental health through sport" conceptual model. *Systematic Reviews, 12*(1), 102.

Elbot, C. F., & Fulton, D. (2007). *Building an intentional school culture: Excellence in academics and character.* Thousand Oaks, CA: Corwin Press.

Eldridge, J. A., Palmer, T. B., Gillis, K., Lloyd, R., Squires, W. G. Jr., & Murray, T. D. (2014). Comparison of academic and behavioral performance between athletes and non-athletes. *International Journal of Exercise Science, 7*(1), 3–13.

EY Global. (2020, September 23). *Why a female athlete should be your next leader.* Accessed at www.ey.com/en_au/athlete-programs/why-a-female-athlete-should-be-your-next-leader on January 4, 2025.

Ferraresi, M., & Gucciardi, G. (2020, August). *Team performance and audience: Experimental evidence from the football sector.* Accessed at www.researchgate.net/profile/Massimiliano-Ferraresi/publication /344106744_Team_performance_and_audience_experimental _evidence_from_the_football_sector/links/5f526a86299bf13 a319f78ce/Team-performance-and-audience-experimental-evidence -from-the-football-sector.pdf on January 4, 2025.

Fortune Business Insights. (2024). *eSports market size, share, and industry analysis by streaming type (live and on-demand), by revenue streaming (media rights, advertisement, sponsorship, ticket & merchandise, game publisher fees, and others), by gaming genre (real-time strategy games, first person shooter games, fighting games, multiplayer online battle arena games, mass multiplayer online role-playing games, and others), and regional forecast, 2024–2032.* Accessed at https://www.fortune businessinsights.com/esports-market-106820 on January 4, 2025.

Fredricks, J. A. (2012). Extracurricular participation and academic outcomes: Testing the over-scheduling hypothesis. *Journal of Youth and Adolescence, 41*(3), 295–306.

Friedman, H. L. (2013, September 20). When did competitive sports take over American childhood? *The Atlantic.* Accessed at www.theatlantic.com/education/archive/2013/09/when-did-competitive-sports-take-over-american-childhood/279868 on July 31, 2024.

Fujita, K. (2006). The effects of extracurricular activities on the academic performance of junior high students. *Undergraduate Research Journal for the Human Sciences, 5*(1), 45–58.

Furda, M., & Shuleski, M. (2019). The impact of extracurricular activities on academic performance and school perception. *Excellence in Education Journal, 8*(1), 64–90.

Gamarra, M. P., & Girotto, M. (2022). Ethical behavior in leadership: A bibliometric review of the last three decades. *Ethics and Behavior, 32*(2), 124–146.

Garfin, D. R., Silver, R. C., & Holman, E. A. (2020). The novel coronavirus (COVID-2019) outbreak: Amplification of public health consequences by media exposure. *Health Psychology, 39*(5), 355–357. https://doi.org/10.1037/hea0000875

Gillies, R. M. (2023). Using cooperative learning to enhance students' learning and engagement during inquiry-based science. *Education Sciences, 13*(12), 1242. https://doi.org/10.3390/educsci13121242

Gordon, J. (2007). *The energy bus: 10 rules to fuel your life, work, and team with positive energy.* Hoboken, NJ: Wiley.

Grabmeier, J. (2023, April 24). *No need to load up on extracurricular activities, study finds.* Accessed at https://news.osu.edu/no-need-to-load-up-on-extracurricular-activities-study-finds on July 31, 2024.

Gruenert, S., & Whitaker, T. (2015). *School culture rewired: How to define, assess, and transform it.* Arlington, VA: ASCD.

Guhn, M., Emerson, S. D., & Gouzouasis, P. (2020). A population-level analysis of associations between school music participation and academic achievement. *Journal of Educational Psychology, 112*(2), 308–328. https://doi.org/10.1037/edu0000376

Guo, D., McTigue, E. M., Matthews, S. D., & Zimmer, W. (2020). The impact of visual displays on learning across the disciplines: A systematic review. *Educational Psychology Review, 32*(3), 627–656. https://doi.org/10.1007/s10648-020-09523-3

Gurley, D. K., Peters, G. B., Collins, L., & Fifolt, M. (2015). Mission, vision, values, and goals: An exploration of key organizational statements and daily practice in schools. *Journal of Educational Change, 16*(2), 217–242.

Harvard Medical School. (2024). *Exercise can boost your memory and thinking skills.* Accessed at https://www.health.harvard.edu/mind-and-mood/exercise-can-boost-your-memory-and-thinking-skills on January 7, 2025.

Heath, D. (2020). *Upstream: The quest to solve problems before they happen.* New York: Simon & Schuster.

Heitzeg, N. A. (2009). Education or incarceration: Zero tolerance policies and the school to prison pipeline. *The Forum on Public Policy.* Accessed at https://files.eric.ed.gov/fulltext/EJ870076.pdf on January 7, 2025.

Heitzeg, N. A. (2016). *The school-to-prison pipeline: Education, discipline, and racialized double standards.* Westport, CT: Praeger.

Hemmeter, M. L., Ostrosky, M., & Fox, L. (2006). Social and emotional foundations for early learning: A conceptual model for intervention. *School Psychology Review, 35*(4), 583–601. https://doi.org/10.1080/02796015.2006.12087963

Hernández-Mendo, A., Reigal, R. E., López-Walle, J. M., Serpa, S., Samdal, O., Morales-Sánchez, V., et al. (2019). Physical activity, sports practice, and cognitive functioning: The current research status. *Frontiers in Psychology, 10,* Article 2658.

Hillman, C. H., Erickson, K. I., & Kramer, A. F. (2009). Be smart, exercise your heart: Exercise effects on brain and cognition. *Nature Reviews Neuroscience, 9*(1), 58–65. https://doi.org/10.1038/nrn2298

Honor Society. (2023, June 2). *The impact of extracurricular activities on academic success.* Accessed at https://www.honorsociety.org/articles/impact-extracurricular-activities-academic-success on January 5, 2025.

Hoque K. E., Wang, X., Qi, Y., & Norzan, N. (2023). The factors associated with teachers' job satisfaction and their impacts on students' achievement: a review (2010–2021). *Humanities and Social Sciences Communications, 10*(1), 177. https://doi.org/10.1057/s41599-023-01645-7

Horn, T., & Smith, A. (2019). *Advances in sport and exercise psychology* (4th ed.). Champaign, IL: Human Kinetics.

Howard, B. (2023, September 12). *The "why" of high school activities and athletics programs.* Accessed at https://www.nfhs.org/articles/the-why-of-high-school-athletics-and-activities-programs on July 31, 2024.

Huck, C., & Zhang, J. (2021). Effects of the COVID-19 pandemic on K–12 education: A systematic literature. *Educational Research and Development Journal, 24*(1), 53–84.

Hungerford, M. W. (1878). *Molly Bawn.* London, England: Smith, Elder & Co.

Hwa, Y.-Y., Kaffenberger, M., & Silberstein, J. (2020). *Aligning levels of instruction with goals and the needs of students (ALIGNS): Varied approaches, common principles.* United Kingdom: Research on Improving Systems of Education. Accessed at https://riseprogramme.org/sites/default/files/2020-11/RISE_Insight_ALIGNS.pdf on January 5, 2025.

Jekiel, C. (n.d.). *The importance of celebration in organizations.* Accessed at https://leanleadershipcenter.com/the-importance-of-celebration-in-organizations on January 5, 2025.

Jing, H. (2023). *Developing global awareness for global citizenship education: English language teachers' beliefs and practices in China.* Singapore: Springer.

Johnson, D. W., & Johnson, R. T. (2008). Cooperation and the use of technology. In J. M. Spector, M. D. Merrill, J. van Merriënboer, & M. P. Driscoll (Eds.), *Handbook of research on educational communication and technology* (3rd ed., pp. 401–424). New York: Erlbaum.

Johnson, W. (2022). Celebrate to win. *Harvard Business Review.* Accessed at https://hbr.org/2022/01/celebrate-to-win on January 5, 2025.

Jorgensen, J. (2023). *Why teachers and students should celebrate their successes: Boosting confidence and building momentum.* Accessed at https://www.jeremyajorgensen.com/why-teachers-and-students-should-celebrate-their-successes-boosting-confidence-and-building-momentum on January 5, 2025.

Jugl, I., Bender, D., & Lösel, F. (2021). Do sports programs prevent crime and reduce reoffending? A systematic review and meta-analysis on the effectiveness of sports programs. *Journal of Quantitative Criminology, 39*(3), 333–384.

Karaman, P. (2021). The effect of formative assessment practices on student learning: A meta-analysis study. *International Journal of Assessment Tools in Education, 8*(4), 801–817.

Kennedy, J. F. (1962, August 17). *Remarks at Pueblo, Colorado, 17 August 1962.* Accessed at https://www.jfklibrary.org/asset-viewer/archives/jfkpof-039-038#?image_identifier=JFKPOF-039-038-p0001 on January 4, 2025.

Kennedy, K. E., & Walls, J. (2024, October 29). Social-emotional well-being for high school students: Guidance for school and system policy and practice. *RAND Corporation.* Accessed at https://www.rand.org/pubs/research_reports/RRA3377-1.html on January 4, 2025.

Kight, T. (2020). *E + R = O*. Accessed at www.acalltoexcellence.com/ero on September 26, 2024.

Kniffin, K. M., Wansink, B., & Shimizu, M. (2015). Sports at work: Anticipated and persistent correlates of participation in high school athletics. *Journal of Leadership and Organizational Studies, 22*(2), 217–230.

Kolhar, M., Kazi, R. N. A., & Alameen, A. (2021). Effect of social media use on learning, social interactions, and sleep duration among university students. *Saudi Journal of Biological Sciences, 28*(4), 2216–2222. https://doi.org/10.1016/j.sjbs.2021.01.010

Koutsandréou, F., Wegner, M., Niemann, C., & Budde, H. (2016). Effects of motor versus cardiovascular exercise training on children's working memory. *Medicine and Science in Sports and Exercise, 48*(6), 1144–1152. https://doi.org/10.1249/mss.0000000000000869

Landry, A. T., & Whillans, A. (2019). The power of workplace rewards: Using self-determination theory to understand why reward satisfaction matters for workers around the world. *Compensation and Benefits Review, 50*(3), 26–35.

Leibtag, F. (2023, November 14). The power of celebrating success in the workplace. *Forbes*. Accessed at https://www.forbes.com/councils/forbescommunicationscouncil/2023/11/14/the-power-of-celebrating-success-in-the-workplace on January 5, 2025.

Lemola, S., Räikkönen, K., Gomez, V., & Allemand, M. (2013). Optimism and self-esteem are related to sleep: Results from a large community-based sample. *International Journal of Behavioral Medicine, 20*(4), 567–571. https://doi.org/10.1007/s12529-012-9272-z

LibQuotes. (n.d.). *Joseph de Maistre quotes*. Accessed at https://libquotes.com/joseph-de-maistre/quote/lbm2s1d on January 7, 2025.

Lin, L., Parker, K., & Menasce Horowitz, J. (2024). What's it like to be a teacher in America today? *Pew Research Center*. Accessed at https://www.pewresearch.org/social-trends/2024/04/04/whats-it-like-to-be-a-teacher-in-america-today on January 5, 2025.

Lindsay, A., & Byington, T. (2020). *Physical activity improves brain and cognitive functions.* Accessed at https://extension.unr.edu/publication.aspx?PubID=2921 on January 4, 2025.

Lipscomb, S. (2007). Secondary school extracurricular involvement and academic achievement: A fixed effects approach. *Economics of Education Review, 26*(4), 463–472.

Loveless, B. (2025, January 1). *Guide on extracurricular activities for high school students.* Accessed at https://www.educationcorner.com/k12-extracurricular-activities on January 4, 2025.

Maag, J. W. (2009). Resistance to change: Overcoming institutional and individual limitations for improving student behavior through PLCs. *Journal of the American Academy of Special Education Professionals.* 41–57. Accessed at https://files.eric.ed.gov/fulltext/EJ1137313.pdf on February 20, 2025.

Mallett, C. A. (2016). The school-to-prison pipeline: A critical review of the punitive paradigm shift. *Child and Adolescent Social Work Journal, 33*(1), 15–24.

Mandadi, A. (2022, April 15). There is no evidence to state that Bill Gates made this statement about choosing a lazy person to do a hard job. *FACTLY.* Accessed at https://factly.in/there-is-no-evidence-to-state-that-bill-gates-made-this-statement-about-choosing-a-lazy-person-to-do-a-hard-job on September 30, 2024.

Marlett, D. (2021, August 25). *Why do school improvement plans, initiatives, and implementations fail?* Accessed at https://learningfocused.com/why-do-school-improvement-plans-fail on July 31, 2024.

Maxwell, J. C. (2007). *The 21 irrefutable laws of leadership: Follow them and people will follow you.* New York: Harper Collins.

Mayol-García, Y. (2022, July 26). Girls take lessons, join clubs more often than boys but boys play more sports. Accessed at www.census.gov/library/stories/2022/07/children-continue-to-be-involved-in-extracurricular-activities.html on July 31, 2024.

McCarthy, K. (2000). *The effects of student activity participation, gender, ethnicity, and socio-economic level on high school student grade point averages and attendance.* Accessed at https://eric.ed.gov/?id=ED 457173 on February 20, 2025.

McCarthy, R. F. (2014). *The effect of athletic participation on the academic achievement of high school students* [Doctoral dissertation, Northeastern University]. Northeastern University Library Digital Repository Service. https://repository.library.northeastern.edu/files/neu:rx915b88r/fulltext.pdf

Mehdi, S. (2018). Impact of sports on academic achievement: Evidence from recent literature. *Impact Journals, 6*(8), 149–156.

Meltzer, L. J., McNally, J., Wahlstrom, K. L., & Plog, A. (2019). Impact of changing middle and high school start times on sleep, extracurricular activities, homework, and academic engagement. *Sleep, 42*(1), A328–A329.

Miller, C. (2024). *Does social media use cause depression?* Accessed at https://childmind.org/article/is-social-media-use-causing-depression on July 31, 2024.

Mintz, S., & Rutter, M. P. (2016, October 20). *The curricular and the co-curricular* [Blog post]. Accessed at https://www.insidehighered.com/blogs/higher-ed-gamma/curricular-and-co-curricular on February 20, 2025.

Moore, K., & Ehrle, J. (n.d.). *Children's environment and behavior: Participation in extracurricular activities.* Washington, DC: Urban Institute. Accessed at https://www.urban.org/sites/default/files/publication/70131/900869-Children-s-Environment-and-Behavior-Participation-in-Extracurricular-Activities.PDF on July 31, 2024.

Moore, S., & Newsome, K. (2019). Management by exception? The Taylor Review and workforce management. *New Technology, Work and Employment, 34*(2), 95–99.

Moran, J. P. (2017). *The impact of extracurricular activity on teacher job satisfaction* [Doctoral dissertation, Youngstown State University]. Accessed at https://etd.ohiolink.edu/acprod/odb_etd/etd/r/1501/10?clear=10&p10_accession_num=ysu1492182067273518 on January 7, 2025.

Morgan, H., Bush, A., & Bowles, H. (2022). *Active for employment: Enhancing employability through sport and physical activity participation: Report for the Sport for Development Coalition.* Bath, England: University of Bath.

National Academies of Sciences, Engineering, and Medicine. (2023). *Promoting learning and development in K–12 out-of-school time settings: Proceedings of a workshop—in brief.* Accessed at https://nap.nationalacademies.org/read/27885/chapter/1 on January 5, 2025.

National Federation of State High School Associations. (2014). *The case for high school activities.* Accessed at www.nfhs.org/articles/the-case-for-high-school-activities on July 31, 2024.

National Federation of State High School Associations. (2024, September 10). *Participation in high school sports tops eight million for first time in 2023–24.* Accessed at https://www.nfhs.org/articles/participation-in-high-school-sports-tops-eight-million-for-first-time-in-2023-24 on November 15, 2024.

National Gang Center. (2020, November 24). *Risk factors.* Accessed at https://nationalgangcenter.ojp.gov/spt/Risk-Factors/FAQ on July 31, 2024.

NCAA. (2021). *Student-athlete activism and racial justice engagement study.* Accessed at https://www.ncaa.org/sports/2021/7/29/ncaa-student-athlete-activism-and-racial-justice-engagement-study.aspx on January 5, 2025.

NCSA College Recruiting. (n.d.). *How to use Twitter for college recruiting.* Accessed at https://www.ncsasports.org/recruiting/contacting-college-coaches/how-to-use-twitter on July 31, 2024.

O'Donnell, A. W., Redmond, G., Gardner, A. A., Wang, J. J. J., & Mooney, A. (2023). Extracurricular activity participation, school belonging, and depressed mood: a test of the compensation hypothesis during adolescence. *Applied Developmental Science, 28*(4), 596–611. https://doi.org/10.1080/10888691.2023.2260745

Olmstead, L. (2022, November 5). *Resistance to change: 7 causes & how to overcome them* [Blog post]. Accessed at https://whatfix.com/blog/causes-of-resistance-to-change on January 5, 2025.

O'Neill, J. (2000). *Smart goals, smart schools.* Accessed at https://ascd.org/el/articles/smart-goals-smart-schools on February 20, 2025.

Osmun, R. (2024, November 13). *Time management and sleep.* Accessed on https://eachnight.com/sleep/time-management-and-sleep on December 24, 2024.

Pill, S., & SueSee, B. (2017). Including critical thinking and problem solving in physical education. *Journal of Physical Education, Recreation and Dance, 88*(9), 43–49.

Posselt, J. R., & Lipson, S. K. (2016). Competition, anxiety, and depression in the college classroom: Variations by student identity and field of study. *Journal of College Student Development, 57*(8), 973 989.

Price, M. (2021, May 12). *The importance of formative assessment and responsive teaching in the post-COVID era.* Accessed at https://my.chartered.college/impact_article/the-importance-of-formative-assessment-and-responsive-teaching-in-the-post-covid-era on January 5, 2025.

Provini, C. (2013). *Why don't professional learning communities work?* Access at www.educationworld.com/a_admin/professional-learning-community-pitfalls-best-practices.shtml on January 6, 2025.

Purdue University Global. (2020). *What is servant leadership?* [Blog post]. Accessed at https://www.purdueglobal.edu/blog/business/what-is-servant-leadership January 5, 2025.

Quoteresearch. (n.d.). *Quote origin: Choose a lazy person to do a hard job because that person will find an easy way to do it.* Accessed at https://quoteinvestigator.com/2014/02/26/lazy-job on July 31, 2024.

Raiyn, J. (2016). The role of visual learning in improving students' higher-order thinking skills. *Journal of Education and Practice, 7*(24), 115–121.

Reason, C. (n.d.). *The relationship between new money levies and winning football teams in Ohio* (Unpublished study).

Reason, C. (2009). *Leading a learning organization: The science of working with others.* Bloomington, IN: Solution Tree Press.

Reason, C. (2015). *Stop leading like it's yesterday!: Key concepts for shaping today's school culture.* Bloomington, IN: Solution Tree Press.

Reason, C. (2017). *Creating the anywhere, anytime classroom: A blueprint for learning online in grades K–12.* Bloomington, IN: Solution Tree Press.

Reason, C., & Reason, C. (2011). *Mirror images: New reflections on teacher leadership.* Thousand Oaks, CA: Corwin Press.

Resilience. (n.d.). In *APA Dictionary of Psychology.* Accessed at https://dictionary.apa.org/resilience on January 4, 2025.

Riddell, R. (2020, March 11). *Curricular counsel: What makes a 'transformational' school?* Accessed at https://www.k12dive.com/news/curricular-counsel-what-makes-a-transformational-school/573519 on January 4, 2025.

Ritz, I. (2006). *Playing for an active community: Sports participation and civic engagement.* Sociology honors projects. Accessed at https://digitalcommons.macalester.edu/cgi/viewcontent.cgi?article=1000&context=soci_honors on February 20, 2025.

Rix, K. (2022, November 15). The benefits of mental health programs in schools. *U.S. News & World Report.* Accessed at https://www.usnews.com/education/k12/articles/the-benefits-of-mental-health-programs-in-schools on January 6, 2025.

Ryan, R. M., & Deci, E. L. (2000). Intrinsic and extrinsic motivations: Classic definitions and new directions. *Contemporary Educational Psychology, 25*(1), 54–67.

Sabo, D., Miller, K. E., Melnick, M. J., & Heywood, L. (2004). *Her life depends on it: Sport, physical activity, and the health and well-being of American girls*. East Meadow, NY: Women's Sports Foundation. Accessed at https://search.issuelab.org/resource/her-life-depends-on-it-sport-physical-activity-and-the-health-and-well-being-of-american-girls.html on March 5, 2025.

Sagie, A., Zaidman, N., Amichai-Hamberger, Y., Te'eni, D., & Schwartz, D. G. (2002). An empirical assessment of the loose-tight leadership model: Quantitative and qualitative analyses. *Journal of Organizational Behavior, 23*(3), 303–320.

Salehin, R. U. (2024, May 22). 13 problem-solving activities & exercises for your team [Blog post]. Accessed at https://www.onethreadapp.com/blog/problem-solving-activities on January 5, 2025.

Santayana, G. (1905). *The life of reason or the phases of human progress*. New York: Charles Scribner's Sons.

Schulenberg, J. (2015). The social context of police discretion with young offenders: An ecological analysis. *Canadian Journal of Criminology, 45*(2), 127–157.

Sepanik, S., & Brown, K. T. (2021, November). School-community partnerships. *MDRC, All4Ed, and The Education Trust*. Accessed at https://files.eric.ed.gov/fulltext/ED616007.pdf on March 11, 2025.

Serviss, J. (2022, May 13). *4 benefits of an active professional learning community* [Blog post]. Accessed at https://iste.org/blog/4-benefits-of-an-active-professional-learning-community on January 5, 2025.

Shafer, L. (2018, July 23). *What makes a good school culture?* Accessed at https://www.gse.harvard.edu/ideas/usable-knowledge/18/07/what-makes-good-school-culture on December 23, 2024.

Shaheen, S. (2023, October 23). *How school culture shapes student success* [Blog post]. Accessed at www.t4.education/blog/how-school-culture-shapes-student-success on January 31, 2024.

Shimaly, J. (2023, August 21). *From field to boardroom: Championing women in sport.* Accessed at https://www.ey.com/en_ca/women-fast-forward/from-field-to-boardroom-championing-women-in-sport on January 4, 2025.

Shuck, B. (2023). *10 powerful questions that inspire creativity and innovation* [Blog post]. Accessed at https://www.biworldwide.com/research-materials/blog/10-powerful-questions-that-inspire-creativity-and-innovation on January 7, 2025.

Sissons, B. (2022). What is emotional health and well-being? *Medical News Today.* Accessed at https://www.medicalnewstoday.com/articles/emotional-wellbeing on December 24, 2024.

Sitrick, M. (2018, June 6). *Mike Sitrick's 10 rules of engagement to fix any scandal.* Accessed at www.sitrick.com/mike-sitricks-10-rules-of-engagement on July 31, 2024.

Skiba, R. J., Arredondo, M. I., & Williams, N. T. (2014). More than a metaphor: The contribution of exclusionary discipline to a school-to-prison pipeline. *Equity and Excellence in Education, 47*(4), 546–564.

Smith, C. (2014). Time and money: Parents placing kids in specialized sports do so at a price. *The Dallas Morning News.* Accessed at http://res.dallasnews.com/interactives/club-sports/part1 on November 1, 2024.

Sneck, S., Viholainen, H., Syväoja, H., Kankaapää, A., Hakonen, H., Poikkeus, A.-M., et al. (2019). Effects of school-based physical activity on mathematics performance in children: A systematic review. *International Journal of Behavioral Nutrition and Physical Activity, 16,* Article 109.

The Social Institute. (2023, November 3). *The top 5 strategies to avoid digital distractions in the classroom* [Blog post]. Accessed at https://thesocialinstitute.com/blog/the-top-5-strategies-to-avoid-digital-distractions-in-the-classroom on February 20, 2025.

Sportanddev. (2022, July 29). *How Title IX changed the landscape of sports.* Accessed at www.sportanddev.org/latest/news/how-title-ix-changed-landscape-sports on July 31, 2024.

Sportsmanship. (n.d.). In *Merriam-Webster's online dictionary.* Accessed at www.merriam-webster.com/dictionary/sportsmanship on July 31, 2024.

Stensland, P. J., Taniyev, O., Scola, Z., Ishaq, F. J., Wilkerson, Z., & Gordon, B. S. (2019). The ties that bind: Examining Division I athletics as a social anchor. *Journal of Issues in Intercollegiate Athletics, 12*(1).

Stewart, G. J. (2019). The impact of servant leadership on school climate and teacher retention. *International Journal of Business Management and Commerce, 2*(5), 1–5.

Stirling, A. E., & Kerr, G. A. (2012). The perceived effects of elite athletes' experiences of emotional abuse in the coach–athlete relationship. *International Journal of Sport and Exercise Psychology, 11*(1), 87–100. https://doi.org/10.1080/1612197X.2013.752173

Tafesse, W. (2022). Social networking sites use and college students' academic performance: Testing for an inverted U-shaped relationship using automated mobile app usage data. *International Journal of Educational Technology in Higher Education, 19*(16).

Tang, Y., Wang, T., & Liu, L. B., & Li, Q. (2020). Teacher job satisfaction in high-performing systems: A multi-level study of teacher, classroom, and school factors using TALIS 2013 surveys. *Asia Pacific Journal of Educational Research, 3*(1), 17–43.

Taylor, F. W. (1911). *The principles of scientific management.* New York: Harper & Brothers.

Terada, Y., Merrill, S., & Gonser, S. (2021, December 9). The 10 most significant education studies of 2021. *Edutopia.* Accessed at https://www.edutopia.org/article/10-most-significant-education-studies-2021 on January 5, 2025.

Tharayil, S., Borrego, M., Prince, M., Nguyen, K. A., Shekhar, P., Finelli, C. J., et al. (2018). Strategies to mitigate student resistance to active learning. *International Journal of STEM Education, 5*(1), 7 https://doi.org/10.1186/s40594-018-0102-y

Thompson, D. L., & Thompson, S. (2018). Educational equity and quality in K–12 schools: meeting the needs of all students. *Journal for the Advancement of Educational Research International, 12*(1), 34–46.

Thouin, É., Dupéré, V., Dion, E., McCabe, J., Denault, A.-S., Archambault, I., et al. (2022). School-based extracurricular activity involvement and high school dropout among at-risk students: Consistency matters. *Applied Developmental Science, 26*(2), 303–316. https://doi.org/10.1080/10888691.2020.1796665

Troseth, G. (2023). *How does technology affect kids' social development.* Accessed at www.childrenandscreens.org/learn-explore/research/how-does-technology-affect-kids-social-development on January 17, 2024.

TrueSport. (2024, March 19). *7 ways athletes can show leadership in the face of resistance.* Accessed at https://discover.sportsengineplay.com/issues-and-advice/7-ways-athletes-can-show-leadership-face-resistance on January 6, 2025.

U.S. Department of Education. (2024). *U.S. Department of Education's 2024 Title IX final rule overview.* Washington, DC: Author. Accessed at https://www2.ed.gov/about/offices/list/ocr/docs/t9-final-rule-factsheet.pdf on July 31, 2024.

University of San Diego. (n.d.). *The benefits of youth sports in child development* [Blog post]. Accessed at https://pce.sandiego.edu/child-development-through-sports on July 31, 2024.

Unterschutz, C. (2016, May 23). *Extracurricular activities—The history and benefits of involvement for youth.* Accessed at https://www.linkedin.com/pulse/extracurricular-activities-history-benefits-youth-unterschutz on July 31, 2024.

VanDerBill, B. (2021, June 22). *What to do about depression in students.* Accessed at https://psychcentral.com/depression/depression-in-students on January 5, 2025.

Vasilopoulos, F. (2022, July 15). The importance of physical activity for learning and wellbeing. Accessed at https://theeducationhub.org.nz/the-importance-of-physical-activity-for-learning-and-wellbeing on January 6, 2025.

Venkataraman, S., & Dheivamani, A. (2021). Impact of extracurricular activities on secondary level students' academic performance. *International Journal of Advanced Multidisciplinary Research, 8*(10), 43–47.

Vidal, C., Lhaksampa, T., Miller, L., & Platt, R. (2020). Social media use and depression in adolescents: A scoping review. *International Review of Psychiatry, 32*(3), 235–253. https://doi.org/10.1080/09540261.2020.1720623

Vincent, K. (2023). *10 ways out-of-school time programs can bridge opportunity gaps and boost student success* [Blog post]. Accessed at https://www.rightatschool.com/blog/10-ways-out-of-school-time-programs-can-bridge-opportunity-gaps-and-boost-student-success on January 5, 2025.

Vogels, E. A., Gelles-Watnick, R., & Massarat, N. (2022, August 10). Teens, social media and technology, 2022. *Pew Research Center.* Accessed at www.pewresearch.org/internet/2022/08/10/teens-social-media-and-technology-2022 on July 31, 2024.

Wadley, J. (2012, September 10). *High school sports participation lowers major crime and suspensions.* Accessed at https://news.umich.edu/high-school-sports-participation-lowers-major-crime-and-suspensions on January 5, 2025.

Wallace Foundation. (2021). *Out-of-school time programs paving the way for children to find passion, purpose & voice.* Accessed at https://wallacefoundation.org/report/out-school-time-programs-paving-way-children-find-passion-purpose-voice-paving-way-children on January 5, 2025.

Wang, W., Li, W., & Yao, J. (2024). The relationship between participation in extracurricular arts and sports activities and adolescents' social and emotional skills: An empirical analysis based on the OECD social and emotional skills survey. *Behavioral Sciences, 14*(7), 1–19.

Willink, J., & Babin, L. (2017). *Extreme ownership: How U.S. Navy SEALs lead and win.* New York: St. Martin's Press.

Women's Sports Foundation. (n.d.). *Title IX.* Accessed at https://www.womenssportsfoundation.org/advocacy_category/title-ix on March 11, 2025.

World Health Organization. (2024a). *Adolescent pregnancy.* Accessed at https://www.who.int/news-room/fact-sheets/detail/adolescent-pregnancy on January 7, 2025.

World Health Organization. (2024b). *Physical activity.* Accessed at https://www.who.int/news-room/fact-sheets/detail/physical-activity on January 7, 2025.

Xu, A. (n.d.). *Use extracurricular activities to improve communication skills.* Accessed at https://simplysoftskills.org/use-extracurricular-activities-to-improve-communication-skills on July 31, 2024.

Yellowbrick. (2023, November 11). *Mastering the art of storytelling in sports branding* [Blog post]. Accessed at www.yellowbrick.co/blog/sports/mastering-the-art-of-storytelling-in-sports-branding on July 31, 2024.

Youth.gov. (2023). *Civic engagement.* Accessed at https://youth.gov/youth-topics/civic-engagement-and-volunteering on January 6, 2025.

Zarrett, N., Veliz, P., & Sabo, D. (2018). *Teen sport in America: Why participation matters.* New York: Women's Sports Foundation. Accessed at https://www.womenssportsfoundation.org/wp-content/uploads/2018/01/teen-sport-in-america-full-report-web.pdf on January 5, 2025.

Zumeta, L. N., Oriol, X., Telletxea, S., Amutio, A., & Basabe, N. (2016). Collective efficacy in sports and physical activities: Perceived emotional synchrony and shared flow. *Frontiers in Psychology, 6,* 1960.

INDEX

A

academic impact of activities and athletics, 12–14, 39–40
accountability, 86, 109, 126
acknowledgments and winning or losing with grace, 158
action orientation, 127–128. *See also* professional learning communities (PLCs)
action plans
    program evaluation standard and, 82, 84–85
    taking action to improve the program, 160–161
activities and athletics. *See also* examining athletics and extracurricular activities in K–12 education; understanding the past, present, and future of activities and athletics in school
    athletics, prioritization of, 31–32
    building your school culture and, 52
    community building, reliance on for, 33–34
    esports, 40–41
    expectations for growth and development opportunities, 40–41
    "front porch focus" of, 55–56
    gender discrimination and, 32–33
    impact of on learning, 12–14, 39–40
    participation, low levels of, 67
    social networks and, 33–34
ACTs. *See also* learning communities for ACTs
    loose-tight leadership and, 107–110
    preparation and support of, 137–138
    reflecting individually as, 108
    reviewing with assistants and, 108–109
    sportsmanship and integrity standard and, 88
    standards for hiring, 79–82
    visions of the program and, 97, 98
advisory boards, 110
agendas, 140–142
align
    about, 95–96
    case study: harmonizing the rhythm between Mr. Black and Mr. Brown, 112–113
    case study: strumming up success with Riverview's orchestra program, 104–106
    case study: the disjointed journey of Riverton's music program, 97–98
    case study: the success story of Pinewood High's theater program, 100–102

conclusion, 117
fundamentals of the Rally model, 2
identifying challenges of, 96–98
Rally in action, 114–117
responding to the challenge with Rally practices, 99–114
where are we now, 97–98
assessments, formative assessments, 182–184
Atomic Habits: An Easy and Proven Way to Build Good Habits and Break Bad Ones (Clear), 51

B

balance and celebrations, 179
behavior. *See also* expectations
  behavior, attendance, and graduation, 16
  building a positive school culture and, 45
  crime, aggression, and antisocial behavior, 19
  Lincoln High School, living the culture, 46
  sample rules for respect, 88
  sportsmanship and integrity standard and, 87–90
bottom-up alignment, 103, 106. *See also* Rally practices for alignment
boundaries, 152
branding, 194–195
bullying and fighting, 131

C

career readiness and skill transfer, 21
celebrations. *See also* you're never done celebrating
  big-c celebrations, 187–190
  small-c celebrations, 181–187
  taking action to improve the program, 161
  team celebrations, 184–185
  transformational vision and, 157
  why we resist celebrations, 176–177
  winning or losing with grace and, 157–158
ceremonies, 185–187
change and raising the standard, 68–69
civic engagement, 21–22

civility, setting a civility standard, 139
Clear, J., 51
club sports and activities, 34–35.
  See also activities and athletics
collaboration. *See also* professional learning communities (PLCs)
  ACT learning communities and, 136–137
  being intentional with other programs and, 111–112, 114
  collaborative initiatives, 162
  collaborative leadership, 154–155
  community and parent support standard and, 87
  cooperating to see benefits, 112
collective inquiry. *See also* professional learning communities (PLCs)
  about, 123–125
  collaborative teams and, 126–127
  innovation and creativity and, 125
committing to the process and the plan, 186, 187
communication
  and ACT communities, 134, 135
  with the community and parents, 85, 86, 87, 109–110
  expectations, 45
  and formative feedback, 182
  getting information back to the programs, 166–167
  reviewing with assistants and ACTs, 108–109
  and student leadership, 158
  and team sports and activities, 21
community
  community and parent support standard, 85–87
  community building, reliance on activities and athletics for, 33–34
  community celebrations, 188–190
  community engagement, 25, 179–180
  community service projects, 155, 161–162, 189
  cooperating to see benefits, 112
  leading in the community, 161–163
  sharing with the community and parents, 109–110
competencies for leadership. *See also* leadership

demonstrating excellence in practice and preparation, 158–159, 163
leading in the community, 161–163, 164
optimism and positive energy, showing, 151–153, 163
positive influence, observing and celebrating evidence of, 150–151, 162–163
servant leadership and, 153–155, 163
taking action to improve the program, 159–161, 164
transformational vision committed to growth, 155–157, 163
using student leadership programs to teach the eight competencies, 164–168
winning or losing with grace, 157–158, 163
continuous learning, 126, 127, 128–129. *See also* professional learning communities (PLCs)
cooperating to see benefits, 112
Covey, S., 99
critical thinking and problem solving, 13–14

D

daily actions and school culture, 44
de Maistre, J., 86
decision making, 134, 154–155
defining school culture. *See* school culture

E

empathy, 21, 154, 155
engagement
　and benefits of athletics and activities in K–12 education, 24–25
　and challenges of leading through students, 148
　community and parent support standard, 85, 87
　and leading in the community, 162
　teacher engagement and activities and athletics, 138
equity
　of access, 38–39
　gender discrimination and, 32–33
esports, 40–41

event + response = outcome (E + R = O) (outcome formula), 151
examining athletics and extracurricular activities in K–12 education. *See also* activities and athletics
　about, 11–12
　academic impacts, 12–14
　after graduation, 20–22
　benefits to teachers, 22–24
　benefits to the school, 24–25
　conclusion, 26
　mental and emotional well-being, 14–19
expectations
　building a positive school culture, 45
　excellence in practice and preparation, 159
　for growth and development opportunities, 40–41
　Lincoln High School, living the culture, 46
　participation expectations standard, 71–73
　program or activity commitment standard, 76–79
　sportsmanship and integrity standard, 87–90
extracurricular activities. *See also* activities and athletics
　athletics and, 31–32
　gender discrimination and, 32–33
　history of, 30–31
　use of term, 32

F

Facebook, 192. *See also* social media shout-outs and social networks
fans, poor fan and parent support, 68
feedback, 160, 181–182
feeder programs, 103
fitness, 13, 20–21
formative assessments, 182–184
"front porch focus" of activities and athletics, 55–56

G

gender discrimination, 32–33
goals
　about, 50

benchmark goal sheet, 71
case studies, 53–55, 120–123
collaborative teams and, 126
cooperating to see benefits, 114
learning communities for ACTs and, 137, 138
mission, vision, values and, 51, 52, 120
participation and expectations standard, 71–73
planning action, 84–85
process goals, 82–83, 85, 160–161
progress monitoring and, 83–84
SMART goals, 50–51, 53–55
transformational vision and, 156
GPA outcomes and college attendance, 14
growth mindset, 45, 46

H

halftime recognitions, 189
head coach and advisor representatives, 136
homecoming parades, 189
Hungerford, M., 89

I

inclusivity, 178
influence, observing and celebrating evidence of positive influence, 150–151, 162–163
Instagram, 191–192. *See also* social media shout-outs and social networks
intentional design and developing school culture, 46–47
intrinsic motivation, 45, 46
introduction
  activities, athletics, and academics, 1–2
  fundamentals of the Rally model, 2–3
  organization of this book, 3–7

J

Jorgensen, J., 175

K

key performance indicators (KPIs), 3

L

lead through students
  about, 147
  conclusion, 172
  fundamentals of the Rally model, 2
  identifying challenges of, 147–149
  Rally in action, 168–172
  responding to the challenge with Rally practices, 149–168
  where are we now, 149
leadership. *See also* competencies for leadership
  collaborative leadership, 154–155
  leading in the community, 161–163, 164
  loose-tight leadership, 107–110
  opportunities and challenges of leading through students, 148–149
  small-c celebrations, 184, 186–187
learning communities for ACTs
  about, 119
  case study: the unified vision of Rivertown's girls soccer program, 120–123
  conclusion, 145
  establishing a collaborative learning culture, 119–130
  fundamentals of the Rally model, 2
  identifying challenges of, 130–131
  Rally in action, 142–145
  responding to the challenge with Rally practices, 132–142
  where are we now, 132
Lincoln High School. *See also* defining school culture
  case study, 47
  living the culture in, 46
local government, 189–190
loose-tight leadership, 107–110
love, definition of, 153
loyalty and activities and athletics, 36

M

meetings
  case study: harmonizing the rhythm between Mr. Black and Mr. Brown, 112–113

establishing the norms of the ACT learning community, 140
implementing the elements of an effective ACT learning community, 136
progress monitoring and, 83
mental and emotional well-being
  about, 14–15
  after graduation, 20–22
  behavior, attendance, and graduation and, 16
  crime, aggression, and antisocial behavior and, 19
  depression, 18–19
  resilience, 17–18
  stress management and sleep, 16–17
mentorship, 156, 158, 160, 162
mission. *See also* professional learning communities (PLCs)
  about, 48–49
  aligning and, 96–97
  building your school culture, 51
  case study: Springfield's amazing marching band, 53
  shared mission, vision, and values, 120, 123
modeling, 45, 46, 154, 159
motivation, 45, 46, 154

N

native school applications, 192. *See also* social media shout-outs and social networks
negative training, 69
neglect, 45
norms of the ACT learning community, establishing, 139–140

O

open enrollment culture, 36, 74
OST (out-of-school time) programs, 12–13
outcome formula (event + response = outcome), 151

P

parents and families
  club sports and activities and, 34–35
  community and parent support standard, 85–87
  mission and vision and, 96
  poor fan and parent support, 68
  sharing with, 109–110
  understanding family demands, 110
participation
  cooperating to see benefits, 112
  raising the standard, 67, 71–73
  small-c celebrations, 183
peer learning, 159
peer mentoring, 156
pep rallies, 2, 3, 188
pivoting, 68–69
positive energy, process for maintaining, 151–152
positive influence, observing and celebrating evidence of, 150–151, 162–163. *See also* competencies for leadership
positive reinforcements, 134
post-game debriefings, 157–158
practice and preparation
  competencies for leadership, 158–159, 163
  pregame festivities, 189
  small-c celebrations, 185
professional learning communities (PLCs). *See also* learning communities for ACTs
  about, 119–120
  action orientation, 127–128
  collective inquiry, 123–127
  commitment to continuous improvement, 128–129
  results orientation, 129
  shared knowledge, 129–130
  shared mission, vision, and values, 120, 123
program offerings
  identifying challenges of raising the standard, 67–68
  program evaluation standard, 82–85
  program offerings standard, 73–76
  program or activity commitment standard, 76–79
  sample school offerings survey, 74–75
  taking action to improve the program, 159–161, 164

unresolved competition between programs, 131
progress
  program evaluation standard, 83–84, 85
  small-c celebrations, 183–184
public presentations, 109
public representation, 162

R

raise the standard
  about, 63–64
  case study: the forgotten fields of Driftwood, 64–66
  conclusion, 92
  fundamentals of the Rally model, 2
  identifying challenges of, 64, 67–69
  Rally in action, 90–92
  responding to the challenge with Rally practices, 70–90
  where are we now, 70
Rally model. *See also* align; lead through students; learning communities for ACTs; raise the standard; you're never done celebrating
  fundamentals of, 2–3
  Rally of your own, 203–205
  setting the stage for, 10
  staging the Rally, 61
Rally practices for alignment. *See also* align
  about, 99
  align programs from the bottom up, 103, 106
  align programs from the top down, 99–103
  being intentional with other programs, 111–112, 114
  practicing loose-tight leadership with continuous review, 107–110
Rally practices for celebrations. *See also* you're never done celebrating
  about, 180–181
  big-c celebrations, 187–190
  small-c celebrations, 181–187
  social media shout-outs, 190–195
Rally practices for leading through students. *See also* lead through students
  about, 149
  implementing the eight leadership competencies, 149–164
  using student leadership programs to teach the eight competencies, 164–168
Rally practices for learning communities for ACTs. *See also* learning communities for ACTs
  about, 132
  establishing the agenda around the vision, 140–142
  establishing the norms of the ACT learning community, 139–140
  establishing what an ACT community in the school really is, 132–135
  implementing the elements of an effective ACT learning community, 135–139
Rally practices for raising the standard. *See also* raise the standard
  about, 70–71
  community and parent support standard, 85–87
  participation expectations standard, 71–73
  program evaluation standard, 82–85
  program offerings standard, 73–76
  program or activity commitment standard, 76–79
  sportsmanship and integrity standard, 87–90
  standards for hiring ACTs, 79–82
recognizing and rewarding effort, 159
recruitment, 32–33, 37, 38, 192
reflection
  reflecting individually as ACTs, 108
  transformational vision committed to growth, 156
relationships
  building a positive school culture, 45
  Lincoln High School, living the culture, 46
  showing optimism and positive energy, 152
reproducibles for
  align, 220–227
  leading through students, 236–243
  learning communities for ACTs, 228–235
  raising the standard, 208–219
  you're never done celebrating, 244–255

resource allocation, 159, 178–179
results orientation, 129.
    See also professional learning communities (PLCs)
reviewing with assistants and ACTs at other levels, 108–109
rewarding students
    positive reinforcement, 134
    recognizing and rewarding effort, 159
    working together, 184, 186
role-playing scenarios, 158
rules
    collaborative teams and, 126
    norms of the ACT learning community, establishing, 139–140
    sample rules for respect, 88

S

Santayana, G., 29
schedules and scheduling
    case study: harmonizing the rhythm between Mr. Black and Mr. Brown, 113
    collaborative teams and, 126
    cooperating to see benefits, 112
    social media shout-outs and, 194
    stress management and sleep and, 17
school culture
    about, 43
    benefits of athletics and extracurricular activities, 24–25
    building a positive school culture, 45
    case study: intentional design for positive culture, 47
    case study: lack of plan leads to toxic culture, 47–48
    case study: Springfield's amazing marching band, 52–55
    conclusion, 59–60
    how culture is built, 48–56
    Rally in action, 56–59
    what school culture is, 43–47
school loyalty, 36
schoolwide awareness, 111
servant leadership
    competencies for leadership, 153–155, 163
    leading in the community, 161–163
service projects, 155, 161–162, 189

shared knowledge, 129–130.
    See also professional learning communities (PLCs)
showing optimism and positive energy, 151–153, 163. *See also* competencies for leadership
showing up, 183, 186, 187
Sitrick, M., 191
SMART goals, 50–51, 53–55. *See also* goals
Snapchat, 193. *See also* social media shout-outs and social networks
social anchors, 33, 34
social media shout-outs and social networks
    about, 190–191
    activities and athletics and, 33–34
    creating a consistent brand, 194–195
    knowing what tools to use, 193–194
    platforms reach the right audience, 191–193
    understanding the reasoning behind social media celebrations, 191
sportsmanship and integrity standard, 87–90
stress
    cooperating to see benefits, 112
    emotional well-being and, 14, 15
    stress management and sleep, 16–17
struggle, 183
support
    community and parent support standard, 85–87
    poor fan and parent support, 68
    preparation and support of ACTs, 137–138
    servant leadership and, 154

T

teachers
    ACT learning communities and, 138
    benefits of athletics and extracurricular activities, 22–24
    job satisfaction and engagement in school life, 23
    story of Ahmad, 23–24
team celebrations, 176, 184–185
team optimism and rigor, 184, 186
TikTok, 193. *See also* social media shout-outs and social networks
Title IX, 32–33

top-down alignment, 99–103. *See also* Rally practices for alignment
toxic school culture, 47–48, 67, 131
transformational vision committed to growth, 155–157, 163. *See also* vision

U

understanding the past, present, and future of activities and athletics in school. *See also* activities and athletics
  about, 29
  conclusion, 41
  desired future, 37–41
  past, 30–34
  present, 34–37

V

values
  about, 49–50
  aligning and, 96–97
  building a positive school culture, 45
  case study: Springfield's amazing marching band, 53
  core value evaluation survey, 80–81
  shared mission, vision, and values, 120, 123
  tips and strategies for building your own intentional school culture, 51
vision
  about, 49
  align programs from the top down, 99–100, 102
  aligning and, 96–97
  case study: Springfield's amazing marching band, 53

establish the agenda around the vision, 140–142
  optimism and positive energy and, 152
  raising the standard and, 69
  shared mission, vision, and values, 120, 123
  tips and strategies for building your own intentional school culture, 51
  transformational vision, 155–157, 163
volunteer projects, 189

W

whole-school activities and celebrations, 188
winning or losing with grace, 157–158, 163

X

X (formerly known as Twitter), 192. *See also* social media shout-outs and social networks

Y

you're never done celebrating. *See also* celebrations
  about, 175–176
  conclusion, 200
  fundamentals of the Rally model, 2
  identifying challenges of, 177–180
  Rally in action, 195–199
  responding to the challenge with Rally practices, 180–195
  where are we now, 180

Wait! Your professional development journey doesn't have to end with the last pages of this book.

We realize improving student learning doesn't happen overnight. And your school or district shouldn't be left to puzzle out all the details of this process alone.

No matter where you are on the journey, we're committed to helping you get to the next stage.

Take advantage of everything from **custom workshops** to **keynote presentations** and **interactive web and video conferencing**. We can even help you develop an action plan tailored to fit your specific needs.

Let's get the conversation started.

Call 888.763.9045 today.

solution-tree.com

Up to the Challenge
Jay Jackson

This timely resource lets educators take a deep dive into helping students build character to confront and overcome challenges. With passion and purpose, author Jay Jackson blends personal challenges and achievements to equip teachers with tools to improve student resilience.

BKG076

Bolstering Student Resilience
Jason E. Harlacher and Sara A. Whitcomb

Move beyond the buzzwords surrounding social-emotional learning and focus on three fundamentals for successfully supporting your students. This book illuminates the why behind the work and offers proven strategies for building positive, supportive classrooms.

BKL063

The Tactical Teacher
Dale Ripley

Positively influence the behavior of even your most challenging students. In *The Tactical Teacher*, author Dale Ripley shares a plethora of tactics, ranging from persuasive dialogue to environmental details, proven to improve classroom behavior and increase student learning.

BKG025

Coaching Competitive Sports
Tammy Heflebower and Logan Heflebower

Writing from experience as both athletes and school athletics coaches, authors Tammy Heflebower and Logan Heflebower detail specific attributes and behaviors of effective youth sports coaches and the knowledge, skills, and intangible assets they must help student athletes develop.

BKL073

Solution Tree | Press

a division of Solution Tree

Visit SolutionTree.com or call 800.733.6786 to order.